# Burnt Bread
# and
# Chutney

## GROWING UP
## BETWEEN CULTURES—
## A MEMOIR OF AN
## INDIAN JEWISH
## GIRL

# Burnt Bread
# and
# Chutney

### GROWING UP
### BETWEEN CULTURES—
### A MEMOIR OF AN
### INDIAN JEWISH
### GIRL

# Carmit Delman

One World
Ballantine Books • New York

A Ballantine Book
Published by The Ballantine Publishing Group

Copyright © 2002 by Carmit Delman

www.ballantinebooks.com/one/

Library of Congress Cataloging-in-Publication Data:
Delman, Carmit.
Burnt Bread & Chutney : Growing Up Between Cultures—A Memoir of an
Indian Jewish Girl / by Carmit Delman.—1st ed.
p. cm.
"A Ballantine book"—T.p. verso.
ISBN 0-345-44593-7
1. Delman, Carmit. 2. Jews—United States—Biography. 3. Jews, Indian—
United States—Biography. 4. Jews, Indian—Israel—Biography. 5. Jews—
India—Biography. 6. United States—Ethnic relations. I. Title: Burnt bread
and chutney. II. Title.

E184.37.D45 A3 2002
973'.04924'00092—dc21
[B]
2002022855

Manufactured in the United States of America

First Edition: September 2002

10  9  8  7  6  5  4  3  2  1

*In memory of Nana-bai,*
*beloved wife and mother.*

# Contents

# Acknowledgments

Thank you to Anita Diggs, Dan Smetanka, and Jennifer Rudolph Walsh, for their kindness and wisdom. Thank you, also, to Bernice Stern, Mark Lisanti, the dear friends and family who have always believed in my work, and my teachers at Brandeis University and Emerson College—especially Dewitt Henry and Bill Donoghue. Most of all, I owe eternal love and gratitude to my parents and siblings, for everything that lies behind our shared story and this interpretation of it.

# Author's Note

Of all Jewish communities to have sprung up, mushrooms and dandelions in odd corners around the world, perhaps most obscure are the three Jewish communities in India. The ancient Jews of Cochin (now called Kochi). The Baghdadi Jews. And the Bene Israel—the Children of Israel—from western India and Bombay (or Mumbai). This last group, the Bene Israel, is said to have the most shrouded history of all. And though there are many theories explaining how it came to be, its true origins may always remain a mystery. This is the community from which my family is descended.

Tradition connects the ancestors of the Bene Israel to the ancient kingdom of Israel, which was once occupied by ten of the biblical Twelve Tribes. According to one legend, a boatload of people left that region somewhere in the final centuries B.C.E. They sailed across the ocean and were shipwrecked on the Konkan coast of India, far from their initial destination or contacts. Seven men and seven women survived that shipwreck and took up residence in villages along the shore. They and their descendants were cut off from the Jewish world at this point in history until they were rediscovered and reabsorbed many centuries later. So the Bene Israel evolved quite uniquely, without many of the holidays, rituals, and rabbinic rulings introduced meanwhile in the general Jewish Diaspora.

Though they adopted the local language, Marathi, and manners of dress like the sari, along with some of the other Indian customs, the Bene Israel mostly kept to themselves. They maintained the few ancient Jewish rituals which could be passed on, such as the Sabbath day or Shabbat, circumcision, basic prayers, and laws of kosher food. They were skilled in oil pressing, and the community grew throughout the generations, even building up its own stock of folklore and customs. This Judaism absorbed an Indian essence which emerged in the prayer melodies and rituals, the fasting, pilgrimages, and castelike patterns that distinguished full-blooded Bene Israel from those who were products of mixed unions.

In recent centuries, the Bene Israel began to move from the villages to the great city of Bombay for its many work opportunities and the chance to serve in the British army. There they established synagogues, schools, orphanages, journals, burial grounds, and many kinds of societies and charities to foster Jewish life. Because they were not persecuted by non-Jews for their beliefs the way that Jews in other countries often were, the Bene Israel achieved a solid relationship with the general Indian community and succeeded in the military, medicine, and the arts. They faced another kind of discrimination, however, because once they reconnected, the dark color of their skin and their centuries of isolation sometimes led other Jewish communities to look down on them and question their Jewish purity.

The Bene Israel had always longed to return to Israel. In recent times, as Jews internationally came together to create the modern state of Israel, many young Bene Israel immigrated there, too, to help build the new land. This began the movement of much of the community to Israel, leaving fewer and fewer Jews in Bombay and in the other two Indian Jewish communities with each passing year. In the end, all that transpired could be tracked in the mixture of names in any given Bene Israel family, which might include Biblical, Indian, European, and modern Israeli variations.

And my own family? Where do we sit in all these passing generations? My mother and her mother and all the mothers going all the way back up are descended from one mother who crawled out of the ocean like an amoeba, salty after that ancient shipwreck. They lived in India for hundreds of years until my mother, as a child, along with other relatives and Bene Israel youngsters, went to live, learn, and work in Israel as part of the Youth Aliyah movement. She married my father, an American Jew of Ashkenazi (Eastern European) descent, and then followed him to the United States. But after all this time of missing a Jewish homeland in our very genes, now that a modern state actually existed, we could not just dismiss it. My parents, this time with four children, picked up again to try and live in Israel for good. Later, we ended up coming back to the U.S. But that move topped off the many layers of influence in me: Judaism, India, America, Israel.

What follows is my story, and the story of my family. This work of creative nonfiction is not a perfect account, and it would surely be told differently by every other person involved. It does not attempt to represent a larger community or culture from my limited experiences. It is just my one humble version of all that has happened, tinted by poetry, time, wistfulness, misunderstanding, and the could-have-been, should-have-been holes of history and memory. Some details and identities have been altered for this book and to protect the privacy of the people I love. But I hope that I have been true here to the essence of our lives.

# *Foreword*

*T*he day I saw Nana-bai eating hot dogs, I knew that she was dying.

Nana-bai never ate hot dogs. As a rule. For many years when I was a child, I did not even realize such a thing as a hot dog existed. At that time we lived in a red brick Ohio home. With lemon walls. With oak chests crammed full of hand-carved toys. With an apple tree and a vegetable garden gated off in the backyard. Each spring I sat on an overturned pail and watched as Daddy painted the gates a fresh layer of green. Afterward, he tightened the wiring with pliers. And everything seemed to begin and end within these gates.

Then, one summer day, barbecue smells beckoned me into the neighbor's backyard. Mommy, Daddy, Gertie, Tzvi, Batsheva, and I were downstairs, cleaning out the basement, when I first smelled something wonderfully smoky through an open window. I pretended to have to go to the bathroom and made my way upstairs. But once out of sight, I ducked past the bathroom and slipped out to our backyard instead. There, peering at the neighbors through the twining blanket of leaves and gate wire, I spied a slowly smoking grill, some plastic chairs, and a wicker patio table loaded with paper bowls of food. The neighbors milled about, eating, talking, filling their plates again and again at the table as they passed in and out of the porch screen door.

Amidst the ongoing movement, one bony old man sat stolidly by the table, sunning himself. He stretched his legs out into the grass, like two blue-veined French breads, fanning himself furiously with a newspaper. When a bumblebee buzzed over the open ketchup jar, he swatted at it. Every now and then, he took a gentlemanly sip from a dripping beer, and allowed himself a peaceful belch. I scratched at an ant crawling up my arm and from behind his oversized orange sunglasses, this man spotted me through the rustle, a foraging animal in the brush. He lowered the sunglasses on his nose and signaled me over with a finger, so I wormed my way between the gate wires, ducked under their sprinklers, and tiptoed to him at the table.

Up close, the piles of food seemed to glisten before me with mayonnaise and meatiness, and for a moment I stopped, breathless for sheer admiration. Then, as though I would not understand his words, the old man nodded and pointed to me, then to the food, then back to me. Given the go-ahead, I stuffed my mouth full of chips, haphazardly grabbed at whatever lay nearby, and raced back to our own yard. Only then did I take a good look at the hot dog specimen in hand. It was a beauty. Baby pink, branded from the grill, already striped by mustard, and nestled in a soft bun.

I wandered into our kitchen, climbed up into a chair, and poised myself to take a bite. Just then Nana-bai emerged from the pantry. I worried she would scold me for not staying to help the others in the basement, but she did not. "Aiaa," she warned omi-nously instead. "That's not real food." She set a sack of potatoes on the counter and dipped her finger into a steaming pot on the stove above me. As usual she was stirring, chopping, frying up some-thing curried and homemade for a family meal. I felt her standing over me, then one brown, gentle palm on my shoulder. Using the spatula in her other hand, she poked suspiciously at the hot dog in question.

Who was this ancient specter in our home, this Nana-bai, with her prophecies, with her dishtowel—so spotted and smelling from sauces—over one arm? Her given name was Ruthie; Nana-bai was just our term of endearment for her. But this woman was—depending on the day and with whom you spoke—sometimes one of the many great-aunties, sometimes matriarch, sometimes baker of cookies, sometimes bearer of secrets, and also, at the end of it, sometimes just a mystery. Nana-bai was kin, and she was very old, so obviously if she needed somewhere to live, just as other uncles and cousins had done before her, she could come to us. And she did.

"Not real food?" I asked her. I was intrigued at the possibilities of not-real. I imagined my hot dog opening a hundred eyes and talking to me, or growing into a giant beanstalk, or disappearing in a smoky poof after just one bite. Taking a cautious, deep breath, I sank my teeth into the hot dog, watching it for any sudden moves. But I found that it just lay there rather mundanely, allow-ing itself to be quietly chomped, morsel by morsel, until nothing remained.

On guard from behind me, Nana-bai seemed almost as disap-pointed as I was when no chaos erupted from the hot dog. She nodded her head, conceding defeat to a nemesis who'd managed to best her—till next time, anyway. And despite this fact, almost as if determination alone would prove it wrong, she told me again, "Nai. It's not real food." Wielding the spatula squarely before her, she returned to the cooking and proclaimed, "Even with mustard, even with chutney. By G-d, I would not eat this thing for all the gold in the world."

This was not the first time G-d found Himself summoned up with such resolve in our family. Uttering this one syllable was a crutch, a habit in our home's language—beginning with Nanabai, seeping down through my parents, and finally infiltrating the children. So we called out to Him in surprise or anger or pleasure, automatically. And every day, in just this way, we petitioned Him, thanked Him, made Him stand as witness to our declarations. Secretly I worried that we might be crying wolf, or taking His name in vain, which the Torah itself warned against. And I wondered if we weren't being overly bold, expecting G-d to find the time for our petty worries. With the world outside our home so big and frightening that we children almost never even went across the street—and then only if someone strong and all-knowing could hold our hands—surely He had bigger problems to deal with. Did He really need to have a part in our squabbles, our pleas for a sunny day, for a good plumber, for fewer bills, for high grades at school, for a 25-percent-off sale? Probably not. So, always a reasonable child, I tried to brace myself for the worst. And I decided that when He turned his attention to me, and all I could tell Him was something frivolous and flighty, I would just have to understand if he looked at the clock and said, I haven't got time for this. But still, hopeful, we called upon Him as easily as if he lived down the road. For good measure and just in case, the way other people will cross their fingers and knock wood and toss salt over the shoulder. Because who knew: someday even such a thing as a hot dog might, in fact, require divine intervention.

On principle the many other aunties, grandmas, great- and great-great-grandmas in our family took the same stance as Nana-bai on hot dogs. A kind of culinary bravado which asked boastfully: Why should I eat that thing that has been made by strangers and machines, when I could cook something so much better myself from scratch? They, too, were gravely mistrustful of what might be tainted, dirty, unkosher, gristly, or watered down in such packaged foods. And yet, when they thought no one was looking, they eyed whatever odds and ends I bought with found nickels and managed to scrape up at the neighbors: bologna slices or string cheese. They toyed hesitantly with the edges of their saris or dug their hands into housedress pockets. Then, finally, they succumbed to these temptations, sheepishly picking and nibbling at the curiosities. "Just a bite," they would say, and then grimace as they swallowed, confirming these things were indeed the scandal they'd suspected.

Only Nana-bai was different. She never once in her life brought herself to eat something like a hot dog out of plastic. A hot dog was a hot dog, no matter who was looking or not looking. Until that day years later, when I returned from university to see her in the hospital. There, at the edge of reason and death, as a woman I could barely recognize, she consented weakly. And while I watched in disbelief, a nurse gently cut the pale boiled meat into chewable pieces and fed her as though somehow this was ordinary.

After Nana-bai died—but long before the outrage that would someday haunt her passing—I claimed an old suitcase of junk that had belonged to her. It was brittle, painted in a bean-hued green, and I am not sure exactly what I expected to find inside. I lay the suitcase flat on the floor and tried to snap open its locks with just my hands. But they had rusted stuck, so I brought a butter knife in from the kitchen and wedged it through, prying at the plastic edges. The hinges cracked finally, the suitcase folded out before me, and at once I was startled by its mustiness, its rubber-banded stacks and fat stuffed books, the old boxes, letters, and newspaper cutouts. Here was the essence of generations, the legacy of the Indian Jewish community of Bombay.

It was a mess and I began to move quickly into the piles, opening, touching, flipping through pages. I found a box of ash crumbs collected after an Indian dignitary was cremated. A worn book of psalms. A pile of pictures neatly razored out from magazines over the decades. A booklet scribbled with a convoluted family tree in Marathi. It was clear that there was no kind of order my twenty-something years could possibly impose upon all these things that were collected in almost a century of living. I had existed alongside this my whole life, but now I saw that I knew almost nothing about it. Had Nana-bai been around I would have asked her. And she would have been delighted to tell the stories, to see that they were of interest to my generation, to be lost in the remembering herself. But she was gone and I was frustrated. So very soon I began to research the history of Indian Jews on my own.

Through my makeshift study, I was able to piece together the fuzzy bits of history. I could follow along the various steps of the lineage and journey. But still the names and dates were meaningless, sitting silent, barren, unanswered. What more could I need, I asked myself one day weeks later, dissatisfied though I was surrounded by piles and piles of facts. I rummaged some more through the original suitcase, poring over pages I had flipped past, turning a small wooden box between my fingers. I looked more carefully through a stack of photographs which till then I had only skimmed. Suddenly, as I was toying with the lining of the suitcase, my hand slid into a flat silken pocket along the inner lid, and from inside it I pulled a booklet that I had never seen before. It was a diary.

I knew it was Nana-bai's. I knew the penmanship if only from birthday cards that she had often written me, her words round and slanted and always ending with this: May G-d give you long life, health, happiness, and the best husband, please G-d. Amen. But here as I began to read that handwriting, it played out in strange, gorgeous cursive trails of the mind. Things I had never even known about Nana-bai. Ideas and subjects I never could have guessed she was interested in or thinking about.

She wrote about her childhood as one of fourteen children. About living in India under British rule. About her husband and her own children. She recounted stories she had heard about her grandparents and their grandparents. She wrote about the years she lived with us when I was a child. What furniture she sold off when she moved between countries. Her medical problems when she was elderly. What she cooked. How much money she gave to people in the family. She wrote about how the Jewish holidays were uniquely celebrated in Bombay. How she survived the 1973 war living in Israel. There were also sections in the diary entitled "Facts to Know," in which she had written chapters of factual information on many diverse subjects. A summary of the history of Israel. The water bodies of the earth. British parliament. The chronology and ages of people in the Bible, beginning with Adam. Well-known quotations. Births and deaths of famous people. Other miscellaneous things: Who climbed Mt. Everest. When the world's first postal stamps were issued. In what year the phonograph was invented.

This diary was the book that stopped me. Something about its thorough neatness, the very strange fact of its collection, caused me to finally sit down by the suitcase in absolute wonder. There was something stunning here in the existence of it: quests and revelations, traces of my ancestors, secrets even. It was suppressed and intelligent and trying to leave a mark somewhere, if only on a piece of paper.

How did this book happen? Did Nana-bai write it in secret? What convinced her that her thoughts and daily goings-on were important, when the culture around her believed the contrary of women? Did she do it from boredom or excitement? Rebellion against the family or duty? Was she content or judgmental or proud or angry or tired or happy?

These were the questions I had to answer. They could not be found in the histories alone, and yet somehow they were reflected in my own life. In the blend within my face of my father's button nose and round cheeks, and of my mother's syrupy colors and eyes. In how my mother could tell me, "If you were walking down the street in Bombay, everyone would immediately know you were my daughter." And how my father could at the same time say, "You look exactly like my Aunt Rose from Brooklyn."

For so long I had quietly resented my family, the mix of cultures, the awkwardness that arose. The un-American sense of fashion. The way strangers looked at my father and I walking together, assuming that because I was brown and he was white, I must be his young girlfriend, not his daughter. The way my father was seen by the Indian side as a prized token of the white people, and my mother, in his circles, could be eyed coolly, because she was not Ivy League–polished and cardigan-clad. The way, even, that it seemed my only true allies were my brother and sisters, since my authenticity as a Jew was mistrusted by Jews, and as an Indian by Indians.

Both my parents were Jewish and they raised me as a Jew. In

making a biracial marriage in the 1970s, they did not see themselves as radicals. But theirs was probably the ultimate protest. They simply lived their lives and chose mates without regard to details like skin color. They searched only for another kindred soul, and a shared belief in G-d and old-fashioned family principles. This was what they passed on to me. Because for them, the religious belief and framework were more powerful and true to a person's soul than the culture of color alone. This is who I was on the inside.

But from the outside, no matter what the gradations in my mixed heritage, the shadow of Indian brown in my skin caused others to automatically perceive me as Hindu or Muslim. They could not imagine that I was Jewish because I did not look like a typical American Jew. And they attached to me a view of the world that spoke to my color only. Still I trekked through life with the spirit of a Jew, fleshed out by the unique challenges and wonders of a combined brown and white tradition.

Now, reading through Nana-bai's writing, I wondered if inside the resentment, suppression, confusion, and embarrassment, there could in fact be something breathtaking and true. For her and for me. The histories I had dug out from texts began to seem unimportant when put up against such things as what she thought about kissing, her goals, the people she admired most in the world, when and why she called upon G-d. And all that lay behind the foods she loved and the foods with which she feuded. There were so many stories in just her life alone. And what about all the lives before and after her? The mothers and the daughters that had bred her, that had bred me, that I myself would breed? I sat there fingering the crinkling, yellowed diary with new energy now and lost in thought.

Possessed by the details, I began to try and piece together

Nana-bai's legacy. When I could not find what I needed in her diary, I searched for it in the scraps and photos and letters from the suitcase. Or else in the memories of others in the family. Though sometimes people became tight-lipped over the most hushed of the secrets. And certain details no one now living ever knew to begin with. And after all that, when still there were gaps, I could for my part only reconstruct and imagine what long ago happened to her, filling in the blanks clumsily, earnestly trying to understand. So this was what the suitcase would give me in the end: the need to discover all these stories. Because somewhere, I felt sure, I would find myself in there, too.

PART ONE

# Portions of Pleasure

*I was teacher for five years at Bene Israel Home for Destitutes and Orphans. There were twenty boys and twenty girls, between ages nine and eighteen, who had no one to look after them. We had for them a classroom and beds, and for every Passover and New Year, all the children used to get new clothes, white shirts and pants for the boys and white dresses for the girls. Some of the teachers used to cane their students, but not me. I loved them and told them Bible stories, so they were very good with me.*

—NANA-BAI'S DIARY, PAGE 30

When the matchmaker first came for Nana-bai, he had a very reasonable proposition. As the late afternoon sun poured down, he seated himself, along with her mama and papa, in the shade by the house to discuss it. All three watched and waited quietly while Nana-bai brought out clean, damp hankies for them to refresh with. Then she served them tea and sweets and churda in small bowls. Usually there were servants to do such things. But this was a ceremony. And in these moments of serving the food and drink herself, Nana-bai's mannerisms and efficiency were demonstrating whether she was, in fact, fit to be a wife and mother and daughter-in-law. The matchmaker watched her as a merchant. Her mama watched her, sharp-eyed for details of crumbs and spilled drops. Her papa watched her with a soft heart. But Nana-bai only kept her eyes downcast throughout, her simple braids tucked behind her ears. She was twenty-four years old, and already it was embarrassingly late for a matchmaker.

The matchmaker took a thoughtful sip of tea as Nana-bai retreated to the house. Like any wily businessman, he usually tried to dispose up front with any illusion that might threaten the deal at hand. As if to say, yes, these vegetables are somewhat bruised, but they have plenty of good meat on them still, and let's face it, how much are you even offering me in return? He and his wife kept an account of the unmarried boys and girls in the community, biding their time and sizing up their bargaining points. Crossed eyes. Albino coloring. Stutterer. Elephantiasis of the legs. Strange birthmark on the face. If in meeting with any other family, he was presented with such a girl as Nana-bai, he would have said immediately, "Let us speak plainly. She is not a beauty. And she is very dark-skinned. And she is old." Then knowing the parents were anxiously waiting for him to continue, he would remain silent a few moments too many. For dramatic effect, he might also lean back in his seat and stretch a bit. A small man with weak arms and an unusually large stomach, when the matchmaker walked through the streets, he knew very well he looked awkward, even ugly. But in discussing brides and dowries at the very center of a transaction, he was exactly in his element, and appeared, he imagined, to be powerful and calculating.

But now he was not dealing with just any family. And as papa cleared his throat, the matchmaker saw that already he had been silent too long. He straightened up in his seat just a bit. "Sir. Your daughter is blessed to come from such a respected family. Everyone in this city admires you, sir, for your prosperity in the printing press, for your generosity towards the synagogue, for quietly taking so many orphans from the Bene Israel community to be your own adopted children. From all of my heart, I believe she will be a lucky bride for the right man." He looked around him at the sprawling house, and at their automobile—yes, an automobile, when even in Britain such a thing was a rarity.

Mama saw with disgust the way his eyes roved over their richness. She cringed at his sniveling mannerisms and greediness. But the matchmaker was required, to make a marriage sound. There had to be ceremony in everything, of course, but especially for something as serious as this. Mama had heard of two Jews from somewhere in Pune who married without a formal matching. It had been decided upon—if such a thing was even possible—by just the young man and woman. There had been no matchmaker. The parents themselves were barely involved. Good G-d, that kind of thing was not even really a marriage. The entire family was shamed because of it. And mama only shook her head sadly when she heard of this, because she knew no one from a good family would ever marry the children from that union.

"What is your proposal, sir?" papa said, not rude but pointed.

"There is a man who has come here just recently from the Jewish community in Cochin. His name is Moses. He oversees the school for orphans where your daughter teaches, and he himself has asked about her. Yes, what joy!" The matchmaker looked intently at mama and papa, as if to share their joy, and then upon seeing that they sat stone-faced, to try and prompt it.

"Kai-bug! But he is from another city, another community," mama said softly.

"Now, now," the matchmaker answered automatically, shaking his head and holding up his hands as if to let them dry. "I know you must be thinking, what can we know about this stranger? What do we know about his background? But he is a good man and educated. There are no cases of deformity or insanity in his family. He himself has told me how much he respects your daughter's cleverness with writing and books. And," he added, trying to be delicate, "he is willing to, ahem . . . overlook any shortcomings of maturity or otherwise." His fingers tapped one another nervously, allowing mama and papa to think.

"Are you willing to stand by this man, this Moses' reputation?" papa asked severely.

"With all due respect, sir," the matchmaker bowed his head slightly, "have I ever failed you before? Of all your fourteen children," he continued grandly, "I have matched ten of them. Ten. Look at your son Samuel. And your eldest twins. Look at the youngest girl you took in, Rebecca, now married to Solly five years because of me. And today they all prosper enough to have their own homes, and you have many beautiful grandsons and granddaughters from them. Think of it." Having delivered the words he knew were his proof, the matchmaker discreetly turned away. As he watched the servant's children playing nearby, he allowed the parents to consult quietly together.

"This man seems to have a genuine interest in her," papa said.

"Haa. And we cannot be too choosy now," mama agreed.

"True. She is twenty-four already."

"Yes," mama said, warming to the idea. "Yes, we are very fortunate in the end, that this Moses arrived from Cochin. Finally our daughter's cleverness has come to something."

When mama and papa informed Nana-bai of the engagement, she was surprised and pleased to learn that the man in question was Moses, the man from Cochin, whom she had often seen looking at her in the orphan's school. Now, when Nana-bai caught a glimpse of Moses, she blushed and modestly hid her face behind a corner of her sari. Certainly, she decided to herself, flustered, those bold eyes could never have come from here in Bombay. But when she prepared herself for the school day, she was more careful that her braids were tied smoothly and free of bumps. As she spoke to the orphans, held their small hands, she was especially gentle, and more aware than ever of the warmth and softness of their skin, the fragility of their bodies. Even at night, while drifting to sleep, she wondered: What would he say to me now? What would he do to me now? Wouldn't he enjoy if I prepared such a curry for him as I made tonight?

One day during lessons, the assistant who worked for Moses knocked on the door and came into Nana-bai's classroom with a letter for her. It was from Moses. "He asked that I give this to you and wait for a response."

"Kai-bug!" As her students read quietly to themselves, Nana-bai took her note to a corner and slowly tore the rice paper open. Inside it said just this, in neat print: "Are you agreed?" Such a pointless gesture, to ask this question, if she was agreed to their engagement. In fact, she had no right to agree or disagree at all. But still, he had asked it, and this made her catch her breath. She folded the paper up and put it into her handkerchief pocket, to take home and save, pressed tightly between the pages of a book. Then she took a new sheet of paper and wrote on it in round script letters: "Yes." That was their exchange.

Just a few days after the engagement was officially announced to the community, Moses was denounced as a drunk. A messenger boy had discovered him in his home, asleep over his books and papers, with an empty cask of wine at his desk. Soon everyone knew about it. Old men gossiped about him at the synagogue. Wives shook their heads over him as they fed their babies together. Even the Bene Israel newspaper ran a barbed editorial declaring that certain educators in the community seemed to have a thirst for far more than knowledge.

"The marriage is off," papa told Nana-bai. "It is because of the drinking."

"What?" she cried out in disbelief. "Because of the drinking? What if he was just tired? Or reading late into the night? What if it was just one drink? Is there something wrong with that?"

"I am surprised you even ask this," said papa stiffly. "That is unacceptable."

"I promise you, papa," Nana-bai cut in. "I am strong and I will teach him to never drink again."

"Maybe she is right." Mama proposed this now, under her breath. "We worried no one would marry her before. But now, after this—a broken engagement—her name will be ruined forever. She will be tainted. She will certainly never marry now."

"I have worked hard my whole life," papa said proudly. "And I should hope the good name I have built for my family will continue to stand as a strong reference behind her—no matter what. In any case," he added, "we cannot bring on such a shame to our family. We cannot."

Mama looked at him worriedly, but then she nodded her head and closed her eyes in resignation. Seeing this, Nana-bai begged him again to reconsider.

"Nai. It is already done," he told her with finality. "I have asked the matchmaker to end it."

Just then, a great bustle was heard moving through the house. Into the room came Rebecca and her husband, Solly, and their many toddling children. Rebecca had on all her gold jewelry and a new yellow silk sari, and as she approached Nana-bai she twirled in it slightly, waiting for a murmur of admiration. "We are going to the theater," she told her. "And the children's ayah has fallen ill. So I knew you would be a dumpling for me and watch them. Haa? It would be so good of you."

Nana-bai placed a hand on Rebecca's shoulder, holding herself up for a moment in the flurry. "Do you know?" she choked. "My engagement. My engagement is off."

"Kai-bug! Oh, my dumpling. You may never find another husband again. That is terrible," Rebecca told her, scratching at an invisible smudge on her sari. She leaned in confidentially and whispered, "I have heard, though, that he was a drunk. That would have been a disgrace for us all. So you will soon feel relieved that you did not marry him." She patted Nana-bai's hand and paused a moment, as if to let her sincerity sink in. Then she continued. "I know what will make you feel better, though. Taking care of the little ones this evening. They were so excited to come see their auntie, weren't you, dumplings?" She turned to her children who stood clustered around their father a step away, while he watched the exchange between the women. Solly was a brittle, unsmiling presence among their young faces. A hard intellectuality spread out from behind his spectacles and his long poised fingers. As though on signal, the children ran happily toward Nana-bai and fell onto her and pulled on her legs. "Thank you, dumpling," Rebecca told her, taking Solly's arm as they left. She made a kissing sound to her over the shoulder.

"Aiaa!" As they closed the door behind them, in the first and last moment she was ever unhinged, Nana-bai gave a terrible cry of grief. It was so loud and anguished, like the graceless braying of an animal, that her mama and papa were startled out of their seats. Even the children scurried away for a moment, frightened.

Usually, Nana-bai was soft-spoken, timidly obedient. But now there had been a man, a smart man who saw something in her, and she had seen something in him, too. And before she was able to visit him alone, speak to him up close, close enough to smell his scent even, it had all been taken away.

"Well, Ruthie," papa said severely, ruffled at being made to jump in this way. "Well. It is done," he told her firmly, as he and mama settled back into their chairs once more. And now, as Nana-bai took a seat across from them, quiet, defeated, gathering the children back into her lap, something whispered to her of what lay ahead, and she trembled.

*"The man who gives pleasure is as charitable as he who relieves suffering."*                        *—George Moore*

—Nana-bai's diary, page 44

*T*he first moment of pleasure I remember was a taste of peanut butter.

I remember other early pleasures, of course. I hung by my knees from the apple tree. I went scuba diving at the bottom of the bathtub. I chewed on my thumb. And all these things were pleasurable. But my parents had assembled a careful nest of rules inside our home—to shelter us from the world and to mold us with unity, respect, and old-fashioned healthy priorities. So, naturally, the most remarkable pleasures, like peanut butter, lived outside these.

When I put my ear to the settling floorboards of our home, I heard rules over everything. Over wind chimes. Over Mommy's pancake-batter whisking. Over late-night giggling. Over the dog barking. Over doors creaking. The rules told me: Before your elders, sit and be quiet, listen and learn; be unified, be friends and protectors first for your brother and sisters, not random boys and girls in the neighborhood; don't watch shoot-ups and kissy television because they will fill your mind with nonsense, with bubbameinses. Especially, I heard: Frivolous sweets are forbidden. Chocolate and pink breakfast cereals and cake and ice cream, even Halloween candy, were automatically suspect in a way that made my young self feel suddenly awakened to the injustices of the world. Somehow though, peanut butter managed to slip through the cracks. This sweet, creamy, crunchy stuff was not only used in all manner of chocolate cups and snack cakes, but—by some oversight in our house or a twist of nutritional logic that I could not understand—it was also put onto sandwiches and kept freely in large tubs in our very own kitchen.

One day, my big sister Gertie and I swiped a jar of peanut butter and ran into the bathroom with it. A moment later, in the hallway, I heard my younger brother Tzvi padding around, suspicious for sensing some bit of mischief in which he was not involved. And baby Batsheva crawling by, scratched at the closed door, curious, simply because it was closed. They, too, would have enjoyed this treat, but Gertie and I instinctually knew the success of our mission depended upon efficiency. Inevitably there would be casualties. So we grimly cut our losses and worked wordlessly then, listening for any adult sounds from the hall, bare feet planted on the cold blue tile as though ready to run at any moment. We were careful to not leave telltale marks on silverware or bags of bread. We screwed open the jar and dug in with our fingers, clawlike, into the peanut butter, emerging with handfuls that we sucked clean. It was divine. I flipped over the toilet cover, climbed up, and stood atop it triumphantly, puckering with the peanut butter grip in my mouth. It was Jif, still cold from the refrigerator, and I remember that even after we snuck the jar back and washed our hands, I continued to smell peanut butter traces from underneath my fingernails.

The first moment of pain I can remember was when I broke my leg.

This was not, obviously, the only pain from my youth. In all my adventures, inevitably, I was cut, scraped, bruised, poked, and torn quite regularly, often achieving feats of astounding acrobatics along the way. On one occasion, I even managed to get one of my limbs caught up inside a moving bicycle tire as it passed me randomly on the road. But, of all these instances, my broken leg stood out to me, since the hurt was so tremendous and since, in the end, I brought it on myself.

It was the tail end of a cold winter, and all I wanted to do was hurry up the warm weather. So I reached into the back of storage and pulled out a pair of sandals from last summer. "It's time. It's *definitely* warm enough," I insisted pointedly to Mommy, as if insistence alone could shape the reality, as if spring were a deity to be bargained with or tricked. I put on a wrinkled T-shirt and shorts, too, and dragged Gertie out into the weak white sunlight.

"I'm telling you. Come play inside. It's not sandals weather," Mommy called after me. But I ignored this and my own goosebumps, and raced into the backyard despite her. "Ach, she's a stubborn girl." Then she threw up her hands when inevitably Tzvi and Batsheva followed our exodus.

We tied one end of a jump rope to the gate, and Gertie held the other end, turning it for me. Tzvi had scoffed at our play, saying jumping rope was for girls. So when Batsheva plopped down on the ground near us to watch, he felt outnumbered and promptly scooped her into a red wagon and wheeled her away into the garage. I stood, chilly, just outside the loop made by the rope, expertly watching the red and white stripes turn and beat the ground in rhythm, readying myself for the perfect moment of entry. I gave a small hop under the rope, feet tucked into my knees as it slashed the ground, and we started to chant. "Teddy bear, teddy bear, turn around. Teddy bear, teddy bear, touch the ground. Teddy bear, teddy bear, go upstairs. Teddy bear, teddy bear, say your prayers."

Suddenly a sandal strap loosened, and its leather, still stiff from basement storage, slipped out from under me against the frosty pavement. My feet came down at a strange, clumsy angle, and I hit the concrete, snapping bone hotly. As I cried and screamed from an agony I could not believe existed, Gertie, Tzvi, and Batsheva approached me with faces of absolute wonder. And, not yet knowing the gravity of the situation, Mommy heard some seemingly generic noise from inside the porch where she and Nana-bai polished the brass pots. "See?" she called to Daddy, drinking coffee in the kitchen. "I told you *something* would happen."

Day to day, I just lived my life, and I never thought outright about such ideas of pleasure and pain. Until years later, when I reached high school and read *Narcissus and Goldmund* by Herman Hesse. I was in English class, and Mr. Pinnell was discussing the first part of the book, which we had been assigned for homework. An avid reader, and a little too proud of myself, it seemed to me that in just those few beginning pages, I had already harnessed the entire novel. So, at my desk, I flipped ahead through the chapters. My pencil point finally, randomly stopped on a page and a passage. And from its scramble of words, Hesse's hero emerged and confided to me, softly, this bit of his thoughts, that the look on a woman's face during orgasm is just like the look on her face as she struggles to give birth.

At first I breezed through the lines. Then I read them and reread them and underlined them with my pencil, stunned. I was fascinated by this idea. Not only because of the artistic layers and beauty in this picture. Of contorted lines, closed eyes, cheeks tightened expectantly, extremes overlapping and unfolding into each other as a body, arched and poised in grace then surrenders to something animal. But also because it captured the intangible quality at stake. That no matter how much someone else rejoices for me in my pleasure, or comforts me in my pain, in the end I am alone. During those achingly vulnerable magnified moments when pleasure or pain runs its course, just my one body is there, a slave to it, self-consumed, answering to my own particular set of nerve endings.

A home's set of rules will sometimes go so far as to dictate and nurture specific responses to pleasure and pain. The mix of cultures in our house deemed that a degree of hearty stoicism, both to pleasure and pain alike, was the true test of one's self. My parents had learned from the generations before them to sacrifice and toil feverishly until the end, without luxurious 401(k) plans and early retirement. And this was what they passed on. "Work hard and don't complain about the small things," we were always told. My parents took this line from the middle of comfortable Ohio because both, at the very core of their souls, harbored a dream. The tough, laboring, ideological dream of Zionist pioneer settlers. All that propelled the men and women who had come to Israel in the early twentieth century and raised a nation from the sand with just their sweat.

My father grew up in Cleveland, and all his life he was

surrounded by Jews who tried to neatly shed their ties to the Old World. They changed their telling names, Kleinberg and Horowitz. They put up Christmas trees in their home—for decoration, and to keep up with the neighbors. That was all he knew of Judaism. But then one day, he picked up a copy of a book by Leon Uris called *Exodus*. It told of a different breed of Jews. Jews who were once pale and beaten in Europe's ghettos. Who migrated to the land of Israel, planted trees, shot guns to defend themselves, and transformed themselves into heroes. And this picture, this surprising twist, inspired him to unprecedented feelings of loyalty, pride, and ideological yearning for a new kind of Judaism and Israel.

My mother, on the other hand, instead of just reading about this dream, actually spent her childhood living it. Transplanted from India to a still-crude Israel, she worked the budding desert, attempting to spring a civilization. Milking cows. Picking tomatoes. Serving in the army. Building homes. Eating, when there was nothing else to eat, just bread and salt and being satisfied. And for her, once the glamour faded, it left a hardcore belief in the country she was creating. Having actually lived the hardship, however, she was not so much an idealist. She was more the type to seize any small morsel of happiness in the present, and push the trials of the past behind her. "Make lemonade from lemons," she always said, not like a cliché but like she had come to this conclusion herself one day working out in the lemon groves.

One a dreamer, the other tried and proven; for both of my parents, the land of Israel was at the base of everything good and honest and strong in the world. It was a place where Jews, for so long nomads and victims, might finally live free. A place where all people could be equal. Where their own kindness, and their unshakable faith in the kindness of others, might finally find a home.

Nothing could be more important than contributing to such a place. They hoped that at some point our family would move there to be a part of this, to live simply and heartily on the Israeli frontier. And though in the end they only had four kids to offer the cause—instead of the ten they once dreamed about—for much of our young lives, we as a family were in training for this.

As part of the preparation, ours was not a family of conveniences. We did not own appliances like hairdryers, dishwashers, air-conditioning. When we traveled, we never bothered with the excessive luxury of public transportation. Instead we drove our own clunky car for days cross-country, waving off the flu or the chicken pox. Then we cramped six people, plus Nana-bai sometimes, onto one king-size bed in a motel room. Why buy a box of tissues, special, when you could just stuff a wad of clean toilet paper into your pocket? Why take a cab ride when you could easily walk twenty wintry city blocks? When there was work to be done around the house, we never hired anyone to help us unless the plumbing or electricity breaks were life-threatening. Why pay someone to mow the lawn or wash the car or move heavy furniture when there were plenty of strong souls in the family who could do it? We did this work, not for an allowance as other children might have done, but from expectations of family duty and for the ethic of getting our hands dirty. Once, so we could experience farm life though we lived in the city, we even bought a live goose and fattened it up in the basement for a week. Then we took it to the kosher butcher to slaughter and pluck ourselves. In truth, sometimes our preparation for pioneering was medieval.

But, because of all this, for years the slur Jewish American Princess did not even click in my understanding. To me, being Jewish meant rolling up your sleeves. A rugged sort of living and healthy minimalism. It was closely connected to a peasant life. Very remote from the wealth and opulence that were implied in this American slang.

Beyond my parents, the ethic of hard work was especially passed down through Nana-bai. Though my parents' grand ideal drove the direction of our family, in the day to day details it was Nana-bai who brought it to life.

When I looked at photographs of Nana-bai, I saw a woman in her nineties, with a thin, hard body and clear skin. She wore the wrinkles of age and delicate sari around her in majesty. She peered at the camera evenly, certainly, with a pleasant look on her face but without a smile. "See?" I heard her telling me. "It is not necessary to be loud and vulgar and laughing. Hoo hoo hoo. Ha ha ha," she exaggerated for me, as an example. "Nai. But be solemn and serious. That is good."

Not to imply we couldn't enjoy, of course. "I was turning somersaults until just a few years ago, you know," she often reminded me in a way that seemed vaguely challenging. As though after hearing it, I myself needed to turn somersaults on the spot, to prove that I could enjoy, too. And Nana-bai throughout her life had a profound weakness for chocolate ice cream. But above all, there had to be a mode of womanly decorum maintained. Somersaults were practiced in private. And even her pleasure in ice cream was admitted to reluctantly, almost joking that she did not really like it, denying that *she* should be the cause of a half gallon Breyer's purchase.

This same philosophy was applied to pain, too. Often I saw Nana-bai cooking in the kitchen, picking up heavy, hot pots with just a thin dishtowel, as though she did not feel the burn through its cloth. Sometimes as she worked at the stove, drops of scalding oil splashed her arm. But she just wiped these away and continued stirring, only running her arm under water when there was enough time. How could she do that? I wondered to myself. Just one drop of hot oil on my arm brought tears to my eyes as I flew to nurse it under the faucet. She felt the pain, of course. But there was work to be done, a meal that had to be prepared. So she put the pain aside.

An impressive discipline to try and live up to. Feeling all, both good and bad, but never cracking one way or the other. This kind of strength helped sustain Nana-bai in the larger pleasures and pains of her life, too. But growing up in a different country, I was never able to truly emulate her. Perhaps there was less balance in my life. Perhaps my pleasures and pains were not as simple as hers. Or maybe they were just easier to come by. At the heart of it, though, there were moments when I had no cool dignity about me at all. When I was at the whim of these sensations, and I showed myself raw. There were things I couldn't just suck up and get over and control. I had not yet found that hardwire will in me. Surely, it was in part my nostalgia that colored in her culture of silence with quaint, unattainable dignity. Still, I often wished that I had some of Nana-bai's no-nonsense presence for myself.

Because when it came to my own life, pleasure and everything briny-hungry-earthy delighted me and frightened me. Pleasure lived regally within the intimate cupboard drawers of my body. It lay nestled somewhere between slinky tights, panties, slips, and bathing suits that still smelled faintly of seaweed and clam shells. For all pleasure dictated—muse, want, touch—it lacked only the scurry of barefoot slaves, the rustle of peacock feather fans. So I paid pleasure its due homage myself, arranging and rearranging the smorgasbord of soft cloths surrounding it, now setting the silks like a blanket of succotash, now layering the colors like a finger-painted birthday cake. Humbly I followed pleasure's inexplicable summons. And I tried to do it hushedly.

But once when I was in college, some man, a stranger, eyed me and pegged me from the start. "You are obviously a creature of pleasure," he said. Maybe this was a compliment, or some attempt at seduction. Still, all I felt at that moment was vaguely suspicious that my skirt was too short. Or that I had not an ounce of mystery left about me.

"No. I'm not," I told him in my embarrassed, ruffled self-defense, spiriting quickly away. He had seen something I would not face.

On the other end of this spectrum, I was deathly afraid of fire. If I were Nana-bai, I would have gotten over this fear long ago. There would be meals to make over an open gas flame. And there would be no patience for making fusses, or for trying to pinpoint the exact psychological moment of childhood that marked the origin of this fear. And yet, because I was me and not Nana-bai, I did not use matches. And even when I blessed the Shabbat candles, I used a foot-long lighter that stretched the flame a safe distance from me.

The most horrific thing in the world for me to think about was the slow melting death of a person on fire. Fire came to me in my nightmares, from scenes in movies. And I imagined the tiny burns I had felt in an instant touching a hot radiator, multiplied infinitely all over my body. Not just through skin, but through hair and flesh and organs. This fear made the sour taste of vomit come to my mouth. And in my very depths, I knew I could lose my humanity to fire, shamefully selling even G-d and my loved ones, if only I myself might escape.

These were the pains and pleasures that made me silly, giddy, weak even. They did not possess the sense of proportion that they would have had in Nana-bai's life. And knowing that, I felt like a doll on clumsy wooden legs, trying to keep in its muppet-stuffing. But still, it was just this contrast between my life and hers that drove me to wonder. To remember peanut butter and tripping over a jump rope with a vividness that marked me. To ponder the pains so deeply. And especially to cling to the pleasures. Because someday, when I grew old myself, these were probably the things I would try to pass on. And very likely by then, I, too, would seem to be a relic in my good intentions.

*Fact: Tea leaves grew in China and were discovered for use thousands of years ago by emperor when leaves accidentally blew into boiling water. In 1667 they started using tea in England.*

*One Lipton tea bag may be used, pressed, and saved for three cups if looking to pinch pennies.*

—NANA-BAI'S DIARY, PAGE 12

*T*he greatest daily pleasure of my childhood was tea time. From the soft shell of warm blanket and pillow, my afternoon nap rolled into half-awake luxury, then abruptly snapped at the sound of the teakettle whistling. I rubbed my eyes and stumbled into the kitchen where Nana-bai waited patiently near a fragile china cup and saucer, both spotted by chipped green flowers. She turned off the stove and poured the cup full of boiling water. Then she screwed open an old gold-colored Brooke Bond Tea canister filled with different kinds of tea bags. She dug right past the fruity tea bags, of course, choosing the same old-fashioned Lipton tea every time and submerging it in the scalding water. The liquid turned a deep clear auburn. She stirred in milk and two spoons of sugar. Then she had a piece of toast on the side, to spread with margarine and dip in the tea every so often. Tea time was never so much an American pastime. But Nana-bai brought it from British India into our home. So it became part of our culture, too. And when Nana-bai prepared her tea, my brother and sisters and I clamored to share in the mysterious ritual of it, begging for sips of its perfection.

Eventually, when I grew older, I became too big to take sips from her cup of tea. It would have been awkward to take a warm cup away from an old woman's lips; clumsy, crass, unnatural even. So, instead, I tried to recreate her perfect tea myself. I experimented with bags and bags of Lipton. Then, unsuccessful, I turned hardcore with black tea and iced tea and crazy herbal varieties. But none of them ever tasted quite right. And finally I gave up trying to orchestrate something so delicate.

When I was a child, Nana-bai happily made fresh tea for us, of course. But in our own mugs tea never was as extraordinary or magical as when we drank it in molten gulps from hers. It is possible that the tea we drank alone was not as tasty as Nana-bai's for very unmagical reasons. Maybe as Nana-bai partook, she knew just how long to dip her toast in the tea, so the toast melted and the tea became buttery. Maybe, when she made these separate cups, she let her tea brew more strongly. Or else she added extra sugar to ours. More likely, simply the victory of commandeering someone else's treats was what exhilarated our senses.

Still, the bites and sips she offered from her own cup were so delicious, it was as if we were no longer devouring such plain ingredients as tea and toast, but something else entirely. I genuinely wondered if there was some enchantment at play. If with one snap of Mary Poppins' fingers, Nana-bai literally transformed dry bread and hot water into some delightful cake-and-cream concoction. The kind of concoction that, in stories, paupers sold their souls for. Or that erupted from magical bottomless pots which would cook and cook and not stop cooking until a secret spell was uttered. At that green age, it would not have surprised me in the least.

During the bubble in my childhood when tea's pleasure was everything, the world was formed as much by reality as by the imagination. Directions for crossing the street, and concepts like war and honesty, were as significant and true as lullabies and nursery rhymes. These were magical years in which there seemed to be no reason why Monopoly money should not buy real-life groceries. The melody tinkled from a windup toy was as grand as the music of an orchestra. And dolls and jack-in-the-boxes were as much my friends as Gertie, Tzvi, and Batsheva. At school, I colored in pictures of Noah and his ark, and learned about the sinners of Soddom and King Solomon's wisdom. And these adventures seemed, word for word, to inhabit my life.

This side-by-side existence of fact and fiction was fueled by the usual fairy tales read to me at night from cardboard picture books. I made wishes (always in sets of three, of course). I practiced curtsying with serious diligence in case, as I every day expected, I should soon be called to court to dance alongside kings and unicorns. Earnest and practical, I even followed some of the most important lessons daily: When going through the forest, be sure to leave a trail of stones, not breadcrumbs. Check where your secret passageways lead and that your apples are not poisoned. And never ever assume that a frog is just a frog.

Beyond witches and spells, what took root in me most deeply and pleasurably were the Jewish-tinged folk tales that came down through my family—both from the Indian side and the Eastern European side. These stories were starkly different. Their characters, some in saris and others in heavy fur coats, often eyed each other suspiciously from the dark corners of my mind. Every now and then, one or another reached a bullish rage and pushed to the front of my thoughts, demanding priority. But then at other times, both sides surprisingly intertwined, like in a fantastic cartoon where cat and dog are suddenly lovers in a backdrop of rainbow whirls and kazoo whistles.

From my father's family came tales in the tradition of *The Wise Men of Chelm* and *Fiddler on the Roof.* Stories of men in the shtetl, trying to capture the moon in a barrel or loving their daughters too much to let them grow up. These stories were practically institutionalized. And charming, too, with their thick, glossed books to back them up.

From my mother's side came stories of Indian Jews. These were never so polished or wry. Never with the tangible libraries behind them. But they were substantiated instead because they were straightforward and earthy. And in them, where a woman's modesty was always being tested, where animals and plants and moons matter-of-factly came alive, the lessons were both simple and large.

One of the stories from Russia that touched me most was passed down to my father from my great-great-great-grandmother Anna. "It was Easter time," my father would begin, as I slipped under the bed covers and propped up against a pillow. "And in honor of the holiday, priests had riled up the peasants with anti-Semitic cries. Cossacks got drunk on vodka singing songs against Christ-killers. And now they were all tearing through the villages in a loose pogrom, killing Jews and burning their homes.

"Anna quickly gathered her eight children together and escaped into the nearby forest. They searched and searched the thick greenery for a place to hide, but they found nothing. Finally, just as they were becoming desperate, they discovered a small hole that led back into a hidden underground cave. It was not large. But it was out of the way, and would fit the whole family if they squeezed. So one by one they crawled in, helping the very young children, trying to cover up the tracks behind them. Then they waited in the darkness for hours—many long hours—keeping the babies as quiet as possible.

"Soon they heard the sounds of approaching horses and foot-steps. Anna and her children closed their eyes and held their breaths, praying the strangers would not notice the hole and ride by. Even the babies knew not to make a noise. But eventually, stomachs turning, they heard one deadly voice calling for a halt. Above, shuffling bodies and voices came closer, circling the cave. 'Look,' someone said, rough. 'There may be Jews hiding in there.' The men stood around the hole discussing this for a few moments. But then, as if by some miracle, they did not climb down. They trudged back to their horses and rode off instead.

"What happened?" my father often asked me at this point in the story, as though I did not know. Then he told me. And each time I was amazed as if, in fact, I had never heard it before. "In the time that Anna and her children had been hiding in the cave, a spider had spun a web over the opening."

"If any Jews were inside," one of the Cossacks reasoned, not ea-ger to scuff his newly polished shoes to no end, "they would have broken the web on their way down. Let's not waste our time. There's no one inside." Soon after, the family dug its way out of the cave and went home. Anna and her children survived. And all their descendants—including myself—were given life because of that one spider. That spider who, with all the space in the world, chose to spin a web over those critical few inches, in the hours when a handful of Jews waited quaking below.

This story was magical. But as I grew older, I began to feel suspicious. One day, owlish and a know-it-all—like a vigilante out to uncover the truth behind the tooth fairy—I confronted my father. "Daddy, we learned in Torah class that that exact same spider story happened to David from the Bible, when he was hiding from King Saul. I think our great-great-great-grandmother Anna must have made it up that this story happened to her. I think she just *copied* it from him," I told him, skeptical, folding my arms across my chest.

"I don't know," he said thoughtfully, undaunted by my tough line. "It could have happened twice." Then he shrugged. "That is the story she told me. Besides, I remember that out of gratitude after that, she never killed a spider for the rest of her life."

I thought guiltily about all the spiders I had killed simply because they took me by surprise in my closet or on the porch. Well, I decided to myself, if she did that, then I could at least *try* to believe. And so I tried.

Some nights Nana-bai tucked me into bed and I heard her stories instead. "Make sure you brush your teeth," she clucked. "Did you choose a pajama to wear?" She knew that often in the heat of summer, I tried to sleep with no bedclothes on at all. I crawled into bed and pulled the sheets up to my chin, hoping she would not notice. Then a square of bare back slipped out. "But it is not good to have just bare skin inside your sheets," she worried. "It will make you dream." So she took a pink nightgown from my drawer and helped me poke my head and arms through it. "There. Tsangla. Good." Then she began her story. "I heard this from my Eliza auntie when I was a little girl. And she heard it from her grandmamma when she was a little girl. Her grandmamma came long ago from the village by the ocean where the whole thing must have happened." She named the village for me then as if I would make a connection. But I waved it off impatiently and a moment later forgot it. What could that mean to me? Greedy, I only wanted the story.

"Once there was a young husband and wife. He was handsome and hardworking. She was light-skinned and faithful. They had a small, clean home, and just enough food to live happily. They even had a beautiful saffron-colored dog who had wandered out of the wilderness. When he first appeared, the wife fed him a bone of chicken. And since then the beautiful saffron-colored dog had followed them everywhere and guarded their home at night. But one thing was missing for the couple: they did not have any children. The wife prayed to G-d every day, asking for babies, especially for sons. But years went by and she did not become pregnant. People in the village started looking at her with pity, shaking their heads. Her mother-in-law began whispering furiously against her. 'My son's wife is such a barren and sickly girl, she would be better off dead.'

"Finally the wife decided to go ask for the help of a wise old woman who lived just outside the village. The old woman took the wife's hands and sniffed her skin and felt her stomach. This is what she told her: G-d gives us what we need. The wife returned to her husband and told him with peace and confidence: G-d gives us what we need. When the villagers pointed at her, she said: G-d gives us what we need. Especially when her mother-in-law poked her bitterly she assured her: G-d gives us what we need. The wife was confident that she would have a baby. And soon in fact she began to grow rounder and rounder. Haa. Now if ever she walked through the village with her husband and their beautiful saffron-colored dog, her stomach went before her importantly.

Villagers nodded and smiled at her and said: G-d should favor you with a boy. Even her mother-in-law saved the good pieces of meat for her to eat. 'For my grandson,' she said caressing the wife's stomach.

"During spring, the baby was born. He was the fattest, most beautiful baby anyone had ever seen, and all the Jews in the village came joyfully to celebrate his circumcision outside their small house. They cut off a little bit of skin down there and as he cried out healthily the village burst into cheers. The new mother took her baby into the house to soothe him and put him to sleep in his cradle. Then she and her husband received warm wishes from some of their neighbors, while the mother-in-law ushered their other guests to a board full of food."

Here in the story, Nana-bai digressed. Sometimes as she was telling it, there were all kinds of savory meats offered, chicken and fish and lamb. At other times, there were only sweets, fruits, cakes, jellies. No matter which version she was telling, as she described the foods' tenderness and spices, the way guests mixed with each other and took whole handfuls of salted nuts and mango pieces, my mouth inevitably watered. And each time, enchanted and hungry, I was caught off guard when she came to the story's end.

"Just then," Nana-bai would say, without skipping a beat, "the beautiful saffron-colored dog came out of the house to where all the guests were eating and drinking and talking with the family. His mouth was pulled back grimly, exposing his teeth, his fur stood on end, and his face was a mess of blood.

"The soft hum of chatter and food halted in shock at this spectacle, and then the mother-in-law screamed with terror: 'That dog has eaten our baby boy!' In the paralyzed panic that followed, there were cries of anger from the men in the group, and the women began to sob uncontrollably.

"The mother-in-law turned furiously on the wife then: 'How could you leave the boy alone?' Some of the men took up heavy rocks and with several deadly blows managed to reduce the dog to a messy, still pulp. Then the whole crowd rushed into the home to uncover the scene of the horror, to find any remains of the baby. And what did they find? Aiaa. There slept the baby, peaceful in his cradle with a white blanket around him. On the floor below, still half-coiled around the cradle's leg in a twisted pile, was a giant dead snake, broken and ripped bloody. The beautiful saffron-colored dog had killed the snake in defending their baby. But now he, too, was dead. This was what came of foolishness."

When the story ended, I was overwhelmed with sadness for the beautiful saffron-colored dog. Each time, I asked Nana-bai the same questions over and over: "Did that really happen? How could they be so mean? Why did they kill the dog before even finding out what happened? Why did the wife let her mother-in-law push her around? What happened afterwards?"

To all these things, she said simply, "Nai. That's all. That's how it was." Then she kissed me good night and turned off the lights, though I remained wide awake, appalled and doubting, under the covers.

At times I tried to imagine my ancestors, the determined women I'd always heard about, who crafted the stories I lived by. My great-great-great-grandmother Anna, who lived through the spider miracle, who considered herself the final word on most everything. In her old age, I was told, she sat at the table, with a dish of noodles before her, philosophizing for her children and grandchildren about the correct name of the dish they ate: "Well," she'd explain in her heavy accent, "some says kugel. Some says kigel. But I"—here she'd point to herself as the authoritative voice of modernity—"*I* says pudding." In her vehemence, she even pounded the table, causing the silverware to clatter loudly. I figured she'd take the opportunity of having the whole family gathered at a meal to tell the spider story again, reliving the details and exaggerating without a thought. If one surly child, tired of hearing that story so often, tried to break away from the table, she'd probably reach for her cane to catch him with its hook and pull him back. That was Anna.

Nana-bai's Eliza auntie was a power in her own way. She, too, told her story about the beautiful saffron-colored dog over and over for her family in India. But she told it more sedately, gorgeously, with a quiet forcefulness, when she and her daughters were washing the sheets, maybe. While her wet fingers wrinkled in demonstrating the proper way to soap and scrub, she'd describe the fate of the saffron-colored dog seriously, as though she had witnessed the tragedy herself. If a young daughter rolled her eyes at hearing the story yet again, a stern look from Eliza auntie stopped her at once. Perhaps a little less brazen than Anna, however, Eliza auntie would acknowledge that she added the detail of the dog being saffron-colored. "I don't know *exactly* what color he was. But I am certain he was some kind of brown," she would say primly, feeling the need to explain why she took that poetic license, not even knowing why herself. She did not recognize this artist's clay beneath her fingernails. Then, stiff in her petticoats, she returned to hawkishly supervising the sheets. That was Eliza.

Anna and Eliza came from different climates, different prejudices. They had different animals and colors and people populating their stories. Had they known about the joint destiny of their descendants, they might have been frightened by the foreignness. In her Russian village, Anna might have wrinkled her nose at the smell of India heat. In her Bombay home, Eliza would have raised an eyebrow at the Ashkenazi gefilte fish and herring. One outlandish, the other too proper, they certainly would have disagreed with each other's storytelling methods.

And yet, though these women were vastly and obviously different from each other, in essence they were the same. Both women, despite all they calculated in their legacies, could never have envisioned needing to fight for the attention of their descendants, of me, and competing with strange stories over which they had no authority. They certainly did not anticipate Disney. Or television. Or the tempting distractions of elves and fairies and pumpkins that poofed into carriages. They saw that sometimes as they told the stories themselves, their own children and grandchildren made fusses. But they hoped that someday once the stories trickled through the generations, their words would be unquestioned and revered.

So I think that in the end, despite their differences, and the fact that the joining of cultures took place so many years after they themselves lived, my Indian and European ancestors would have, in fact, been allies, based on the stories alone.

I tried to imagine how it would be, if we all three could have somehow sat down at the table together for tea. Anna would drink her tea from a glass, a sugar cube held in her mouth to sweeten the tea as she sipped it down. Eliza auntie, like Nana-bai, would take her tea with milk and toast and all the ceremonies the British managed to reproduce in every corner of the world they dominated, at four o'clock, sharp. I would refuse my own tea and even hot chocolate. I would instead take advantage of this chance to seize upon the pleasure of drinking from their cups as much as I liked.

Then they would take turns telling their stories. Eliza auntie would cringe when throughout her tale Anna pounded a fist for emphasis. As Eliza auntie talked softly and steadily, Anna would interrupt her and demand that she speak up. But still both would prod my hesitation and disbelief, defending each other. Eliza auntie would tell me severely: "Haa. If she says that this miracle happened with the spider, then it must be true."

Anna would say: "Girl, don't drift off, listen to what your auntie has to say." And she would lean forward intently to hear the story herself, so that she might then contribute her own opinion.

Both women would agree with each other long enough to fuss and chastise me for skepticism or scorn. Then, while I willed myself to believe, both would sit back together, stirring their tea, congratulating—and attempting to reassure—one another on the survival of wisdom.

*"Love is swift, sincere, pious, pleasant, gentle, strong, pa-tient, faithful, prudent, long-suffering, manly, and never seek-ing her own; for wheresoever a man seeketh his own, there he falleth from love."*          —*Thomas A. Kempis*

—Nana-bai's diary, page 50

As a child, I was too shy to think outright about the giggling-pointing-oohing-aahing pleasures between boys and girls, but still I grew up with a remarkable example before me: my par-ents seemed to have a blessed marriage. As a child, I watched them share a rare intimacy, woven through with familiar jokes and comfortable silences. They knew each other so well that I never succeeded in playing one against the other in order to, say, be al-lowed to wear nail polish, or play with a boy. "No, you're too young," my father would tell me, not bothering to look up from the newspaper. He wouldn't even have to consult my mother, but simply knew that she would agree on her own and give me the same answer when I slyly sought a second opinion. They were partners, in the old-fashioned sense of the word. Where they both knew and accepted, even expected their roles. That he drove the car and she made him coffee. That he earned the bulk of the family money and she was the one to sit down and write out the bills. Surrounded by latchkey kids and corporate moms, my mother sacrificed her own education and career so his could thrive and she could do the most important work of all: raising the children at home. And in the end, his successes, plaques, and diplomas were as much his as hers. Partners in that way. And they were dancing partners, too. At parties, upon the first notes of music, my parents rose from the table as one, feet tapping, fingers intertwined, thrilled. They danced with such pleasure and synchronized grace that others on the floor would stop their own dancing to watch. Sometimes they argued, even drove each other crazy. And we had our share of illness and hardship. But then they boiled cups of tea and sat to talk, throughout it all, clinging together, continuing to love fiercely and to laugh.

Both my parents are remarkable people. When I was young, they seemed, also, to be perfect. They met when my father spent several months in Israel studying Hebrew at a language school where my mother worked as a secretary. "I signed up for a six-week course," he always jokes. "I didn't know I was signing up for life."

My mother is stunningly beautiful and plays the mandolin. She is a woman who, given yarn and fresh grass and macaroni, somehow will spin her fingers resourcefully and turn these ingredients into something efficient, artful, and possibly even delicious. An ideal hostess in the traditional Indian manner, she would cook for hours behind the scenes, fulfilling every wish of her guests. Every hunger. Every craving. Every itch.

My father, who has traveled the world, is a scholar and an ex-marine. He has always contained so much knowledge that, sitting at the dinner table, I could ask him about anything from ancient

Africa to Shakespeare to obscure tropical diseases, and he would casually launch into a detailed explanation. A dynamic renaissance man, he has always had a genuine interest in all people and all things.

And yet, beyond these elements of what seemed to be mutual perfection, I think now that their happiness comes from something grittier. From their commitment to each other and to family, which was flavored by Nana-bai and her old-fashioned Indian tradition. This ethic was shaped by a history in which couples were betrothed as babies. According to a story Nana-bai told, two children had once been betrothed, but the boy died even before they were married, at age eight. After that, as the girl grew up, she was considered a widow and could never marry again. As if condemned from then on, in order to have enough money for food, she could only work cleaning corpses for the rest of her life. The promise between a couple, in that world, was a bond that transcended even death.

Nana-bai's ethic was heralded on my parents' first date, when she and some of the other family matrons gathered to send them off to the camel races. They were at that time in their late twenties, early thirties, but my mother's fifteen-year-old cousin was in tow as chaperone, of course. And still Nana-bai told them, strict and respectable, laying out the rules, "Go at seven. Be back at nine." Such is the dowry that comes with this girl, she was saying plainly.

The camel-race part of my parents' courtship story at first puzzled me. I myself never went to camel races. I had never seen a camel up close, and I had certainly never heard of couples going out on such dates. Camels, I'd thought, lived sandy and parched, in the universe of the Bible. And yet, after a bit of thought, yes, this seemed to fit easily with my parents. In the Bible, lovers were superhumanly intertwined. Adam and Eve. Abraham and Sarah.

Mom and Dad. I *could* envision them, amidst the camel smells, shading their eyes under the beating sun, offering each other sips of water with ancient wordless chivalry. Camels, in the end, seemed to be natural props in the exchange of my parents' affection and perfection.

Nana-bai's ethic was sealed eventually at my parents' wedding. After the ceremony, she turned to my mother, and said with delight and with finality: "Now go with your husband and don't come back," closing one life for her and ushering her into the next one. They belonged to each other now, and Nana-bai—and the rest of the family—expected absolutism. My parents were lucky because in the midst of what was bestowed upon them, they found that they were, in fact, soul mates.

As a child, I questioned none of this. I did not dig through their perfection to find inevitable small grudges and inequalities and traces of ego. And witnessing my parent's commitment and happiness, I did not connect it with any subtle cultural anchoring. I did not even recognize the fact that it only came at the end of their own private evolutions. Instead I took for granted that every person would bring to a relationship the same kind of investment and morality my parents seemed to have. And though I was in a very different time and land, I expected that this is what I would find when I discovered boys myself.

Hoping we children would one day make happy marriages, too, both Nana-bai and my parents tried to guide us. Relationships are things of gravity, they told us. Dating is to find a husband, not a boyfriend, they seemed to say. Don't date or marry a non-Jew. This for the sake of Jewish continuity, and in honor of all those who perished in the Holocaust, and because despite the love, when things get tough and arguments break out, he'll end up the "goy" and you'll end up the "Dirty Jew." Besides, think of how people in the community would talk. And, anyhow, why would you want your children torn between two religions? This was how we were instructed. And, of course, there was also sex.

Before my parents could even work up the courage to tell me about sex, Nana-bai beat them to it. I'm sure my parents at some point agreed upon a stiff, religious definition for when the time was right. But Nana-bai instead cut straight to the core of it with dramatic stories and widened eyes, exotic bits of advice and Indian superstitions, thinking it was never too soon for a girl to know. I was probably ten years old when she scolded me for acting like a prostitute.

One day in the spring, I was sitting on the front steps brushing my hair. For a time I had refused to brush my hair at all, and the mass would ball up into chunks of messy tangles. So my mother had to cut the whole lot of it off. But a few months before, I claimed to have learned my lesson and promised to brush out the knots faithfully. And now my hair was growing long again. Such a luxury, to draw a brush through all that hair, the feeling of the gentle tugs, the soft bristles against my skin, the smooth slide.

And then at once, a sharp breath sucked in from behind and the squeak of the screen door. "Aiaa! Don't brush your hair out there—come in here now! Do you want people to think you're a spoiled girl? G-d forbid!" A clamp on my elbow, up the stairs, into the house, finally into Nana-bai's room, wondering all the time about what it means to be spoiled. Milk spoils and smells bad. Fruit spoils and turns black. What in the world happens to girls?

"We'll make you two simple plaits," Nana-bai decided as she seated me on her bed. I tasted deeply the smells of her room, ginger and sugar, cloves and dusty handkerchiefs. "Simplicity is the best beauty," she said, taking the hairbrush from me, beginning to run it through my hair herself. "You must not sit on the front steps, arranging your hair." She sliced a thin part down my scalp, concentrating, speaking slowly. "Nai. In India, only spoiled girls, prostitutes, do that. To show the men where to come. To show off . . . it's too easy to become spoiled, if you're not careful and good." Gently poking the hairbrush into my ribs, near nipple nubs that pressed like eyeballs behind my shirt, she lowered her voice and warned: "Even if you think about boys, your breasts will grow bigger."

I pictured the girls in India, the ones who hadn't listened to the warnings, who had become spoiled. And their punishment seemed harsh, really, for making the mistake of opening themselves too much to the world. Doomed to sit, forever exposed on their front steps, enormous, naked breasts resting on their knees like mounds of wet clay. Brushing out their long hair, yards and yards of weedy hair. Too much, I felt certain with my new hard-earned knowledge of haircuts, to ever get out all the tangles.

Nana-bai whipped each plait together between her fingers, and tied them at the bottom with snappy rubber bands so they hung thickly, straight over my ears. "There," she said when she had finished, cupping my cheeks. "Tsangla, tsangla. There, that's beautiful. You should be blessed with the most handsome husband, please G-d."

The deliberate shape which Nana-bai tried to fashion in me did not pare away the physical. Rather, she pulled it all tightly into a guarded, lovely form so that I remember even the very sensations of her molding me. From the time I was a baby, Nana-bai would massage my still-soft bones every day, hoping my face and nose could be worked into the finest features, hoping my hands could be kept narrow enough to slip bangles of glass or gold onto the wrists with ease. She applied concoctions of egg whites, mashed chick peas, and milk and turmeric onto my face to smooth and clean my skin. She slipped me almonds as a treat, because everyone knows that since they are shaped like eyes, they improve your sight; just as walnuts, which are shaped like brains, make you smarter. On special occasions, like Purim, the Jewish holiday of masquerades, Nana-bai allowed me to dress up in paper-light Punjabi dresses, or like a grown lady in her traditional saris. While I stood still with arms raised obediently off my sides, she would draw the many layers of material around and around my body, then over my shoulder, their intricate weaves in deep sea water and sun-blazed colors of silk, a chilly thrill to touch. I can still feel the saris against my skin, her cool wax hands gently covering mine to fold them, pressing my knees together properly, positioning me in modesty.

All that Nana-bai did, which drew so heavily upon the senses and motions of the India she remembered, took on a twist, however, because of the Jewish part. And so the particulars of the physical somehow had to also reconcile themselves with the tradition of a people who define themselves by The Book, by study, and by words.

No matter where Jews have found themselves wandering, stopping, wandering again throughout history in the world, they have carried words with them. A Torah scroll. A holy book. Scribbled notes of commentaries. Or for lack of these, at least a few jagged memories of the words. Words, in some form or another, were depended upon to pass down tradition. To keep a generation in one country tied with several generations removed from it in another. And so, through the connecting course of a river of words and G-d and bodies, Nana-bai's message about sex, as a Jew steeped in the feel of India, turned out to be my parents' message as well, as Jews trying to make a life in the world of America.

The static family value, its desperate appeals to G-d, and its black and white consensus had not changed at all between the generations. Sex is, was, and will be valuable only within the confines of marriage. A woman who is sexual outside of marriage could be seen as a disgrace to her family and a cheap-quality character. My parents did not have access to the same staggering pictures in the Indian landscape that Nana-bai had around her, to make examples of, to physically imbed in me. And yet they were nonetheless able to capture the same sentiment and family interpretation in the Jewish tradition through lengthy talk, piles of words and ideas and more words.

The Torah, in its hard, archaic, thorough words, defined sexuality. It ruled precisely which relationships were forbidden (a man with his father's wife, his daughter-in-law, his sister, his father's daughter, his mother's daughter, his uncle's wife, his brother's wife, his neighbor's wife, another man, an animal). And it described exact punishment for transgressions (death, death by fire, death by stoning, death to the man, death to the woman, death to the animal).

In the same summary manner, my parents spelled out their own decisive views on sex. They had maxims for everything, but especially when it came to sex. For the sake of convenience their words were captured in neat homemade sayings or borrowed clichés to be tossed to me as quick reminders, or folded away into my pocket and memory. "You don't buy the cow, when you can get the milk for free." "Even with women's liberation, the two things that can't be stopped are mother nature and father time: the guy can always walk away, the girl is stuck with the baby."

"Love and marriage are two completely different things: marriage requires stability, love by its very nature is unstable." "Remember the three Rs: respect, responsibility, and the right decision."

I attribute some of this imposed hard line to the remnants of traditional cultures and religion. But really, though, these were just small interpretations of larger worlds. My family's own loving brand of the dynamic between caregiver and child. Good and evil boxed neatly like in a fairy tale, to preserve a norm and a G-d. Most of all, it was there to protect perfection, in all the places where perfection did and did not exist.

*Chapatis:*
*Take 3 pounds whole wheat flour, mix 1-1/2 pounds flour with flat tablespoon salt, some water and two tablespoons butter.*

*Knead it and after one hour take a small ball of dough, and roll it on board.*

*With palm, apply butter on it, sprinkle slightly with flour.*
*Fold it and again to the other side.*
*Roll dough in round shape of 10 inches in breadth.*
*Keep pan on stove. Let it get hot. Put bread on, then turn on other side. Fry in teaspoonful butter.*

—NANA-BAI'S DIARY, PAGE 23

*P*leasures—and the bar on them—were sometimes wrapped up in the larger principles of our household. More often, though, our pleasures lay in disguise, in things we could lay our hands on, and in small, unexpected moments.

It was Sunday, and while I lazily tried to avoid my chores, Nana-bai was making chapati bread in the kitchen. Some days I washed the dishes, other days I dusted. That particular day, while Mommy and Daddy were running errands, I was supposed to fold laundry. The afternoon stretched before me endlessly as I thought about the laundry that awaited, and the many starchy static shocks that lay in ambush among the clothes. What could be more tiresome than wrestling with the unmanageable elastic corners of fitted sheets and hunting for pairs in a mountain of single socks?

Straddling the basket of clean clothes still tangled, warm, and smelling of soap from the dryer, I sat in the doorway joining kitchen and den, watching Nana-bai work the dough, listing for her all my reasons why I shouldn't have to work. "I'm sick. I'm hungry. I'm tired. I folded clothes yesterday. I'm gonna fold clothes tomorrow." She said nothing and only pulled off a dough ball in her fingers. She formed it up, then smacked it down lightly against the wooden board, dusting the checkered table cloth around her and rolling it out. "I could be reading instead. I could be doing homework." I emphasized the word *homework* making it long and pointed, so she would understand that my very education was at stake here. Perhaps, I hoped, if I talked long enough, she would finally fold the clothes herself, with the brisk efficiency adults used when fed up with a child's inability to, say, find the jacket hanging quite obviously in the closet. But, it seemed, Nana-bai was not about to cave in.

I grasped for other ideas, other able bodies at hand, scrolling through the qualifications of my siblings. Batsheva was too young, still a baby, so that was not even a possibility. What if I offered up Gertie? She was older than me, fit, strong-willed, skilled at folding, maybe a laundry prodigy. A very reasonable option. "What about Gertie?" I asked decidedly, certain I had hit upon something. "Why can't *she* fold the clothes?"

"She is arranging all the beds upstairs. And then she is going to come down here and wash the pots and pans." Gertie had already been put to work. My plan was ruined.

"What about Tzvi then?" I suggested, trying to pin it on my younger brother.

"He is outside playing."

"Playing? Why does he get to play and I have to work?" I asked, indignant, but I already knew the answer.

With a firm splat of dough to wooden board, Nana-bai said matter-of-factly, "He's the boy."

"That's so unfair. All these clothes in here, they're his clothes, too."

"But you're his sister. You should respect him and do things for him."

No matter how many times I heard this, still my mind reeled with its injustice. "This isn't India," I said angrily. "Things are different here in America. Just 'cause he's a boy, it doesn't make him better. It doesn't mean I have to be his slave." In the good ol' U.S.-of-A.-world outside our house, women expected to be every bit as powerful as men. So I knew that all of American ideology backed me up on this point. And I held it over her, feeling myself to be an angry ambassador, a superhero, even. Nana-bai stood up and washed her hands at the sink. Pulling a pan out of the cupboard, she turned on the gas and set it on the stove to heat. "You favor him," I told her accusingly. "Can't you see you favor him?"

"Aiaa. I love all you kids." She dug into her pocket and pulled out a sesame candy for me. "Here," she pressed it into my hand. I toyed with the plastic wrapper, debating whether or not to accept this peace offering. Finally I unfolded it and popped it into my mouth, begrudgingly, enjoying the way ground sesame turned to a peanut taste between my teeth.

"But you do favor him," I said, unwilling to let go of my stance. "You would have given him three candies if he were here this moment." Nana-bai always kept sesame candies and nuts and dried fruits in her pockets. Every now and then, at odd times, on car trips or after dinner, she took us aside and pulled these out, trying to slip the gifts into our hands on the sly. If we politely refused, she insisted and forced the treats into our knapsacks anyway, shushing us so that we would feel special and no one else in the family would know what had just taken place. Of course, despite her best efforts, these exchanges were usually very obvious. And I could not help but notice that she always gave Tzvi more than she gave us girls. Soniia, she called him. My gold.

"You favor him. Admit it," I demanded.

"He is the boy," she told me simply. "Come, while the pan heats up, I will get you started with the laundry." Reluctantly, I allowed her to take my arm and stand me up. Then she overturned the basket of laundry onto the couch, making a deal with me: "If you finish all the other clothes, then I'll come and help you with the big things, the sheets and towels. Haa?" I agreed and got busy folding, watching her fry the chapati while I worked.

Gertie came downstairs a few minutes later, rolling her round eyes and fuming about her own chores. She and Nana-bai exchanged a few bickering words, then I heard her pound around the kitchen for a bit. Finally she dragged a chair to the sink, climbed up it, and turned on the tap to wash the dishes. Tzvi walked through the room just then, a skinny, barefoot brown boy with glasses. He had a good heart. But when he did not get what he wanted, he threw a tantrum and screamed until the veins on his neck popped out, and Nana-bai, trying to appease him, worried. "It's going to kill him, G-d forbid." Tzvi led a toddling Batsheva out into the backyard with him, her plastic diaper dragging heavy behind her. She adored him.

"Where are you taking her?" I demanded, nosy, and suspicious of the look on his face.

"Outside."

"Why outside?"

"My ball got stuck somewhere, so I need someone small to get it back."

"Where? Back in the rose bushes? Are you sending her into the prickles again?"

"Yeah, so?" he said, quickly pushing her through the door to outside and following in the next step. "She *is* smaller so the thorns won't get to *her*." He closed the door behind them.

I shook out a pair of Daddy's jeans broodingly. This was all because of Nana-bai, I decided. Unabashedly a tattletale, a worrier, and a goody-goody, I knew I would have to make a point of reporting all this to Mommy and Daddy later that night—even though last time it was no help at all. "She's so old-fashioned," I had told them. "She always fills Tzvi's plate first and takes his side in arguments. And she never makes him do any work."

"You have to try and understand her," Daddy had said. Academically, he knew the history involved. He could tell me all about the culture that raised Nana-bai, could compare it to the cultures in Japan and China where he once lived himself. He started to, even, saying, "Picture life in India almost a century ago, under British rule. . . ."

But I had cut in. "What do you know about this, Daddy? She always fills your plate first, too. And she tells Mommy to never argue with you." His life was only made easier by this culture.

"Well, you should count yourself lucky," Mommy had told me. "Gertie is the oldest, so Nana-bai tries to give her most of the work, anyway."

"You kids should be happy to help out in the house. We all have to pitch in and work together here. Even Tzvi helps me out when I fix the car and shovel the snow," Daddy had pointed out.

"Well, can't you say something to her?"

"No, she's an elderly woman and we can't insult her like that," Mommy had said.

It amazed my classmates that Nana-bai had such influence in our home. Their elderly relatives had their own condominiums and lives. They visited for the holidays or my classmates flew down to Florida to be with them for a vacation, meeting for meals and to swim in the pool, then retreating to their separate rooms. The rest of the year they sent holiday cards with twenty-dollar checks. Even when Grandpa from Daddy's side came by, it was only for an afternoon of cake and coffee. He presented us with small noisemakers or illicit Hershey bars and we told him about what was going on at school, then he went home and that was it.

But Nana-bai lived with us all the time. Her values and experiences inhabited our household every day. Her freshly-washed petticoats hung over our bathtub and the house smelled like her spices. While Mommy and Daddy came in and out of our playroom between outside jobs and running the household and errands and budgets, Nana-bai was a constant presence with us, as she cooked and cleaned and involved herself in our every move. Sometimes, if I was scared at night, I even slept in her bed. In her culture, that generational overlap was natural. "Just respect her and help out and don't pay attention to the old-fashioned part of it," Mommy told me. Not so easy.

I knew intellectually that girls and boys should be equal, but the reality around me—dictated and accepted by people I loved, who loved me—was, in fact, otherwise, and therefore more true than abstractions could ever be. I made a fuss, for the principle of my frustrations, but on a deeper level, I resigned myself to it. Still, I could have processed that culture in any number of ways, like my siblings.

Gertie, my big sister, was already bossy and protective of me. My parents insisted that I play with her friends and that I wear her hand-me-downs so I was, inevitably, a reflection of her. Confident in this responsibility, in their trust and in my devotion, she glowed with charisma, and always drew people to her without effort.

Nana-bai's traditions only fired her up in reaction, made her more vocal, more assertive.

Batsheva, the baby of the family, who even as a child was stunningly beautiful, managed to grow up wearing Nana-bai's way of life with proportion, with easy, classic grace. Like a feathered boa around her neck. Without vanities or airs in her perfect skin and coloring, she floated breezily, coolly through such cultural heaviness. And instead she became independent and self-assured in response to it.

Tzvi, the only boy, the remarkable product of a diverse genetic combination—artistic, athletic, musical, a doctor in the making—was expected to fulfill all our family's worldly ambitions. But from the heights of small kingliness, where once just about every demand and tantrum was soothed (my parents even seriously considered adoption when he begged for a brother to play with), he eventually learned to see his role as the boy with a balanced, gentlemanly perspective.

But for me, with my own particular shy chemistry and relationship to the world, I grew up understanding myself firstly by the traditional, often backward, differences between girls and boys. Boys could make the decisions. Girls could only support these decisions. Boys could wander around in public, meeting lots of people. Girls had to stay safely and modestly in the house. Boys could fart and burp. Girls couldn't; they had to be dainty. Boys could whistle. Girls shouldn't, because if they did, I was told, they would grow a moustache. Boys were loud. Girls must be quiet. Just to be near boys or men was inherently dangerous. Women who were violated had often brought it upon themselves from that sort of thing, from going somewhere alone at night with a man, from laughing too freely. If ever I went to play at the neighbors',

I was warned repeatedly about the brothers and fathers. What terrible, perverted, and strange things could the brothers and father possibly do to me, I wondered, almost curiously. Also, I was told to guard my womb. To lift something too heavy might rip me inside, make me infertile. So many people in my family, it seemed, were invested in this part of me. And so I walked around worried, from an ache or a cramp, that somehow I had doomed myself to being barren. And all these ideas infiltrated my mind and bearing. When I went outside our home, I clutched the corners of my dress timidly and spoke in a painfully soft voice. I tried to be clean, safe, agreeable, odorless, and blend into the background.

Years later, by the time I reached junior high, propriety had seeped inside me too deeply. My parents themselves decided I needed to be more assertive, so they enrolled me in karate classes. Entering the studio, I found empowering paraphernalia at my fingertips. Punching bags. Mouth guards. Athletic cups. Sports bras. Donning these, our white-uniformed bodies became almost sexless amidst the grunting and yelling and boxing. I worked my way up to a green belt, kicked in blocks of wood, sparred in tournaments, and won several tall trophies. But still I did not learn to be a fighter or even an artist. Instead, again, I was conscientiously the girl. I tied my ponytail back with gold elastic and wore Chapstick on my lips at practices. I started shaving my legs solely for the moments when I kicked and my uniform slid up my calf. Inevitably, in the exercises we did, my body strove for grace, not power.

There were several middle-aged men in our class who had apparently one day reached age forty-five, looked down over their potbellies, and decided in a moment of revelation to reclaim their manhood. Gathering at the studio, they lounged around in their dungarees. They guffawed about football and snots and what chores their wives had them do last weekend. But a few minutes later, they stepped into the locker room to put on their uniforms. And suddenly they emerged as part of a Kung Fu movie world inhabited by honorable life-and-death battles, hard discipline, and soulful inner balance. It was the grandeur of their boyhood games revived, and they took this code seriously.

With these men, of all men, there might have been an exchange of equals. They might have honored the skill and talent demanded by my green belt, and come at me forcefully, awakening the force in my own body. But in the end, sparring with them, as we paired up then bowed and started circling each other, they held back—and I expected them to—because I was petite and smiled sweetly. Every so often they humored me, allowing me a clear opening to their ribs. And I took it, with a grateful, gentle, backhand jab.

Attaching to the power around me, I adored my karate instructor, Jim. One day Jim came over to me during class to correct my sparring stance. I held my breath as he tugged my knee one way, chucked at my chin, and barked, "Let's feel the strength here." The strength was supposed to be in my stomach, in the sharpness of my moves, in the depth of my voice when I yelled my battle cry and attacked. But the core of this strength instead concentrated on wondering, Had I forgotten to put on deodorant that morning? Did I stink of sweat? Would he notice? He leaned over me, to adjust my arm, and I breathed in his closeness, felt, almost deliriously, the force in his hands as he told me, "Tighten up, that's where the strength is. Try this." Then he leaned closer to impart some ancient words of wisdom which, finally, I was lucky enough to merit. "It should be like you're trying really, really hard to take a shit." As he said this, thousands of years of majestic karate tradition seemed to crash around me, and I stood there for a moment, mouth quivering, utterly bewildered to find I had nothing girly or delicate left to hide behind. Afterward, I could not meet his eyes again, feeling we had done something shameful together.

Gertie finished washing the dishes and escaped back upstairs, snatching a fresh, hot chapati to take with her. When I had finished folding most of the laundry, Nana-bai left another chapati cooking on the stove and came in from the kitchen, as she'd promised, to help me fold the big things. "Here. We'll do it together," she said, holding a sprawling king-size sheet in a pile in her hands. I picked up two corners of it and she picked up the other two corners. Pinching the ends and holding them taut, we walked backwards in opposite directions, stretching the expanse of the flowered sheet between us. We smoothed it and came back together, folding it in half. Then each of us selected two more of the newly formed corners, stepping backward again. Moving out, and in, and out again with the petal-strewn cloth drifting and shape-changing in a maypole dance, we must have taken a moment too long in our reverie because soon the smell of burnt chapati hit us. Hastily Nana-bai set the sheet aside and I followed her as she hurried back into the kitchen to pull a half-charred chapati out of the pan.

"Look what we did!" I gasped, scared from just the smell of burning in our house. But Nana-bai just put a thick spoon of butter in the pan and set a new piece of flattened dough on to cook. I relaxed a little. "Well, at least it's only one lost," I breathed.

"Lost? Nai."

"Well, who's gonna want to eat that one?"

She nodded, looking at the chapati lying limp on a plate and blackened with smoky stripes. "It's certainly not fine enough to put on the table for your brother and father—we'll have to be more careful. But this should not go to waste." Scraping a crumbly layer of the bitter blackness off with a knife, she took an almost-empty jar of homemade mango chutney from the refrigerator and tore the chapati in half. "Here. You and I will just eat this ourselves with a bit of chutney. You'll see it's quite tasty." Digging the spoon inside the jar till the sides shone clean of orange, she emerged, clanking with a heaping teaspoonful. She rolled one-half with chutney, then the other half also and said, "One for me. One for you. Try a piece now. I want you to always remember how it tastes."

Wordless and distrustful of what she offered, I took the burnt bread and chutney from her anyway. Then I ate it, and I was pleased to find that it was good.

Mommy and Daddy came back from running errands late that afternoon. While Mommy put away the groceries, I worked my way through the many overflowing bags covering the floor, chock-full of boxes and cartons and bottles, so I could sit down at the table and tell her all about that day. I told her about Nana-bai, listing everything for her. How I had to fold the laundry and Gertie had to wash dishes and arrange the beds. How she let Tzvi play outside, and even how he dragged Batsheva to do his dirty work, to pull a ball out from the thorns. I *definitely* saw a scratch or two on her leg later, I informed Mommy primly.

She had heard this kind of thing many times before. So now she only sighed, exasperated, and continued stocking fruit in the refrigerator. "Can I tell you a secret?" Then she continued, before I said yes or no. "Every month Nana-bai gives me money for each of you to put into your savings accounts. Not a lot, but some. She'll give me five dollars each for you and Batsheva and Gertie. Then she'll give me ten dollars for Tzvi, the boy." Mommy paused to let this sink in. "Each month I tell her, Nana-bai, I'm not going to do that, be unfair to my children like that. And I tell her I'm going to divide the money up equally between them. And I do that. Each month, it happens the same way." Mommy began folding the empty grocery bags away, to save and reuse.

"So you see?" I said, hopping up. "That proves it. She does love him more."

"No," she told me. "That proves she loves you all the *same*. Look, she's an old woman and she is stuck in her ways and you can't expect her to change too much. Who knows what she is thinking? That the boy will need money when he grows up and that after the dowry, the girls will be taken care of when they're married? I don't know," she paused. "Anyhow, sure, she divides up the money unevenly, because that's the only way she can do it. But in the end she knows I will equally distribute it among you four. And, if you ask me, I think that is why she continues to do this every month. She can't be fair herself, but she knows I *will* be."

Mommy finished restoring the kitchen to order silently then, while I sat back down at the table, thinking about this, gnawing on a piece of chapati. Eventually, once she was done, Mommy dished herself a plate of leftover cauliflower curry with a dollop of chutney on the side. Then she chose a chapati to warm up on the stove. I watched her and without even knowing about the burnt bread Nana-bai and I had shared that very day, Mommy also purposely weeded out the most browned, the most crusty, the most imperfect and raggedly shaped chapati in the stack. And that was the one she took for herself.

*Fact: In 1775, George Washington was appointed Commander-in-Chief of the Colonial forces.*

*Fact: Third president of the United States was President Thomas Jefferson, who knew seven languages.*

*Fact: The Statue of Liberty arrived in New York City aboard French ship called* Isere *in June, 1885.*

—NANA-BAI'S DIARY, PAGE 19

*T*he unexpected nature of pleasures for me did not end with burnt bread. In those days, strangely, I also loved riding around in our clunky, run-down station wagon. Riding in a station wagon always made me feel American. The truth is, officially I have always been an American. I'm a citizen. I was born here and raised here for most of my life. And yet, growing up, I sensed that our home, and its exotic smells and languages, set us apart from something else. Something vague and elusive that seemed to exist inside our neighbors' homes, in histories and storybooks and television sets.

I peered through the painted gates of our yard and saw these things. They celebrated Christmas; we celebrated Chanukah. They ate macaroni-and-cheese or TV dinners; my mother made curry instead. Theirs was a universe which might tornado into Oz. I could only watch that in the movies. They were *in their very genes* descended from colorful pieces of history and heroism that

55

would never have anything to do with me. From barbarian Celts and Robin Hood and European royalty and Pilgrims and Scarlett O'Hara and flappers. And when I heard that lineage and complicated richness evoked in orchestra music and the grand rising and falling of violins, I ached to the point of tears. Because in those worlds I was only the slave, the gypsy, the heretic, the outcast. I felt left out of the clichés that seemed to mold the spaces beyond my home—the church steeples, the crumbs of apple pie, and chips of picket fence—that defined America for me: freckled, Christ-believing, quaint. And yet, when I was young, piling into the station wagon with my family and driving right into the midst of it all, I somehow always felt that I, too, was an American in that America.

"Come on. We're going for a ride," my parents often said to me.

"To where?"

"Just for a ride."

We drove out into mossy woods to hike or watch the leaves turn autumn colors from the softness of a picnic blanket. Then we got back into the car and drove on. To old estates of the Vanderbilts and Roosevelts, to Amish country and to farms where we tapped the trees for maple syrup and picked grapes and bought real churned butter. Sometimes in the car we were bored or drifted in and out of sleep or argued or read quietly. But throughout, the country that we glimpsed outside the rolled-down windows and that we tumbled into when the car doors finally opened, somehow smelled of *Little House on the Prairie* and flannel, tales of Johnny Appleseed, homemade biscuits, and the smoky breezes of burning hickory wood. I had had whiffs of these things before and as we drove, I could pick them up from even the barest hints, make of them emblems. They were exactly what America was supposed to be.

What did it mean when I was growing up to have strong ties to elsewhere, to non-America? It meant that I heard even the very language with a different ear. "Simplicity" pronounced as "simple city" with an Indian lilt, so that when Nana-bai reminded me "Simplicity is the best beauty," I truly believed it must be a tourist's hot spot. Or body parts identified not in English, but from the very first in Hebrew baby talk. "Tusik" for fanny and "pupik" for bellybutton. There was a specific posture, a humbleness, a dipping of the head for emphasis—all of which originated in a land with a very un-American relationship to bodies and language. There was also a foreign definition for basic behaviors, in which success was not about the individual, but rather about the family. In which politeness was attentiveness almost to the point of subservience. In which superstition, old prejudices, and hierarchies in relationships between men and women, old and young, were as good as law.

Things like arcade games, Underoos, Cabbage Patch Kids, even the movie *Star Wars* were seen as part of some other culture. We did not partake of them. So we had a little less to talk about with people who did. There was always an awareness of "here" vs. "there," "now" vs. "then." Though my mother was naturally beautiful, I looked jealously at the mothers of my friends who went to have their hair permed, with their long red polished nails, and painted lips and cheeks.

The plenty of this country always seemed sketchy and precarious, too. Though there was never a severe lack of food, still we had to eat everything on our plates so that nothing would go to waste. Spoonfuls of jelly scraped from the sides of an almost empty jar. The last of the salad, wilted and wet in the bottom of the bowl. The ends of the bread. Once, at a warehouse closing, we found a hot bargain price on rolls of cloth. So we bought them and Nana-bai cut and sewed a huge batch of underwear for Gertie and me. It would save money in the long run, we were told. When she finished, we had dozens and dozens of pairs of stiff bright pink underwear with red and yellow and green colored fish on it. Forever starchy, they didn't feel like underwear should, and the thick elastic peeped out at the hem. But the supply lasted us for almost ten years, so it was chalked up as a good deal.

Maybe if we had connected deeply to the general Indian community, our family identity might have been more straightforward, a clear-cut piece of American immigration. But we were Jewish also and general Indian culture was another sphere entirely. For a while, I studied traditional Indian folk dance. In that time, the rhythm of the dances, the shared sweat and practice seemed to be a bond between me, the one Jewish girl, and all the other Hindu girls. In an old studio room, we learned to fold our palms, to fan our fingers, to widen our eyes dramatically and pound our heels in rhythm. And I felt myself to be just as one of the others, dark-skinned, reaching far back into droning music and stumbling forward into grace.

At the holiday party though, when families came together in the studio to exchange presents and wish each other happy holiday, I was suddenly aware that none of the other Indians in that room would have guessed what holiday I celebrated when I went home. I stood around with the others, eating pink glitter cookies, fidgety for not dancing. And suddenly it seemed the connection to just India was not enough to stand alone between shy girls. How could I explain to them all I learned in Torah class? They had never even heard of Indian Jews.

Eventually I lost interest and stopped dancing. But driving along in our station wagon, I continued to watch the Indians on the streets around me. Bundled up in saris, looking out from dark eyes and auras of strangeness, I saw that they were like me, but still very unlike me. And they, too, did not seem entirely at home in America. With my own suspicions and awkwardness, I did not need to ally myself to this, too.

Maybe if we had been accepted at face value as regular Jews, the sense of America would have been more natural. But from the earliest age I remember feeling different, even from the American Jewish community. So that brand of Americana, with New York's Lower East Side of Yiddish and bagels and lox so thick in its veins, seemed unattainable to me also. Because of my father, it was bio-logically half of me. He was raised in it and passed it on to us with pride. We had our share of traces back to Ellis Island—to young Russian Jewish immigrants working as tailors or in scrap yards, making it in the tough American urban neighborhoods, running errands for mobster front-shops and men named Corky and Louie High-Tower.

They did what they had to do in order to make ends meet. One day, Grandpa Izzy and his friend even put together a makeshift hot dog stand outside a factory, working from the back of the car with just a pot of water and a small burner. But at the lunch bell, hungry laborers meaning business poured out of the factory, lined up for hot dogs, and knocked on the car windows, impatiently surrounding it. The two were overwhelmed by the crowds and worked themselves into a frenzy. Frantically and ceaselessly, like a machine smoking in overload, Grandpa Izzy pulled hot dog after hot dog from the pot, slapped it into a bun with a fingerful of mustard, then passed it to his friend who took the customers' few cents in exchange. Faster and faster, one hot dog, then another, as more and more people lined up. "Izzy," his friend called out over his shoulder, sweating from the rush. "How the hell are you cooking them so fast?"

And without even stopping for a moment Grandpa asked, "Who's *cooking* them?"

We had these stories, too. But when my father married my mother, in love with her and in love with the Orient, he embraced the entire world that came with her. Besides, the home is often more flavored by the culture of the mother as she presides over the kitchen. And so that other life seemed to be a package deal, which I could admire from afar, but which I could never take part of inconspicuously.

The Hebrew Institute, which I attended as a little girl, taught me that there was one correct Judaism and it was white. This was never part of any explicit curriculum plan, of course. They even made overt efforts to draw our family in, fully Jewish and part Indian as we were. But nonetheless, most everyone else was white, and my sister Gertie and I were the oddballs out, and we knew it.

A little girl on the playground, teasing me, once said that I looked like chocolate milk. I went home, upset, and reported this, tearfully, to my mother. She asked, "Well, what do you like better? Chocolate milk or white milk?" Chocolate milk, of course. And presto, I had a smart answer ready for that girl in the playground. But I did not get the chance to use it because she never mentioned chocolate milk or white milk or any kind of milk again. She'd already made her point.

Even twenty years later, a woman who had once been another girl on our school bus still knew of us two sisters. Not because we had ever been friends or even spoken. But rather because her mind had imprinted an impression of two small dark girls getting onto her school bus. An ordinary encounter like this should have slipped naturally away into the memory abyss that houses the millions of nameless, faceless people brushed past in a lifetime. Instead this encounter was remembered poignantly even decades later, so it could not have been ordinary at all.

The Hebrew Institute also taught me that correct Judaism was scrupulous in its observance of the commandments. Kippot on the men's heads. Modest coverings for the married women. Boys and girls separate. My family, combining two different Jewish cultures, was still figuring out what it wanted to observe and not observe. And clearly just this act of questioning demonstrated that we were in the wrong school to begin with.

Once, riding on the bus for a class field trip, the girl sitting in the seat next to me decided to make up her own rules. "You know," she instructed me, expertly, "we're supposed to turn our faces away if we pass a church because it's Christian. Or if we pass a McDonald's because it isn't kosher."

I nodded as though this were obvious. And casually following her lead, I went through the motions of turning away vehemently at the next McDonald's. Then I got to wondering, was only McDonald's blackballed? Or was it Wendy's and Burger King, too? And what about all the other restaurants, I worried then. The other nonkosher ones that were not so obviously labeled. I tried to watch her surreptitiously and read her motions. But sometimes she turned away and sometimes she forgot, so I wasn't sure what I was supposed to do.

To play it safe, I kept my eyes straight ahead of me after that. I pretended to study the creases in the forest green plastic seat cover in front of us. But all the while I speculated about what this girl would say if she knew that my father liked to drive along in the city and point out just these kinds of things through the window. "See kids, look at that beautiful Russian Orthodox Church," he'd say. "Doesn't it look just like a great big onion?" Then he'd tell us the story behind its architecture. Or even more, what if she knew that with our looser rules on kosher food, my family often went to McDonald's? That I had even seen someone not two feet away from me eat up a baconburger? I was painfully aware of the gaps between me and this girl and all the other girls like her. I felt them everywhere. Most especially though where Shabbat was concerned.

Shabbat is supposed to be a joyous time. A chance for family and rest and good food and songs. But it is also forbidden to use musical instruments or money, to drive, or start fires, or use electricity. In our house, even though we celebrated and made merry, we also broke every rule in the book.

Friday evening, once my mother lit the candles and made the blessings, she cooked up a whole tableful of spicy curry. After we ate, my father would bring out his guitar and play Jewish songs that often moved me to tears for missing an Israel I had not yet seen. We danced around in our living room. The kind of dancing that is unconscious of itself, and knows only music and movement.

During the Shabbat day we drove downtown to the open-air farmer's market to do the week's food shopping. Wandering through the stalls, we bought fruits and vegetables. Some of the vendors knew us after a while, like Cookie. Every week, she joked to us, "Oh no—you again!" And she slipped us cherries to sample, and smoked meat sticks. Sometimes, on the way home, we'd visit Daddy's friends the Chins. The family worked in a warehouse, buying, selling, and shipping Chinese foodstuffs. The adults would talk while we played with the Chin children. We'd suck on rolls of plum candies and run around between huge vats of bean sprouts in water and vases of 1,000-year-old eggs. It seemed to be a carnival of groceries.

When we finally got home at the end of the day, we cooked lasagna, watched *The Muppet Show*, and flopped into bed. This was our Shabbat, and while I loved it, I knew that we were doing it wrong. Because every time we drove our station wagon by the Hebrew Institute neighborhood, where people hurried about to pray at shul or go to lunch, we ducked down in the backseat of the car so that no one would see us.

Gertie and I were once invited to spend Shabbat at the home of the Lender family from school. While she packed up my dresses, Mommy had told me that they lived in a nearby neighborhood. But as it turned out, they lived so far away from the markets and the music and the Chins, they may as well have been in mythical Minsk or Lublin somewhere. We stayed the Friday night with the Lenders and passed the next long Shabbat morning in their shul, too. Afterward, walking back to their home, I held Mrs. Lender's hand, enjoying the spring day. Suddenly, up ahead, I saw a wide, gorgeous tree spread out like a flirt draping its immense green leaves over the sidewalk. As we passed by, I plucked off one huge leaf that brushed my cheek, waving it with absolute delight for Mrs. Lender. "Look what I've got," I told her.

She only shook her head disapprovingly and said: "You can't tear leaves off of trees on Shabbat." I did not believe, or even understand for a moment, that anything in this could have been wrong. I expected my big sister to swoop over and set everything straight. To defend our way of life where picking pretty things off trees *any* day of the week was okay. But she did not, deep in conversation as she was a few paces away. And I began to see—and remember from class—the Torah-sense in all this. So I threw down the leaf, embarrassed, and continued walking, red-faced.

We sat down to lunch at their home, and the table before us was full of things I had heard of but never tasted before. Here was Luchshen kugel. Tzimes. Cholent. Even the names caught in my throat, and only sounded right in a way I could not imitate. In a soft question that wasn't really a question. "You want some? Of course you want some." Beans and meat that had simmered. Potatoes and noodles. Sweet carrots in a thick sauce. For me, a traditional Shabbat meal had always been elaborate Indian dishes. And I was used to the quick fire of their chili powder and chutney. So the heavy pastiness of this new food took me by surprise. But still it felt wholesome, and I continued to think about it as I sat in the back of the station wagon returning home that night. I began to wonder if there had been an authority there which resounded through the closed circles of Judaism. An authority that we in our mixed household could not know. I thought about this again and again throughout the years. Especially as we moved from one congregation to another and found, in each one, that even a minority population needs to set aside a minority of its own.

Maybe if we had belonged to just one community or another unquestionably, America would have been a land like any other. But we did not have a close-knit sect of our own. So instead, when we drove around in our station wagon, I looked out the window at the country passing by and saw its fictions in my head. And I told myself, willing it, that since I wasn't wholly anywhere else, maybe there were pieces of me in that America.

In all the history of automobiles, station wagons have never been fashionable. They were always the whales, the watermelons, the pregnant women. The clumsy transition between a horse-and-buggy and a minivan. My father liked the heavyweight security of station wagons. He counted also on the bit of extra space they offered to make long trips more efficient for our big family. "Let's do a head count," he would say, as though we were a large platoon. "1, 2, 3, 4, 5, 6. Okay, that's everyone. Let's go!" We have owned station wagons in many varieties. Long and fat. Small and neat. Brand new. Slightly used. Used to the point of collapse. Brown, green, turquoise, white, red. One had Chevy written across it. Another had slabs of woodlike paneling along the sides. Each was braced for extra pounds with sturdy racks atop.

Even today I recall exactly what a station wagon that my family had spread itself out in felt like. It had an air of coffee, gasoline, clean bare feet, exhaust, and oranges and apples packed for the road. As we drove, our station wagons rattled and dragged their innards along the road, clanking. On hot days the seats felt like baked plastic. On frosty days before the heat cranked up, they were cold metal liquid against the skin. Some had cracked mug trays. Others had clean rubber mats on the floor. Undoubtedly, if one felt around, there would be pens and coins under the seats, chewed-up gum gobs in the ashtrays, old papers, a sock or two, an umbrella, bottles of coolant and oil. All had messes of maps in the glove compartment.

The fact of the road and its hurried feel—dashing by in yellow dotted lines, in big square trucks and quick stops for gas—allowed for a change in the rules. Usually, at home, our food was sensible. It was cooked in heavy green pots, allowed to simmer for long hours, and then set out on the table where we all sat. It was wholesome, and we washed it down with cold water. But traveling produces a heightened need for food at odd, random hours to hold off boredom and keep up energy. This does not necessarily run by routine or clock, nor can it be fully planned for. Instead it emerges from the primitive nomadic sense of our biologies, and there is no denying it. And so, while driving, we were at liberty to eat unregulated novelties. We picked up bags of potato chips and ice cream at rest stops. We pulled into fast food drive-thru windows to order from familiar television faces. From Ronald McDonald and the brainy-looking man who oversaw the entire business of Kentucky Fried Chicken. What a treat to throw out words that seemed to permeate the lives of all other Americans. Happy Meal. Coca-Cola. We'd pass these delicacies around in the station wagon, warm and greasy, or in icy plastic cups. Offering each other a bite and slurp, we were suddenly generous in the plenty of many paper bags. This food was not kosher or spicy. But it came with bendy straws and toys and ketchup bags on the side. And that was enough.

Along the way my father taught us to sing folk songs that had seeped into American culture. With heroines named Clementine and Oleana and Waltzing Mathilda. We clapped and sang in rounds. "Oh Mr. Johnny Rebeck, how could you be so mean? I told you you'd be sorry for inventing that machine. Now all the neighbors' cats and dogs will never more be seen. They'll all be ground to sausages in Johnny Rebeck's machine. Bang!" Soon we were joined in the station wagon by other simple American presences. "A man by the name of Bill Hall, who had a goat and that was all." Or charming Billy Boy, who boasted again and again, "My wife can bake a cherry pie, she's the apple of my eye, she's a young thing but cannot leave her mother." And of course there was my favorite companion, "My uncle Mort, he was sawed off and short, measured but five foot two. But he sure was a gi'nt when he filled up his pint with that good old mountain dew." They all brought with them the odor and the twang of farms, a lumberjack's code of honor, and rosy cheeks. For a while they would ride along with us, clicking their boots to the music, passing around a pipe, joining in for a chorus or two. I would look out the window. And with a belly full of Burger King, with the visions of green hills and store fronts and bridges flicking by, I felt graced by such company. Because in those moments, there was no passing of time, no differentiation. The wagon trails of the pioneers, the tarred up highways rolling by, and even the barefoot pilgrim's paths in India and Israel and me were all one long delicious generic road. And my family in our station wagon was as American as any other out there.

These were proven American. And still I felt more so myself from just rubbing elbows with them. I felt this even though I was told to love all that made me out of the ordinary here. The color of my skin. The continual touches of other lands and beliefs in me. I felt this because there was still sometimes a need to be simply ordinary. To not have to explain what it means to be an Indian Jew, or who came where, and when, and why.

On paper, I would never be the norm in any one community. But buckled in, watching out the window, I could imagine myself blended in. And I felt that I was made more authentically American and historically grounded, by spending just a little bit of time with these visions. With a deeply rooted, rich smelling America, that had no complex outer ties. A nonaccented, blond-haired, blue-eyed, pork-chops-and-apple-sauce America. A Girl Scout's America.

A gin-drinking, tobacco-chewing, Betsy Ross–and–Buffalo Bill America. I delighted in these possibilities. In the spirits. The flavors. The stars and stripes. But though I always seemed to be alone in it, pressed up against the car window, it never occurred to me that these pleasures could, in the end, be merely part of a fiction's America.

*Kheer:*
*Cook half pound rice and mash smooth with ladle in big pot.*
*Pour in half gallon milk and mix with rice pulp and two cups sugar.*
*Keep on high fire for half an hour, then on middle fire.*
*When it is thick, add cardamom and peeled, cut almonds.*
*Pour the stuff in a platter. When it is cold, cut in pieces.*

—NANA-BAI'S DIARY, PAGE 11

One day, when I was seven, everything changed and pleasure—in all its forms—would never be the same again.

Mommy's relatives were in town visiting for a few days. Not just one or two generation's worth of relatives, but three or four even—blurry with all their siblings and children, and some shirt-tail cousins besides. They had come, many from around the country, but most from Israel, like a flock, like a fleet. And we opened our home to them all. My father kidded to them: "We eat steak, you eat steak. We eat wallpaper, you eat wallpaper." In short, whatever we had was theirs to share. "If there's room in the heart, there's room in the house." We stowed their suitcases under every piece of furniture. We had them sleeping in our beds and couches, even on the floor. They wandered around in flip-flops and smoked cigarettes out on the porch. Each night they lingered over fat, delicious meals till way past my bedtime. At any given moment, there was always someone in the shower, howling, "What happened to the hot water?"

One morning, though still early, already the women were waking, dressing, pushing bobby pins into their hair, and gathering in the kitchen to cook the evening's dinner, fresh. We four siblings woke up, too, restless with so many new people in our home and anxious to watch cartoons. But Mommy had told us to amuse ourselves quietly in the basement, and already Gertie was badgering me with a scheme.

"Come on. We can paint my dolls also someday," she said. "But for now I think we should start with yours." As if to entice me, she made drippy circles in the air with her paintbrush. Holding Holly Hobby tightly behind my back, I pretended to consider Gertie's proposal, but all the while I plotted my escape.

Nearby, Tzvi poked at Batsheva in her crib, and the moment Gertie turned to tell him, "Leave her alone," I saw my chance, jumping up and darting out of the room with Holly Hobby breathlessly in tow. "Come back," Gertie called after me. "We can draw her tattoos and makeup and war paint and . . . and *scars*, too." But I just ran up the stairs and into a splash of female sounds in the kitchen—laughter and pots and pans and quiet bickering.

Mommy, at the sink with Nana-bai, spotted me and said, "I heard lots of noise down there. What's going on? Most of your uncles and cousins are still sleeping, so you need to be quiet."

"It's nothing," I told her. Then I slipped away through a group of aunties and grannies by the table who cooed and blew kisses at me.

In this collection of young women and old women mulling about, even spilling into the dining room, they shared skin shades of brown, arches of eyebrow and curves of lip without boundary. But still there were divisions: There were pettiness and there were veiled, barbed comments. Every now and then one woman jealously eyed the gold earrings and bangles of another. Several aunties wore traditional saris. Others wore cutoff jeans and T-shirts. A few members of the family I knew well—like Nana-bai, who at this point had lived in our house for several years. But others I barely knew at all. This was because of our family secret. A secret which for years they fiercely guarded, even from me. Until that day.

I wandered out of the kitchen back through the house, to where Daddy sat in the living room with one of the uncles. As usual, they were talking about the subject that was closest to everyone's heart and mind. Israel. The uncles liked to debate with Daddy. "He is a Ph.D.," they told each other, emphasizing the weight of this. But Daddy, unconscious of the way they heralded him, only wanted good discussion.

The morning newspaper, already exhausted, lay loosely folded inside-out on the floor before him. "Absolutely," Daddy was saying. "Absolutely. Israel is the best place in the world to raise children."

"So? Nu?" the uncle interrupted. "That's what most American Jews say. Now, let's see you do something about it."

"When the time is right," Daddy told him, nodding with certainty. Seeing me in the doorway, he patted the cushion next to him on the couch. "Come sit, sweetie." But I would have rather let Gertie paint every single one of my dolls than listen to a boring adult conversation. So I moved further down the hall, shuffling around a pile of duffel bags and peeping into corners.

Moshe uncle was just stirring in one of the bedrooms. Around him, some of the other uncles and cousins still lay in various stages of sleeping and waking. He sat half covered in his sleeping bag on the floor, stretching and pondering lazily if he should get up. Unlike the rest of the uncles who were always serious, Moshe uncle told naughty jokes I couldn't understand and pulled chocolate drops out of my ears. So when I popped my head into the doorway, and he put a shushing finger to his lips, beckoning me mischievously, I shyly came forward.

"See that travel case in the corner?" he whispered. "If you bring it to me, I'll tell you a secret." Such a small favor in exchange for a secret. I was thrilled at my good luck. I brought him the case, and he zipped it open, rifling through. Eventually he emerged with a toothbrush and toothpaste. He spread the paste on the brush and drew me into his lap so we could whisper quietly. Then, between the stale smells of night and the minty foam from brushing, I finally learned our family secret: "Back in India, long ago, Nana-bai and the girl she grew up with as her sister were married at the same time to the same man. Imagine that." Polygamy. I didn't even know such a word. But this, then, explained our fuzzy family tree that defied all logic. How there could be within our clan, and even within our kitchen, a universe of contradictions. "See," Moshe uncle said, pointing with his toothbrush to demonstrate. "I come from the first wife, the main wife. And you come from Nana-bai, who is the second wife."

Yoni uncle lying nearby, who had been drifting in and out of sleep, upon hearing this revealing conversation sat up with a start. "I can't believe you're telling her this," he berated Moshe uncle angrily. "Though it shouldn't surprise me really. Knowing you." Moshe uncle just continued brushing his teeth with a sly grin, and Yoni uncle pulled me to him. "Look, this is part of the Old World. People here in America won't understand, so no one outside the family needs to know this. Don't tell anyone. Especially not the white Jews." Even Moshe uncle agreed with Yoni uncle on this. In our small circle, it was true, Moshe uncle came from the most important wife. But outside just us, it meant he came from the odd place where there even *was* such a thing as more than one wife. End of story.

Daily we tried to impress the mainstream Jewish community with the fact that brown skin or white skin, we Jews were all the same. But in truth this kind of thing would never have happened in modern Ashkenazi Jewish culture, with its cookie-cutter family units. Polygamy, once a matter of course for the biblical patriarchs, was weeded out over time by rabbinical ruling for Jews of much of the Diaspora. But the Bene Israel were isolated from general Jewish evolution, and influenced by the native cultures around them in India. So, for them, marriage followed different rules—as it did for Jews in other Jewish cultures, like in Yemen too. This included arranged marriages, child brides, and, every now and then, though some schools within the community rejected it, polygamy.

Once I knew the secret, the other uncles and cousins awakening around us felt free to share their opinions on it with me. It seemed to be our own familial fairy tale. Here, it was logical for a man to take two wives from the same household, to keep his small kingdom's resources and wealth pooled tightly. Here, the first and most important wife was beautiful, light-skinned, vain, empty-headed. And here, Nana-bai, the second wife, was dark-skinned, but as everyone insisted to me, begrudgingly respected for her strong will, generosity, and cleverness. I felt invested in these stories. But since I was young and one more generation removed, I was not caught up as they were in the scandal and the politics of skin color and choosing sides. I especially did not want to be bothered by an explanation of the technicalities, the loopholes in the laws of matrimony and adoption that permitted this marriage to take place—even within the most orthodox of standards. I was instead just utterly fascinated.

Most nights the husband stayed at the mansion with his first wife and children. He took them wandering about the city to enjoy fairs and music. He bought gilded toys and jewelry for them. It was pleasurable to adorn them with his wealth, and to show them off to the community with noisy flair. But since they were spoiled by his money, overfed and always needing to feed more, that household was filled with pettiness and arguing. And so the husband turned with other needs to Nana-bai, whom he kept moving from one hovel to another in the slums of Bombay. She worked hard and made tasty meals for him. He went to her to relax and be quietly pampered, to eat greasy chops and drink tea, to have his feet rubbed after work, and to sleep someplace warm without bribery or protest. Sometimes he spoke to her of world-wide matters, and then, for a few moments, he was amazed anew at all her shy knowledge. But then he would be distracted again with wanting his back massaged or his hair oiled. Or with the cruel itch to beat someone.

It was usually the first wife who maddened him, whining for trinkets and making fusses over the servants. But in the end, naturally, he came to the second wife to take out his anger. Black bruises and cuts were less troublesome on the face of someone who was not considered so beautiful and who rarely went into public. Also, when he beat her—now throwing plates, now slapping her face—she did not scream out the window to the neighbors like his first wife did when he tried to beat her. Nana-bai only cried quietly and proudly into her hands, so that no one would know of this family shame. Careful to keep this, too, a secret. In those days, that was the meaning of strength. In the end, of course, as it happens in small communities, all the Bene Israel soon knew about our family. First wife. Second wife. Who was favored. Who was beaten. And they, too, felt free to follow suit with their own snubs, preferences, and indignities.

The separate households that emerged from these two sisters moved on. Living respectable new lives in Israel and America. Pretending to be modern creatures of one whole family. But traces of that part of India lingered just below the surface.

Once, when visiting Jerusalem, I saw a group of the young men in my family, Israelis themselves now, sitting around the television to watch a soccer game like any of the natives. Cracking roasted pumpkin seeds and spitting out their shells. During a commercial, one man leaned back against the chair, stretching, and asked the others: "Did you hear about Jacob's daughter?" Jacob was Bene Israel too. "Did you hear that she is marrying her cousin? Her cousin!"

The others laughed and imitated an Indian accent, exaggerating a bobbing of the head. "Ah Indians. Is nothing sacred with us?"

The family acted also as if there were no lasting divisions. With hospitality. The kind of hospitality that was rooted there in Israel in Bedouin ways, and even in the Torah. Where if someone wandered through, thirsty from the desert, it was expected—only decent and humane and necessary for survival—to bring them in, let them wash, eat, drink, and rest. Just as we had welcomed all of our relatives in America, when we visited them in Israel, they opened their farms and homes to us. They spread mattresses out on the floor and cooked delicious meals for us. They drove us to tour all over the country and presented us with gifts and the cream from fresh cow's milk in fatty spoonfuls. "Stay as long as you like," they told us. And often we did.

How many baths did we take with their children, crowded like hazelnuts among the plastic boats and soap bars? We looked so much alike that, flipping through photographs of us splashing in the tub, I had trouble picking myself and my siblings out from among the others. How often did we sit among their fruit trees or on the porch for barbecues? How often did they bring us to museums? To parks? To the homes of their friends? How many wonderful gestures did they make for my parents? Even helping us, back in the States, to load our furniture and boxes into trucks, then driving with us as we moved across the country. How many times—before then and for years afterward—did I speak to them using the terms cousin, auntie, uncle, lovingly and without qualifications of "half" or "through adoption" or "by marriage"?

But still I saw the family split along an invisible line of stubborn, loving rivalry. Remnants of the old struggle between the wives for their husband's favor and importance. This was what prompted Moshe uncle, in the first place, to take his toothbrush in exchange for a secret of such magnitude. To make a point of telling me the story of the sisters—and delineating precisely, almost gloatingly, who came from the original wife, who came from the second wife.

I once heard a cousin from one side say to a cousin from the other side, laughing at the ancient tangled ways, as though they were so distant now, "My granny was the ugly one and yours was the stupid one. Or no, was it the other way around?" But then, when he returned to his own side of the family, he confided to the others that their granny was insulted.

Years later, again, the joyous event of a family wedding brought out fresh, begrudging comments from opposing sides. Leah auntie whispered to her husband, "How much money do you think they spent for this day? Look at all this chicken. There's chicken roast and chicken dumplings and chicken curry and chicken kebobs. Who needs so much chicken? What a waste. Haa. I tell you, they've always been a bunch of wasters." She shook her head. Then, to prove her own thriftiness and the wisdom of everyone on her side of the family, she folded a few pieces of chicken into her handkerchief and slipped them into her purse.

Later that night, at the same wedding, I even heard one shriveled granny tell another, "Don't you think the bride is a little fat? That whole side has always been fat. Nai? When *I* was her age, I was so thin and lovely. Everyone called me lovely. I had such arms. Such beautiful arms." She held her arms out then—like flags of flesh—recalling how at one time just the sight of their creaminess striped with glass bangles made strangers stop still. Both grannies nodded contentedly over these arms. As though the wrists did not poke out. As though the elbows were not dry and horny. Then, and only then, when they had come to this agreement, could they begin to enjoy themselves.

I didn't just point fingers at others in this. I recognized the presence of what happened long ago still in those closest to me, too. When I was much older, my mother distanced herself from those kinds of relationships and pushed me to find a mate in standard Jewish America. At singles luncheons and dances. "Go, go," she told me, not questioning the ludicrousness of that lonely scene. The prowling looks. The hunger. The résumé exchange. "*This* is how people meet," she said, as though marriages were always made in this way. As though the polygamy happened much longer ago than it actually did. With my best interest in mind, she urged me to find a mate, a nice Jewish professional, who was worlds away from it all. "He should be educated. And healthy," I was told.

"I didn't marry an Indian, but it's your choice in the end. Also," she said, recalling the family history and abuse, "you want someone who respects women."

"You think all Indian men want their feet rubbed?" I asked, thinking of Nana-bai's story.

"It is not whether they want it. It is whether they expect it."

"So you think all Indian men *expect* their feet to be rubbed?"

"No." For a moment she seemed defensive that I was trying to pin her feelings down, to simplify them. "No," she said again. "I'm proud to be Indian, and the whole culture is not like that. But there are parts of the past that I cannot forget." She shrugged, and there was nothing in this to hold against her. Peeling back these layers is an ugly reality of evolution. Resenting the past and fine-tuning the future, and hopefully finding somewhere between these a core of truth. "Really," she sighed, "you just want a mensch." Of all the possibilities, when she finally found a word for the "gentleman" she wished for me, it was not out of her own vocabulary, but rather from the white Jew's Yiddish. Making peace is never simple or finite.

I also saw a manifestation of the polygamy in myself, too, at a low, naked point in my life. Utterly heartbroken in college when the first lover I ever had left me, I became like a character in a cheap movie, wanting to grasp and hurt. I took up with his brother. I never purposely tried to emulate the triangle from generations ago in my family. But even on a biological level, I had inherited some knowledge of the pain that can come from two people sharing this intimacy. All the while watching myself from the outside and marveling that sexy laughter and scattered moles on skin could be so alike between brothers, I touched one as though he were the other, with a determination that was fueled by something larger than just me.

In the end, it seemed possible that the many generations of this family would never move far past an arrogant Indian man who married these two women. One beautiful. One dark-skinned. Certainly all along, I never would have believed it would be revisited as horrifically as it was in the wake of Nana-bai's death. But for good or bad, what emerged from this was our legacy. So despite all the grudges and fierce loyalties, we continued to come together, in a patchwork, to make meals.

The day Moshe uncle first told me our secret, I returned quietly to the kitchen where our overly intimate culture lived in small ways. The woman baring a brown breast to nurse her baby sat unconsciously with her dress hiked up and her legs spread wide before her. Two aunties bickering over why the tea was cold were loudly accused of being troublemakers. And Nana-bai, the one of the two wives who was still alive—widowed so many years later— even now found herself in just the role of second wife. The archaic details of this almost got lost in the modern expanses of kitchen linoleum. There were no outright demands of her. Instead the other women quickly chose the best of the chores for themselves, and it was only expected that she would take what was left, without complaints, even cheerfully. So the aunties from the other side of the family made up a large chatting presence, taking their time folding hand towels and slicing open new bags of spices. And Nana-bai was matter-of-factly left to the smelly job of chopping onions.

Nana-bai detached herself from the rest of the women to approach my mother and me. She wore a thick tan sweater over a sari, with her gray hair in a bun, and she looked at me, kissed me, ancient, from behind thick glasses. "Haa. There are too many people in this kitchen," she declared to Mommy frankly. I knew she was right. And once the cooking got under way, there would be more opinions and spoons at work than any single stew could handle. "Come out on to the porch," Nana-bai told me. She took a bowl of onions and a knife with her. And I followed with Holly Hobby caught up under my arm and a large red onion filling each hand. I took a position at her elbow, so as we stepped down the few porch stairs, she could lean on me. That was the meaning of respect for her, when someone helped her up and down the stairs, holding her elbow, with graciousness and without being asked to do it. Little in the world was more important that that.

"It is good to be with the whole family," she said as she sat down at the porch table and began to peel and chop. "Nai?"

I shrugged, still absorbing my new understanding of our family, playing with a shred of brittle onion skin. "I guess so."

"As you grow older, it will be more and more important to spend time with them and with the rest of the Bene Israel community," she assured me.

"Why?" In all my visions, I saw myself growing up with many things. With G-d and my parents and much-loved siblings and someday a husband. But never once did I see myself as she did, evolving so I could graduate into this small tribe of chutney and squabbles. "*You* don't even spend so much time with them," I pointed out.

"Kai-bug! There is a long history between me and them," she sniffed, defensive. Her fingers continued to methodically chop the onions, but now she watched my face closely. "For you it is different though."

"If it's so important, you should see them more yourself," I cornered her. "What would I do with them?"

Nana-bai sat quiet for a moment, and I worried that I had angered her. But then she put her chopping knife down and began to speak quickly, in a tirade, scared. "You can be a good girl and listen to your mummy. You can comb your hair and learn to cook and clean and arrange your brother's bed each morning. You can get a fine education. Then you can show the family all these things. And when you have a nice husband someday, you can bring him to the community. And then G-d willing you can bring your children." She stopped abruptly after this and went back to chopping onions. "Promise me you'll be a part of them," she said.

Without even understanding fully what she wanted, it felt impossible to me, at best a burden. But I knew I should at least appease her. "Okay," I told her. And if it had been anyone else—someone I did not know so intimately, who did not every day try to form me—I probably would have just left it at that. But she was Nana-bai and she had lived with us for so long that we had history between us, too. So, despite myself, though I smiled at her, I also crossed two sticky fingers behind my back. As an open-clause loophole. As a way to someday back out of my promise.

"Good. Tsangla, tsangla," she said happily, as if she didn't know what I had done.

But Nana-bai always knew everything. And annoyed by her ploy, I continued deliberately. "I'm not everything you try to make me be." I felt certain I was being cruel, jabbing at her most earnest, vulnerable hopes.

But then she surprised me and deflated my fleeting unkindness by nodding agreeably. As if she expected this. "That, too, is good." And then she left it up to me to find a way of doing it all.

Nana-bai did, in fact, try to hold me to my promise. But this was the only time she ever even subtly spoke to our family's peculiarity, which was an ongoing dialogue for the others. At different times afterward, it felt like my whole existence was in reaction to that promise, trying to be what she wanted me to be. On and off, in loops and leaps and lulls, I struggled to come to terms with the problems and pleasures of my unique background, on its own and up against the other cultures around me. But meanwhile, at every single moment, Nana-bai's expectations and my promise to her always continued to shadow me.

# PART TWO

# Houses and Homes

*Saffron Chicken:*

*Take 1 kilo chicken and apply 1 flat tablespoon salt. After an hour, wash the meat.*

*In a flat pot, add six tablespoons oil. When it is hot, add two big onions cut in thin pieces.*

*When onions are brown, add meat and grinded spices: 1 teaspoon chili powder, two fingers ginger, 8 cloves garlic, 12 seeds black pepper, 3 sticks cinnamon.*

*After half an hour, add coconut juice and peeled potatoes cut in small pieces, 4 pieces from each potato.*

*Ten minutes before removing from the stove, add saffron and 1 tablespoon sugar.*

—Nana-bai's diary, page 52

When the matchmaker came for Nana-bai a second time, almost a year after his first visit, everyone knew his offer would be grim. Nana-bai was already marked as a woman with a broken engagement, so more than ever now, her pickings would be scarce. But many other things had changed in the meantime. Great misfortune had found the family.

One summer night, papa's printing press burned to the ground. Word of this had not yet reached him the next morning. So he woke up and went to work as usual, shuffling papers and straightening his stiffly starched clothes. A few hours later, he returned from the charred ruins, covered in soot, his face torn, eyes unblinking and wide. "We have nothing. We have nothing," he repeated over and over.

Without the proper insurance, the family's entire source of income was destroyed and irreplaceable, leaving them with many liabilities. The servants slowly packed up their clothes and led their children away by the hand. The creditors came to take away the family's automobile, then their furniture, then even their pots and pans. Finally an officer of the government, wearing a stuffy western suit and spectacles, came to claim their fine, large house.

A dutiful son-in-law, Solly gave Rebecca's parents a monthly allowance for food and helped them find a small house nearby, where mama, papa, and Nana-bai went to live with their few remaining belongings. So when the matchmaker came for Nana-bai a second time, this is where he found her.

This time, he was all business. Casting aside the formalities of the past deal, and even its regrettable failure, he expected an easy bargain. He did not bother drinking tea or complimenting mama's sari. Instead, after the initial greetings, he briskly and immediately asked to have Nana-bai brought over to him. Coming out of the house where she had been cleaning the floor, she squinted silently into the sunlight and pushed the loose tendrils of hair from her face, nervous. Her hand still clutched an unfortunate rag. The matchmaker inspected her closely, circling and clucking.

"Well," he said to mama and papa after she had returned to the house. "She has not aged well in a year." Papa started to protest angrily, but the matchmaker cut him off. "I am only trying to be honest and reasonable here. So we can all know what to expect. Come, let us walk."

The three of them started together up the road. Mama picked up a stick as they walked and bent it nervously back and forth between her fingers. It was the stiff, rubbery kind that did not break immediately. But she bent it first this way, then that way, and finally it snapped. "I am not even sure our daughter needs to marry now," she told the matchmaker.

Papa agreed with her. "Our circumstances have changed," he said, pained. "We don't even have servants anymore."

"It is good to keep one daughter at home. For cooking and cleaning and helping us as we grow old. Especially since our daughters-in-law do not live with us," she added.

"This is reasonable," the matchmaker said. He paused for a moment, wondering if he could get away with it, then blurted out: "But after the whole incident with that man from Cochin, wouldn't you be able to face the community more happily if she was finally married?"

Here papa stopped dead still, furious, then turning on the matchmaker, caused a yellow dust to rise around him from the road. "*You* told me I could trust your word on that man. That man who turned out to be a drunk. I have tried to tell myself that you could not be held accountable for his mistakes, but now you dare to throw *that* back at me?" The matchmaker quivered, and mama caught papa's hand with her fingers, to hold him back, just in case. She had never seen him so angry.

"Sir. Sir," the matchmaker stepped back, taking an appeasing manner for a moment. "I have already apologized a thousand times to your family for all that took place. Did you not receive the box of fine papayas I sent you when it all happened, to express my sympathies? I feel terribly. And that is why I am here to help. I want to make up for it."

Papa breathed deeply for a moment and eased his clenched fists. Struggling for an even tone, his voice came out tired instead, and he asked: "What is it you want to do here? We don't need any more difficulties."

"I promise, this will all be discreet and simple and contained," the matchmaker began. "Your son-in-law Solly has approached me. And he has offered to take your last daughter as his second wife." Both parents began to speak at once, but the matchmaker cut in over them. "Please, let me finish. Perhaps it would have been better had he come to speak with you himself. But he knew my wisdom and experience with such delicate matters. And he knew also that I, a third party, would be able to best illustrate for you the practical and complicated considerations in this matter."

"He has never expressed an interest in this before," papa said thoughtfully.

"True. But Solly has always known she is clever and a hard worker. Also, recently, with his increased involvement in your family's welfare, Solly thought this might be the most agreeable setup for everyone," the matchmaker told them.

"He *has* been very generous in all our troubles. Though certainly it is not ideal for either of our girls," mama said doubtfully to papa. "But both would be provided for."

Papa looked back down the road, toward the house where Nana-bai waited. "And at least she would have some kind of status in the end. Even as just a second wife."

They spoke quietly a few minutes longer, while the matchmaker rubbed his hands together in anticipation, waiting for the final word. "Are we settled, then?" he asked.

"Yes," papa told him at last.

And so it was done.

Nana-bai and Solly's wedding was a quiet affair. Mama and papa were not wealthy enough to make something lavish now. And even the dowry was just a few symbolic gold coins and trinkets. Just their close family and friends watched the bride and groom in their humble ceremony. Rebecca was there, as expected, tall in a deep purple sari, stiff and covered by a chilly air. The chazan chanted the ancient Hebrew blessings with a hint of Indian drone. He filled a glass with wine. The groom drank half, then handed the glass to the bride and she drank half. Afterward, there was a luncheon and fruit.

"Do you love him?" Rebecca had asked Nana-bai coldly, just moments after papa first informed them. She threw out that word, "love," from the English books they had read in their school days.

"I just hope he will be good to me," she had told her, stunned by it all.

"You two are suited, you know," she had then said, pouting. "In talk and interests, you are like-minded. And both clever. But I will always be his first wife. And I have given him four sons already." She plucked nervously at the edges of her sari. "There is much honor in that."

Afterward, mama had asked them both to join her for tea. Maybe over the familiarity of hot water and honey, she hoped, everything would be as it had always been in the family. But instead there was only silence. So mama began talking. Without stopping, without blinking even, she stirred her tea, and talked to them. About the neighbors. About the fish she bought that day. About the rains. And the two girls who had many years ago played together—one airy and cheeky, the other shy—now could only avoid each other's eyes, numb, as they listened to her prattle.

On their wedding night, Solly brought Nana-bai to a hovel in the crowded middle streets of Bombay. It was just a dark room, in between other dark rooms and the noises and smells of other people living too closely. "This is where you will stay. For now," he told her. He made no excuses for its filth or the fact that very soon she might have to move elsewhere. Seeing this place for the first time at night made it seem that much more weighty to Nana-bai. Even the act of stepping in and closing the world behind her felt like a sinking, decisive force.

That night he came to her in the wedding bed, which she had decorated in a few red flowers and their perfumes. She waited there, as she had been told, naked under the covers, frightened and quiet. He stood over her, then took a corner of the cover and tugged it away just a little as she cowered. One tan nipple tumbled out before him, clumsy. Then he pulled the whole cover off of her, exposing her entire body. Her dark brown skin, the color of nut and snuff and liver, the native black, the un-British burn of her. "Haa," he mumbled, watching, waiting as she remained still and trembling, till he could see the goose bumps form all over her.

Loosening his pants and watching the resignation melt into her features, he came to her thin and hard, burping quietly from the curry, spreading her thighs with both his hands and taking a fleshy calf to wrap around him. Wordlessly on top, he thrust himself into her, breaking through again and again, making her cry out from the pain. Then, finally, with heavy breaths, he pulled out, to rest upon his elbows. Beneath him, she remained frozen, with closed eyes.

Waking up near Solly the next morning, Nana-bai noticed first his toenails. Under the stark new sunlight, they were thick and long and yellow. And nothing could disguise them as they protruded from the sheets. To think that just a few hours ago they had been digging into the bedding as he writhed above her made her feel sick and look next disgustedly at herself.

She peered down at her own body. The soft meat of her ankles. The point of her knees. The neat span of her hips. The length of her arms and fingers. The curve of her breasts. And the stretch of stomach underneath. And then she saw beyond these. Past the paper cuts from books and the roughness of her hands from cleaning. Past even the glass bangles on her arms and the gold rings in her ears. Into the woman that she was, that every woman was, the primitive being. She saw the pores of skin and the fluffy direction of its hair. The yellow gel of fat, like ghee to fry food in. The intestines, shivering, sliding together, purring, rolling as if in moss. The stringy opening-closing red of muscles. The deep browns and greens and blues of organs, churning like freshly mixed paints. And, finally, the meaty mass of womb, breathing heavily as though through thick leather fins in salty water, slick in its liquid like a raw sacrifice to old gods. She knew with a shuddering feeling what would come next from lying with this man of terrible toenails. A bit of warm flesh to nurture-suckle-bathe-feed-dress, a child.

Maybe in some other corner of the world or fifty years later there might have been a way out, to never have to relive that man and that night. Or perhaps, even, there might have been a choice in this moment. To be bold and run off. To defy the family. To divorce. To break the orders of biology that made her who she was and only that. But Nana-bai knew, both resigned and proud, that she would never bring such dishonor to her family. There, then, she could only turn inwards for the possibility of escape. She spread her hands over her stomach where she imagined she felt her womb and its watery rhythms. She decided then, at least I will make this mine. If not through Nana-bai herself, then through her child, everything might be different.

When Solly next came to Nana-bai, she was determined to create a baby. While she plucked a chicken and peeled vegetables for dinner, she could feel this determination first in her body. Her very tissues were ready and primally edgy as she walked about, carefully cushioned and delicate, like she was carrying fragile things inside. And she knew this determination also in her mind, as she looked into a small looking glass to apply a soft, white powder on her face and a dark line of cazer under her eyes. Around and around her body she swirled the many red layers of sari that Solly had bought for her in Pune as a wedding present. She combed out her long hair, too, so that it hung richly to her waist.

After they ate, Nana-bai led Solly to the bed, before he could even think to lead her. He was caught by surprise from this boldness, and leaned up against the wall, smiling slightly as though charmed. Feeling indulgent, he watched her to see what she would do next. She hesitated for just a moment, tripping over her modesty, bewildered at trying to touch a man so as to make him want to touch her.

And then, at once, instinctually, as though it were a veil or the weighty fabrics of afterbirth, she took in hand the loose end of sari that was draped over her shoulder. She held it up above her, arm crooked, the red trail end of cloth poking out from her palm gracefully like a blood-flow loosened from the vein. Beneath this rain of red, she followed the opening of the cloth in circles around herself, allowing the sari to unravel around her. First slowly, and then more quickly, she twirled, womb pounding. And more and more of the red material was loosened around her, baring an arm, a square of waist, a thigh, a leg and then right after, another leg, till she stood, revealed, in just a puddle of red.

Flushed and dizzy, she came to him, fumbling to remove his clothes. With eyes half closed from above, she took his flesh into her hands like a scoop of water, and brought it deep into her own body. Then the rhythms and sounds that had once been inside her seized him and sounded now outside their bodies, in pudding skin on pudding skin and then, finally, in the fall of exhausted limbs.

Afterward, still stunned, even unnerved by her forwardness and his own succumbing, Solly hissed at her, drowsy, and pushed Nana-bai from the bedding onto the cold floor. But Nana-bai began to peacefully drift to sleep, even there, feeling the baby that was already growing inside her in the tiniest of forms.

*I immigrated to Israel and stayed with my niece Leah for 6
months in Netanya. The government gave me $800, but then
she took it from me on account for that I was staying with her.
When I was finally given an apartment, they moved me to be
with all the other immigrants from India and Morocco in poor
city of Acco. They took immigrants free of charge to see all the
places in Israel. Once we had been to Jerusalem near where the
President worked. He saw us from the window and his police-
man came to pull me out from the line because he immediately
noticed me, the only one who wore a sari. I got afraid, but he
gave courage and took me to the President. He asked me if I
was happy there in Israel, and I said yes, but that I would like
to live in the nice neighborhood of Netanya where I had my relations. He told me to write him a letter to remind him. And by
G-d's wish and with the help of the President we had a home in
Netanya.*

—NANA-BAI'S DIARY, PAGE 26

When I was eight years old, I danced on top of bomb shelters. There was nothing of poetic justice in this, in dancing
on the plain cement blocks that capped those underground tun-
nel ways. Instead, as I climbed onto them off the hot road, barefoot, sucking on an orange, and pressing my joy-flexed toes into
the chalky chill, there was only a spinning, delicious relief. I had
never before encountered bomb shelters or orange groves or bold,
barefoot children back home in the United States, but that year
when my parents' Zionist dreams came together and my family
moved to a socialist kibbutz in Israel, I grew to know them intimately. I was plopped down and flexible, and anything in this new
home, even the tough-kid ethic of purposely going barefoot, felt
to me like a storybook adventure.

The kibbutz was poised atop crisp olive mountains at the barbed-wire crack of the border. On one side it saw Israeli cities decorating the ocean in shiny scoops. On the other side wandered ancient Lebanese shepherds. Over the gates drifted the wailing call for Muslims to come to prayer. With the first pink breath of dawn, I would walk to my schoolhouse, drinking in the air of the mountains and the blanket-patterns of the kibbutz. Black roads, red roofs, grass squares, the spots of gates and watchtowers, and the mazelike sparse white strips of the bomb shelters.

The day could only really begin after I'd reached the schoolhouse. In many ways, it was more of a home for me than the building in which my family and I had just woken up together. The schoolhouse held almost all my clothes and shoes, my soap and shampoo. It even had a bed for me to nap in, from the days when children actually slept each night in the schoolhouse. There, the nanny and teachers provided me and my classmates with breakfast, lunch and snacks, all our classes, music and dance lessons. They would also guide us in our small chores at the animal farm, ensuring that even at that age we were part of the kibbutz labor and way of life.

Following the basic socialist principle which takes from each according to his abilities, and gives to each according to his needs, every member of the kibbutz worked to maintain it, even the very young and old. And in exchange, instead of a traditional salary, the community provided for every individual. All jobs were equally important and assigned through a committee chosen by "the people." It may have been, say, Shmuli's job to spend his entire day working in the banana fields or factories. But at the same time it was someone else's job to doctor his children, cook hot meals in the communal dining hall, launder the clothes, and arrange for things like electricity and toilet paper and holidays. So at the end of the day, after Shmuli had done his part, there were a few dollars of spending money in his pocket and a chance for simple leisure. A dip in the pool, or a trip into the nearby city.

Like the bomb shelter, the kibbutz way of life was also born out of necessity. In the crude, early years of pioneers and dangerous enemies, when the community's very existence was threatened daily, it made sense to have one adult watching over all the children, freeing the other adults for the carefully delegated work that would contribute to the whole and ensure survival. When I lived there, though, the threats from the border were rarely serious enough to force us to seek protection. Instead we scrambled up the flat rooftops of the bomb shelters, to rest, cool, sizzle, waltz. Then others joined us and the bomb shelters became a gathering place.

Among classmates on the kibbutz, the relationship was more familial than friendly. The knowledge of being together for life, even on weekends and vacations, allowed the doting favorites or fights, and the lasting divisions that emerged, to all somehow meld into the routine of eternity. At that age we showered in front of one another. We borrowed clothes back and forth, and knew the details of everyone's home lives and refrigerators. This was not something I could have expected or gotten used to in America.

I remember my first day in the schoolhouse at shower time. I was waiting for a turn under the water, wrapped in only a fuzzy towel, which I had pulled tightly up under my nervous chin. Before me, boys and girls from my class were also waiting for their turns. One by one, bored, they began rolling the towels off their bodies freely, winding them up and trying to smack each other with them from behind. Flat chests and skinny legs skipped around the room, yelping at times, laughing gleefully at other moments, after a particularly rich thwack or a skid across the wet floor. I, of course, was self-conscious. Back home, well-brought-up children did not get naked or try to bring out raw welts on their friends' rear ends. These seemed to be wild children before me, with their hitting and spitting. And yet, surprisingly, I was self-conscious, not so much because of the roughhousing, but because I was left out of it. That day, no one was trying to smack me, the new girl, still covered up in a towel and accents of English. I was somehow set apart from the joke.

It turned out, however, that it would be impossible to remain a stranger for very long within such close quarters. Very soon, they knew me and I knew them. And we accepted each other—in all our plain brown nudity, and in our fuzzy, smacking ideas of me-you, mine-yours—for only natural.

Sitting on the bomb shelters during the day was refreshing for our bare feet after walking on hot tar roads. It seemed we trudged purposely, painfully across the places that were melted by the red Mediterranean sun. Just so that we could stumble upon the bomb shelter oases, where the cement soothed us like running streams of cold water. Some shelters had loquat trees and wild pockets of sour grass flowers draping them, from which we could just pick and eat. Between mouthfuls, and as we eased our

battered toes over the chilly concrete, we talked of many important things. And often my international angle gave new light to
our exchanges.

"The thing is that *Sesame Street* in America has Big Bird. He's
yellow and huge, one of the stars of the show. But in Israel, *Sesame
Street* has Kipi the Porcupine instead. Kipi is too silly, and I really
like Big Bird better, you should see him."

Or sometimes great debates would ensue: "Look, I also love
chocolate spread on bread! I wish more people in America knew
about it. But peanut butter and jelly is great too, maybe even better . . . and maybe even healthy! And no one in Israel will even try
it; that's what the real problem is!"

When we congregated on the bomb shelters at night, though,
in the brisk wind, we were not there for our feet at all, and there
was a different tone. There was something pure and full of awe in
how we knew ourselves, sitting at night on top of a mountain.
Like we were floating on a tire in the middle of a black ocean, with
the added blackness of closed eyes. We seemed to be both unimag-
inably tiny and giant at once. And swept away, we would sing
Naomi Shemer folk songs and prayers:

> *Please watch over me my good God,*
> *on the honey and on the sting,*
> *on the bitter and the sweet,*
> *on the garden, on the wall,*
> *on the light and on the children.*

At those moments, under the rain of stars, the very feel of the
surface we sat on conjured up something biblical and frighten-
ingly fleshy. Images of Jewish fighters in those hills, from radio

snippets of the month before, from ancient tales of hundreds of years ago. We heard the stalking of all those hard feet. And somehow we saw no complexity in singing songs for peace on top of bomb shelters. It seemed just part of reality on the kibbutz. As much as the fact that people always left the door of their homes unlocked. No reason, no need for reason even.

*This is what I tell the children about home: "Home sweet home" and "Charity begins at home." G-d willing, they will see this, too.*

—NANA-BAI'S DIARY, PAGE 17

*T*here was a time in my family, before Israel, when even with all the complexities of our mixed cultures, we seemed to be invincible. Nothing could stop us from becoming everything we wanted. Pretty and naked, we children grew up alongside our parents as they grew up themselves, fresh-faced, even bold. My parents walked the earth like mythological heroes, hair streaming behind them and a child on each hip, eating fish from the lakes and sleeping under the stars. We were resourceful and unhurt. Dreamy. Idealistic. Adventurous. And, in the end, whatever my parents did always turned out to be the right thing.

Much of my family's life, however, has been formed by the era after Israel in which this suddenly went flat. We moved to Israel because my father was a Zionist and believed it was the best place on earth for Jewish families. We gave up our whole life in America for this. A home, friends, and a stable income, hoping to be accepted for membership in the kibbutz. To pick bananas, work the land, and build a Jewish country. My mother, more practical for having done this all her life, appreciated the easier, comfortable quality of the world she had recently discovered in America. But she went along with the move anyway. She had lived much of her life in Israel and felt at home there, too. Most of all, she believed in my father's belief.

We moved to Israel because of their grandiose ideals but were forced to return to the United States in the end because of petty bureaucratic details. A property lawsuit we had pending back in America—which we informed the kibbutz about before moving—suddenly, once we were in Israel, became the symbolic issue that struggling political factions of the kibbutz used to try and assert their power. The old leaders had said to us, We understand your case, come anyway. The new leaders now said to them, We don't want their financial problems, you should not have told them to come in the first place. This snowballed and became the factor that prevented us from being officially voted in for acceptance to the kibbutz. Even if all members there were equal, some members, as it goes, were more equal than others.

My father went to the Israel Immigration office, maddened at how our family was caught up in these tangles. The agent he spoke with sat behind a desk littered with glossy brochures saying, Come to Israel! Build the land! Make the desert bloom! "Look," he told her. "This can't happen. Me, my wife, and four kids, we'll soon have no home, no money. Nothing. We left everything behind and came here."

"Nu?" she asked him, coldly playing with the point of her pencil. "Who asked you to come?"

As our time on the kibbutz came to an end, we grasped for other possibilities in Israel. My father applied for a position teaching at the University of Haifa. He was accepted, but my mother, infuriated at the final blow from the woman behind the Immigration desk, said to him, "I'm going back to America. And I'm taking the kids with me." So he came, too.

When we returned to America, Nana-bai did not come back to live with us—while we were in Israel she had found her own apartment. For the rest of her life, aside from her long visits with us, she was settled across the country. I still lived under my half-promise to her on what I would someday grow up to be. But now there were many more immediate concerns. So heavy and pressing were these concerns that my parents never even had the chance to pause and mourn the fall of their Zionist dream.

Instead they needed to find a home, food, work, and health insurance for the family. They were under so much pressure at this time that my father suffered a small heart attack one day while parking the car. And from sheer will—and the knowledge that we did not have enough money to cover hospital bills—he held his chest and waited it through. Then he just got out of the car and carried on as though nothing had happened. None of us were there when it actually took place. We only learned about it years later. But chilled, I imagined him in those moments many times. Leaning up against the steering wheel, pained and patient, wondering if this would be the end. Then when he saw it wasn't, that he would in fact live, he put on his jacket, rolled up the windows, and locked the car doors, relieved that such tiny details could be attended to.

While he looked for a job, we temporarily rented a house and slept on its living-room floor in sleeping bags. Most of our belongings remained packed up in boxes in the otherwise empty rooms upstairs. It amazed me how little space a whole family's existence could take up when confined by cardboard.

Needing secretly to feel more settled in, I drove my mother

crazy, remorselessly unpacking random boxes in the empty upstairs rooms of the house. Things like candlesticks and framed
paintings—adornments for a genuine home, not a temporary stop-
over. "Who took these out? Who put these here?" she'd call from
upstairs, her voice carrying clear and sharp, since there was no
furniture to insulate the noise between these walls and hardwood
floors. Then she'd pound downstairs with a typewriter or a bundle of records she'd found unpacked in an empty closet.

The key to peace at this house was in keeping the curtains
closed. We sat in the middle of a decent neighborhood, with decent families living right next door. G-d forbid they should glance
into the living-room windows at the front of our house and see
our sleeping bags spread out on the floor, no furniture, just a
small black and white TV on a folding chair. It did not bother me.
Children can become accustomed to anything quite quickly. And,
in fact, though we had all the furniture we needed years later, we
kids still sometimes pulled out sleeping bags and lay down on the
floor to watch a movie. But for my parents the living room curtains were the final shield to the rawness of their shames and bur-
dens. And though they did wonderful things in that house, trying
to make us feel like we had safety and routine—making Shabbat
meals, celebrating the holidays—they still years later would come
to tears of guilt when thinking about this vulnerable moment in
our lives.

Family and old friends came by with worn winter coats and
clothes, and huge boxes of packaged foods for us. At first I did not
think of what this meant, accepting provisions, hand-me-downs,
and even money from our gentle benefactors. They mysteriously
materialized in our lives just when we needed them—like straight
out of some Victorian novel. "We've been so blessed," they'd say,
discreetly slipping checks into my father's reluctant hands. "We

wanted to share our blessings with you." Then they'd retreat into the shadows, to let the good they had done live on its own. Coming from the kibbutz, I was appreciative but unruffled. This seemed ordinary to me. Like sharing, not charity. And instead I was excited for a while at the surprises of the things they brought. The fluffiness of a jacket. Even the novelty of their canned goods, since usually everything we ate was handmade. I was thrilled to be able to select dinner from the boxes they'd brought over, like we had our own personal grocery store before us.

But then one evening, when we ate a dinner of spaghetti on plastic plates, to my surprise the tomato sauce was thin and sour. I poked at the noodles with my fork. I was not eating tomato sauce at all, I realized suddenly, accusingly. It was just the closest thing we had, tomato *juice*. Searching now, I spotted two or three more small cans of the stuff in the big cardboard box of groceries. And, all at once, these miniature cans of juice seemed so flimsy and senseless in the world of foodstuffs. Like marshmallows or tins of caviar. Our benefactors probably kept a stack of these tomato juice cans in their basement bar for Bloody Marys. They must have just tossed a few of them into our goodwill package as an afterthought. But here it was our watery *meal*. And that's when I knew we were poor. Not so poor that we could not even put up some show for the world. Not so poor that we had no food at all, or would even compare ourselves to people in third-world-country poverty. But poor enough to fight over the finances of eating a full banana instead of half of one. To reuse disposable spoons not because it was environmentally wise but because it was cheaper. And to take tomato—sauce, juice, whatever—in any form we could get.

When my father finally found a job, we moved again and rented a home in the back country of upstate New York. We could not afford to live in the expensive New York City suburbs near his work. But my parents wanted us to have access to clean living, so he woke up at the icy four o'clock hour each morning to drive the many miles in between. The place we found sat on acres of swampland. It had a riverbed and long stretches of berry fields and skunk cabbage. It might have been picturesque in this scenery. But there was something unsettled there, leading me each night to dream restlessly.

The house itself was deep and dank, with a large fireplace and a maze of small rooms in the basement. The front door faced the back of our property, and the back door, porch, and dirt driveway led out the front. Its floors were covered in linoleum made to look like red and blue oriental carpets. Its doorways had the swinging shutters of Western movie taverns. And its unfinished wooden kitchen table, benches, bunk beds, and couches, handmade, were honeycombed with secret drawers. It was the place where Alice in Wonderland would retire someday, if she grew old and lonely.

I think our family hoped to recapture the freedom of the kibbutz in this house. We wandered through the long grasses, catching turtles and frogs in the river, hiking in the mountains and cornfields. We spent the seasons counting the stars and watching for the river to flood or freeze. But this was a desolate country existence for us, also. I felt as if, till the day I died, I could continue making endless paper-doll rows of snow angels on the stretches of silent, snowy land, and I could continue cowering under the blankets with the Nancy Drew and Bobbsey Twins mysteries I hoarded from the red schoolhouse library nearby. And the world would not know or care anything more about my existence.

Out in the middle of nowhere, we were the first children on the school bus every morning, and the last to get off in the evening. A surreal two and a half hours each way. During these long trips, we got to know our bus driver, Richie, intimately. He had sleek blond hair and dark sunglasses, and as we shared our snacks with him, Gertie and I argued about who would have him for her boyfriend if we were both grown up. (Gertie said that she should, because she was older. I pinched her and insisted that I should, because she had already gotten to kiss a boy.)

That house was an hour and a half away from the nearest synagogue, so, especially as Jews, we felt lost. One time, we found a swastika carved into a fat cigar in our driveway. It must have been left there by one of our neighbors who somehow eerily knew we were Jewish. I tried to picture the person who would do something like this. Some faceless man, but red and whiskered too. Probably on his way to go hunting. It was then, even before dawn, as he drove by our house, that the swastika must have occurred to him, like a vile artistic vision. So he whittled a moment at a cheap cigar with his pocket knife. Then he rolled down the truck window and left his homespun wickedness to greet us when we woke up to get the newspaper. Numbly we crumbled the cigar into chunky grounds and tossed it onto the dirt path at the side. A day later it was indistinguishable from the earth around it.

After we returned from Israel to the United States, I found myself knotty and tongue-tied in new ways. Not only was the culture bestowed upon me through biology strange, but now my own experiences, memories, and leanings were also different from those of other children around me. In the moving and unsettling from house to house to house, I retreated even further into my shyness, confused and absent during the period when tastes, styles, and social graces are traditionally formed. I should have been striking out on my own, carefully assembling the pieces that would some-day evolve into a grown-up me. Like all the other children around me, who had lived in one place all their lives. Whose parents seemed to have as much money as they needed to nurture normal whimsy and experimentation. But because of my parents' shelter-ing strictness in our lives and our tough finances, I remained naively sheltered in our eclectic, often eccentric, potpourri of cul-tures. Some children might have turned bullying or uncaring or jealous. But for me, this was where I began my life as a geek.

I knew very little of the expensive clothing and trendy new col-ors most children my age were steadily learning about and begin-ning to wear. Instead I had only the samples of traditional garb to influence me. The Israeli covah tembel, a dopey pointed hat to be worn against the sun. The modest, often frumpy, long skirts of ultra-Orthodox Jews. The brilliant greens and reds of Indian silks and flashy jewelry. No particular style fit me well. So when I reached into the large boxes of hand-me-downs, the best I could put together was an earnest, studied combination of them all. A triumphant but garish and appalling mishmash. The concept of matching fabrics and colors utterly eluded me—and to some de-gree, will always elude me. In learning fashion, like in learning a language, if the crucial period of potential fluency is missed, it can never come naturally. I missed it, and after that, though I made vague attempts at the elegant bearing a girl can have in heels and a smart suit, or in the fit of a scarf—not even for warmth, but for show—it never sat right with me.

Now, when I try to imagine how I must have seemed to the

other children around me, neatly pressed and color-coordinated as they were, I have to laugh. To them, as I passed by—startling them—in the halls, I probably looked like a pint-size bag lady, caught between the Nineteenth Century and a jazzercise video. My favorite outfit consisted of a bright blue skirt, a shiny peach blouse, sandals and leg warmers in two shades of purple. I wore big red button earrings and barrettes with large bowed ribbons atop my head. I wore stretch pants with stirrups and four different kinds of stripes at once. And checkered shirts and cotton flowers in my hair. Like a suitcase that had vomited its contents. Like all the many colors and textures of my body's intestines and organs had been turned inside out. I was certain I looked good then, though now, when I see pictures of the mess I made of myself in that time, I know the stylish children around me must have suspected I was trying to single-handedly bring down all that was sane and sensible in their designer suede world.

My experience with pop culture was similarly limited. I had heard of pop stars whose records my classmates were beginning to buy. But I knew nothing about them myself. Like Madonna. I had never actually seen her. But I was told she sang sexy songs and wore black fishnet, that she had handfuls and handfuls of cleavage, and probably kissed boys with her tongue—really, what did her father have to say about *that*? But I did not think someone like Madonna actually existed in the real world. I imagined her as more of a cartoon character, like Betty Boop.

Then, one day, a classmate brought Madonna's latest album to school. As she pulled it from her backpack to show her friends, the bright cardboard caught the overhead lights. And in my desk a few paces away, I gasped out loud. There she was on the album. Madonna: shiny and fleshy and sexy. I would not have been more startled if she had actually stepped out of the album, taken form from ears to toes, and given our teacher, Mr. Kappelle, a lap dance right there. The joke—the testament to that wondrous time in my life—is that as I sat there for several long minutes with eyes round in amazement, my surprise had nothing to do with finally witnessing Madonna's raw sensuality for myself. It had nothing to do, even, with finding that she was far more beautiful than I had ever imagined—though certainly she was. It was, in fact, just surprise for the fact that this legendary Madonna was not an ink-drawn, painted cartoon at all. She was *photographed* and that meant that such a woman really existed on this earth.

For a long time, even after I should have been discovering my own tastes, the only entertainment I was exposed to reflected my parents' opinions. We listened to my father's classic Neil Diamond, of course. His lovely candy lyrics about women named Caroline and Cherry and Rosie were planted so deeply in my mind, that even years later in college, my roommate woke me out of a deep sleep to tell me I had been chanting his name from my dreams: Neil, Neil, Neil.

Following my mother, we also listened to a tubby, middle-aged Israeli folk singer named Yehoram Gaon. He sang nostalgic, traditional songs about an Israel of mythology. Of settlers who whistled on their way to work. Who read the Bible while they ate lunch in the fields. We had only the one record of him live in concert. But we listened to it again and again, so that I could imagine him feisty, parading around in a white pantsuit and crooning to the ladies in the audience. We heard it so often that soon I knew all the songs by heart, and even the exact moments in the concert when he stuttered and told jokes.

I might have made up for what was missing if not through

television, which was regulated, then with a steady diet off the modern big screen. But going to the movies as a family was an expensive outing, so we rarely did it. Also there were very few movies my parents deemed appropriate for children. We saw a few drive-ins. And *E.T.* and *The Song of the South*, which my parents carefully selected for screening. But aside from these, the glamour of film was foreign to me. And everything about it seemed wildly frivolous, from the five-dollar popcorn to the Pac-Man arcade games that ceaselessly devoured one quarter per one minute of pleasure.

When my classmates began to go every weekend to see such racy-sounding movies as *Back to the Future* and *Dirty Dancing*, I could not even begin to imagine all the things they witnessed there. The few tastes of this I got for myself, at their birthday parties, were as exciting for me as if I had entered the fantasy, carnival worlds within the actual movies. I returned home from their parties and recounted all that had happened there for my siblings. Like the way a trip to Bali is documented in a journal. I carefully listed everything that took place—step-by-step since it was so foreign. As if I were afraid to forget the details and the local lingo I'd picked up.

At their parties, we ate junk food and looked through stacks of rented videos about college boys or rich Manhattan living or beautiful ladies. Eventually, we decided on one adventure to plug in and watch. We rummaged through the different pizza boxes—onions, extra cheese, mushrooms—selecting drippy slices to sprinkle with red pepper and then consume. Finally we settled down into the plush couches and waited for all that would unroll off the large-screen television. It was sublime. My own eleventh birthday was approaching and, feeling for a moment bold, innovative, even unconscious of the differences between us, I decided that I would have one of these parties, too.

I planned it out weeks ahead of time, down to the finest detail. But somehow what I pictured in my mind could never happen in our strange, lost home, with our meager finances. It could only happen in the homes of my classmates. In their darkened dens and lush carpeting and La-Z-Boy chairs. I should have known in the very beginning that it would never be the same. From just the fact that instead of spending money on stiff, professional invites painted with glitter and balloons like my classmates had, my father drew the invitations himself and photocopied and folded them at work. He sent these out to all my classmates, not necessarily people I liked or wanted. "But it's just good to make these connections," my father assured me. "Build bridges." I should have known it would not go as planned. But when the day came and my parents scurried around to make everything as best they could, I was still a believer.

That day I wore a plaid skirt with a fuzzy striped sweater and two ponytails. Digging through the closet, I pulled out the black plastic shoes I wanted to wear, but they were mud-splattered. I carried them in to my mother, sheepishly swinging them by their straps, knowing well we could not afford new shoes but also that I could not possibly wear them so muddy at my own party.

"Here," she told me. "This is how you can shine them even if we don't have shoe polish." She took a spoonful of butter and with a bit of toilet paper rubbed it all over the plastic. The butter coated the shoe, cleaned it, making it suddenly shiny and slick. I was amazed at the ingeniousness of it. "This is how we used to do it when I was little and we wanted to keep our shoes like new for as long as we could." I took my shoes out onto the porch, buttering them up in the sunlight. I felt delighted with this trick. And somehow it reassured me, too, that the day would be perfect.

Meanwhile, my mother left for the grocery store. I had given her a much-considered list of the foods I wanted. Lots of snacks, potato chips and cookies and cheese puffs and soda. But when she returned, she had bags and bags of the cheap generic snacks. Where were the flashy, scripted, famous brand names I had expected from the commercials? Instead, I saw these packages proclaiming shamelessly in plain white letters: Price Chopper Corn Chips. Unreasonably, irrationally, against all my best judgment and knowledge, I wanted to cry.

I had frantic visions then of canceling the whole party, calling up each classmate one by one to soberly whisper into the phone that there had been an accident. Something too terrible to describe or even mention again, so please don't bring it up, not even in school next week, not ever. They would probably have thoughts of blood and shattered glass and emergency rooms. But so what? Let them think that. I was desperate.

In light of my absurd frenzy that day, it would seem impossible that the executives at Fritos and Nabisco managed to live with themselves afterward, having caused the panic that they did. Had they ever even seen such melodrama? A little girl pacing the kitchen floor. Biting her nails, humming their jingles, and looking for philosophy in their marketing as though it were life and death instead? A tirade of other omnipotent brands flew through my head then, too. The tiny tag on the back pocket of Guess jeans. The Reebok scribble on a sneaker. The Adirondack backpack. The Maybelline lip gloss. The Nature Valley granola bar. What about the big shots behind those companies? Did they know how I searched their products for truth, asking again and again: Are *these* the things that make people cool? Or were they cool before that, and then, as a matter of course, they bought these cool things, as obvious, cool accessories? Which came first, the chicken or the egg, the cheerleader or her Gap miniskirt? Could these things, I questioned seriously, make me more gorgeous and brilliant than their less-well-known counterparts? Of course not, I tried to tell myself firmly, sensibly. But somewhere in the back of my mind, I was fairly certain that, in fact, they might.

In any case, rallying my wits, I knew it was too late to cancel the party. Even under a guise of death and doom. But since I was sure my classmates would look pityingly upon these nameless chips, I hurriedly emptied them into large bowls and threw out the telltale bags so there would be no trace of what we had done. "Please G-d," I thought. "Don't let them notice a difference in taste or crunch or whatever," not certain myself what the differences might be. The soda bottles stood fast against me, however. I could not replace those containers, and their labels proclaimed unabashedly Price Chopper Cola and Price Chopper Lemon-Lime. I set them out on the table and carefully turned their faces to the wall so only the side listing ingredients would face people. Maybe they won't bother reading the bottles, I hoped. Maybe they'll just assume by the color of the plastic that this bottle is Pepsi and that bottle is Sprite.

Since we did not have the money for the extravagance of a pizza lunch, nine dollars per pie, my mother also returned from the grocery store with several boxes of macaroni-and-cheese, fifty-nine cents each. I never had the pleasure of eating this creamy orange store-bought food—but she knew I always wanted to. Just the week before, I had watched a pretty little girl dig into a bowlful of it on television, and I had leaned back into the couch and sighed with audible envy.

On my birthday I helped my mother prepare the macaroni-and-cheese, enchanted by the instant alchemy of yellow cheese powder and butter and milk and boiled noodles. But when she served it out at the table to my classmates, underneath the gaudiness of pink balloons and red crepe paper, I saw them exchange looks. This was not birthday party food. They could pull a box of macaroni-and-cheese from their loaded pantries at any old time. To me, because we never ate either macaroni-and-cheese or pizza, both were equally exotic. But apparently there was a vast hierarchy out there, of which I understood only a tiny corner.

Just as I dreaded, my classmates, like mutineers, began to stir around me, asking, "When is the pizza coming?" "Do you guys have any real Coke?" I took an orange forkful of macaroni, embarrassed, and it tasted chalky to me.

After lunch and a frosted cake we moved to the living room to watch a video. We did not own a VCR, but I had told my father that I wanted to have a movie party. So he went to the store and splurged for me, renting a VCR and a movie for $15. He returned with these things halfway through the party and, to my horror, I saw the video he had rented was something called *The Yearling*. I had never seen this movie before, and did not even know what it was about. But when I pulled him aside, he told me it was a children's classic about a lonely boy and an orphaned fawn. With a sinking feeling I knew it was nothing at all like those exciting movies we watched at my classmates' parties, in which there were beer-drinking contests and fast cars.

"Why? Why?" I asked him, quiet and appalled in the corner. "Why couldn't we get a fun movie, a fraternity party movie or something?"

My father stiffened. "I'm not going to expose you kids to that trash. What would these parents say if they found out their kids were watching the kinds of things that go on in those movies here?"

"But we watch it at their homes," I told him, feeling the mounting realization of defeat at hand.

"Maybe in their homes. But not here." He tried to make me feel better as the tears came to my eyes. "Trust me. It's a children's classic. You're going to love it." But I could only sense the larger-than-life embarrassment before me. His understanding of children was locked in a time that did not account for modern, frivolous enjoyment. He valued only the profound and educational, and he was trying to form my own values that way, too. Still, the core of me yearned for bubblegum snapping and laugh-tracks. And though I did not understand pop culture much better than he did, I knew for a fact it did not include any stories about lonely boys with fawns.

I hoped by some miracle, when the lights dimmed in the living room, the video he'd rented would somehow be magically transformed. Or maybe there had been a mistake at the video store, and another video was rented under *The Yearling* cover. Maybe, in fact, it would be fun and flashy and there would be some kind of rock-and-roll music in the background. But the screen opened, the credits began to roll, and the starkness of the scenery and quietness of the characters soon caused my classmates to stand up, yawn, stretch, and ask if there were any other videos.

What could I tell them? That we had barely enough money for even one video? That I had no say in even choosing that one? I crouched in a corner in the back of the living room, curled up and aching a little with too many cheap potato chips in my stomach. Scratching at the thick butter grease on my shoes, I was suddenly conscious that they were spread, obviously, with dairy. I wished only for it all to be over.

But the orphaned boy and his fawn continued to play on the screen before me as if in persistent mockery of my embarrassment.

And my father just stood there, watching the movie obliviously, his arms crossed with contentment. Meanwhile, my classmates grumbled around me and eventually wandered outside to wait on the porch to be picked up. They checked the clock and called home and tugged at their coat sleeves, impatient to hop into their parents' cushy cars and speed away from the world that was mine.

After the party, I knew I should be grateful, if only for the money spent. My parents had saved up for it, and put off numerous unpaid bills, too. Cleaning up, we carefully set aside the leftovers to eat later. And we even left the decorations up till they wilted beyond recognition, trying to squeeze as much joy as possible from that financial investment. Today, my parents' selfless attempts to concoct stone soup from nothing but rocks and water awe me. I wonder, sometimes doubt, if I could ever find that strength in myself. But at that time, in truth, I was thankless. My birthday party only made it plain for me—and my classmates—that we lived very differently, though in almost any other circle, all these things which I mourned would have been absurd luxuries.

Everything that my parents wanted for us children, in the failed move to Israel, in pristine hopes, and in enormous sacrifice for each box of rotten macaroni, all faded into the background. Instead I padded my shyness with a new layer: resentment. And that was what I fed as I grew into my teens and my parents gave up more and more of themselves, body, skin, soul, and dollars they didn't have, to move us one final time to the sweet suburb of the nearest city so we could be near the local Jewish community. In an ordinary house in an ordinary neighborhood, they thought, we could try and live as an ordinary Jewish family.

It was impossible to see the end of an era while we lived its passing. Certainly, while we plodded through the various points along the way, there was a sense of vast possibility. I did not just suddenly change into a guarded, awkward child. We did not go to sleep one night incapable of mistakes, and wake the next morning a family of grit and bounced checks and sour milk. But somewhere in that time, we lost our invincibility. And one day, upon looking back, the random events seemed to string together with clarity and order, leading us toward a destiny that would never be as pristine or lovely as we once expected. At least, we hoped, it might still be full.

*I never told the family this: When I was living in Jerusalem three years, I went to hospital for eye drops. Afterwards, on way home, I was seeing blurry and falling on the foot path. I requested somebody to help. A Yemenite girl near me took my hand. Then she left me in middle of road. Taxi driver came out from a car and saved me from accident. But I heard that girl laughing with the joke.*

—NANA-BAI'S DIARY, PAGE 67

*M*y father always advised the parents of children who were on the verge of being teens: "Prepare yourselves. You are about to become the village idiots." And it is true. This is how those years are.

When I was in junior high, my parents hoped that happiness secretly lived beneath my teenage angst and selfishness. But it did not. I was just angry. I was also awkward and confused and resentful of girls my age who had somehow emerged unbelievably polished and sunny. Where did they find the poise, I wondered. My parents had taken me out of scholarships in private school and moved me into public school. So I was having trouble adjusting to that larger world. I had bad skin and bunchy clothes and greasy hair and thick glasses and few friends. I was stumped and rendered awkward by the mechanics of tampons and math. I was bullied in class.

"You're ugly," one boy told me every day in French period.

Often, the boy sitting next to him parried with, "Sure. But she's got big tits." I cowered into the back of my chair, feeling hopeless and heavy under my glands. "Big tits. How would you like it if I pinched them?" He made a pinching motion with his thumb and pointer finger. Even as class got under way, he continued to make this motion quietly, so only I could see. I gulped, silent and frightened, pretending to conjugate verbs.

There seemed to be no world beyond that world, beyond me and my troubles. No future, no past. Just a forever of awkwardness and bullies and feeling lost. What were catastrophes around the globe—rioting in the streets and genocide and destruction of the environment—compared to my problems and a boy who liked to pinch? They had nothing on me, I decided.

Self-protective because of this certainty, I tried to wreak havoc on the universe. If only in small ways. I wrote horoscopes for the school newspaper, crafting purposely misguided messages and passing it off as the will of the stars, hoping someone would follow this crooked path of nonsense to hell. Of course, I had no actual idea about how to read the stars and I made no pretense of it. I did not even research what real astrologers had to say. Instead I concocted these horoscopes from my own dark will. "Taurus: You will find the love of your life and then lose him to a redhead," I predicted in my bit. Fiercely unrepentant, I allowed these words of calamity to sit right alongside the bright weekly column highlighting the cafeteria specials.

I was antagonistic and cryptic, poking at those closest to me, and fighting with my siblings and parents. Most of all, I wanted to get far away from everything that was Indian or Jewish because these were the things that I felt branded me as the uncomfortable stranger. They made up the core of my vulnerability. I knew that the curry smell seeped from my very pores, alerting those around me like the musk of a fearful animal.

I wanted to disappear inside a culture—any culture—that was foreign to my family. Nothing elite or impossible. I was past the point of wishing myself into royalty. Nothing even like the plain, white, American, Christian version of our aspiring lifestyle. But something my parents could never plumb in its remote and alien depths, in its sullen, dirty, resigned permanence. Like hillbilly inbreeding or slum cocaine—that deep-rooted and that insurmountable. I wanted something so intense and all-encompassing that it would cancel out what set me apart with its authenticity. If there had been a cult nearby, I would have joined it and perhaps that would have made for a more lofty struggle. But there was no cult handy, so I did the next best thing. I went to the mall.

At thirteen, I demanded that my parents give me at least the freedom of the mall, as it seemed everyone around me had this. They allowed it hesitantly, in random bits and pieces. And in the end I did not quite know what to do with it. When I went to the mall, I did not meet up with anyone there or get a job serving tacos. I did not buy makeup or play arcade games or see movies or try on clothes just for fun. Instead I walked around aimlessly, alone, watching other people walk around with their friends. I bought a soda at the food court and pretended I was waiting for my friends to show up. Sometimes I tried to make eye contact with people, the man sitting next to me on the bench or even a saleslady. I hoped that somehow, between the neon glamour of shoe sales and gourmet pretzels, someone would pluck me out of anonymity.

One day while I was wandering through the mall, I walked past a record store. Its loud speaker was playing a song called "Crazy,

Crazy Nights." Rhythmic and summoning, it spoke to me as only the sounds of mass yearning could. Immediately, I went in and inquired about the song. Then I bought the cassette. It was a rock group called KISS and from that moment on, as I listened to their music over and over again, my life had meaning.

I have never experienced such a thing as love at first sight, before or since. But that is what I had with KISS. Especially the lead singer, Paul Stanley, a shaggy, hairy man with piercing round eyes. His singing stirred something in me—like a growling stomach or an impossibly sexy thought. I wanted to possess him and be possessed by him, get close to him in any way possible—haul stage equipment, do his laundry, become a groupie. Whatever I had to do, I would do it.

I read somewhere that Paul Stanley had had hundreds and hundreds of lovers. Jealous, I wondered, where would such a girl get to meet him? Did he happen to make eye contact with her as she straddled someone's shoulders at a concert, topless and ecstatic and beautiful? Did he point her out to his heavy and have her secreted backstage? The hit-or-miss chance at play here seemed like such injustice to me. How much better if a girl could just queue up for this, like at the deli or the post office. At the front of the line, my beloved Paul Stanley would sit behind a window, shuffling memos, taking claims from old lovers, considering propositions from new ones. And there, before the counter, I would have just as much a chance as anyone to make my case.

KISS had already experienced its heyday years before. In the seventies they were legends and pioneers. They hid their identities behind long hair and crazy makeup. Painted as insatiable lovers and devils, they marched onstage at concerts to immortalize sex and partying with their music. With spitting blood, and wagging tongues, and blasting fireworks.

Yet by the time I first heard them that day in the late 1980s, the KISS insanity had been tempered. Now even *they* took themselves seriously. They scrubbed off their makeup. They slowed down all the paraphernalia. All the lunchboxes and buttons and action figures. So there was no good reason why I should have been seized with KISS then. But I was.

The irony here, of course, coming to KISS at this late stage, was lost on me at the time. Like I was victoriously defeating a fever with the help of leeches and magic spells. And meanwhile, everyone else was just taking aspirin. I had come too late to the hubbub, and still worse, I was clueless of that. And so, my great rebellion, in the end, turned out to be the worship of a bunch of middle-aged men on stage. Who, even musically, were more ordinary for the many similar groups following in their footsteps. All they had left were their raspy voices and platform shoes.

But this did not bother me. This was the first time I had ever discovered a taste on my own, without the tug of my parents. And I was delighted that what I chose was something with such a gigantic and circuslike history. Something that had been bold enough to call itself the KISS Nation and the KISS Army. So, I bought rock magazines and cut out pictures of KISS and Paul Stanley, pasting them up on my walls to form a screen that drew me into their concerts and mayhem. I listened to their music so much that years later I could still sing these songs by heart—and even my family, who had heard these songs so often through my bedroom walls, could sing them by heart, too. I began to mimic KISS and the girls that followed them around, wearing high teased hair and dark eye makeup and lipstick.

But I did not live like KISS at all. I did not have marathon sex or crazy parties. I did not even have friends who did. With the family, it was the same it had always been. Going to synagogue.

Taking long car trips together. Otherwise, just staying close to home. And a severe expectation of morality. So I nurtured this decadent KISS world in isolation. Like a set of fancy porcelain dolls which I could not really play with. I just set them up against the mirror and primped myself alongside them, to make do. Even then, I never took my new, wild, rock-and-roll hair and makeup anywhere far. I just moped around the house with it, and wore it sometimes, shyly, to school.

It must have been comical, I think, to see me like this, seated scowling and painted up at our quiet Shabbat meals. Imitating a lifestyle that had no part of me. I think eventually even I could sense how preposterous this was. Because after all the music pushed and pulled me through, after all the lipstick I caked on, in the end, I was still just a short, Indian-looking girl who had high-sprayed hair. This taunted me and fueled me. And above everything else, I wanted to grab hold of the corrupt glamour of KISS, make it some substantial part of my reality.

The home economics classroom smelled of cinnamon that day. Trudging in wearily beneath a backpack full of textbooks, I considered the projects we were working on. Fluffy snicker-doodle cookies and flannel pillows shaped like animals. How is this home economics, I brooded, nitpicky and inanely targeting my general resentment at the closest thing on hand. Did these teachers really believe that someday a home of my own would be made right by things like cookies and pillows? Wouldn't we, in the end, be better off learning to fix a furnace or tile a roof?

I put my backpack down next to a Raggedy Ann–faced girl at the sewing machine, stuffing and stitching her cat-shaped pillow. I had seen her before, admired her, too. She was a girl who did what she liked. She wore black nail polish and smoked cigarettes outside the school, not hanging around with the popular kids, but bumming matches off them and then retreating coolly to her corner. She seemed to have a quiet dignity about her.

Bashful, I watched her for a moment as she concentrated on the cat's surgery with a thoroughness that made our home economics teacher croon. Carefully she stuffed the cat with large wads of cotton, almost to the point of bursting. Then, with exacting, even stitches, she sewed it stiffly shut. She knew I was watching her. She stuffed and sewed, stuffed and sewed. Then turning up angel's eyes, she beamed at me and confided coolly, "This pussy's gonna be just as tight as mine."

I gasped. Eager to shock and impress, this girl might have been Betty Crocker in a porno, the way she spoke just then. And I, it seemed, was only waiting to be shocked and impressed by someone like her. Because after that, wordless, stunned, I plunked down into the seat next to her, waiting to hear more. "I'm Lynnette," she said mischievously. She sensed my loneliness. And I, for some reason, knew she could lead me into a coveted underworld I would not reach on my own. That was how we became friends.

Lynnette loved KISS too. And she introduced me to heavy metal icons like Ozzy Osbourne and Iron Maiden. She let me borrow her rock concert T-shirts. I liked that they smelled of smoke and sweat. She showed me how to ruthlessly take a comb and tease my hair up even bigger than I already had it—as if my hair could have needed more height. Already it drove my parents crazy, but they allowed me this quirk, so that I would feel I had been granted personal expression. This is how Lynnette advised me: Big hair needs to tower on top and the sides have to fan out like a cobra's hood. The best hairspray is the ozone-killing super-hold. Always carry around a full-size bottle in your purse. I nodded and studied her methods, then followed them meticulously.

Most importantly, Lynnette brought me closer to the actual world only represented by music and hairspray. One night she invited me to go to a party with her. I had never been to a real party before. A party of beer and long-haired boys. My parents never let me do anything like that. Even with Lynnette's nerve by my side, I was still meekly disciplined by their expectations of me. But she pleaded for me to go with her and she promised me her friend Steve would be there. "Steve looks exactly like Paul Stanley," she said enticingly. "I told him about you and how you love KISS and Paul Stanley. He can't wait to meet you."

I knew then what I had to do. I paced my room, and thought out what to say, and practiced in front of the mirror. Finally I mustered up the nerve and asked my parents if I could sleep over at Lynnette's place. Of course, I did not mention the party. They hesitated, and their faces wrinkled as if smelling for danger. But then, making a huge, unprecedented leap of trust, they agreed.

When my father dropped me off at her trailer park, I could see how its shabbiness and dark corners hit him, made him immediately worry I'd be up to no good. Already as he pulled away, I suspected I would never be allowed to sleep over there again. But at least I have tonight, I decided. And its promise seemed endless.

Lynnette helped me with my hair and makeup. She let me borrow a tiny miniskirt with a fat zipper all the way down it, and her high leather boots. The boots were a bit big but I stuffed the toes with toilet paper. While we waited for her boyfriend to drive by and pick us up, we defrosted some chicken rounds stuffed with broccoli and cheese and ate these sitting out on her trailer stoop. With the smell of exhaust and dandelions on the breeze, with chicken grease on my hands, with a party and possibilities before me, I felt, this is what I have always wanted. Rawness. Freedom.

But once Lynnette's boyfriend arrived, everything changed. She smacked her plum lips against his window then circled the car and got into the front seat next to him. I crawled into the back. She told me: "We need to stop by my friend's place first. I've got to drop off her bowl." Why would she need to drop off kitchenware on Saturday night before a party? I sat there confused, but trying to appear laid back.

"Sure," I told her. "Whatever."

But Lynnette's boyfriend saw my face in the rearview mirror. "She doesn't know what you're talking about," he laughed good-naturedly to Lynnette.

She turned around in the seat back to me. "What are you thinking? Soup bowl? Salad bowl?" I only stared at her blankly. "A bowl. A bowl. Haven't you ever heard of smoking a bowl? Weed? Get it?" She laughed and turned back around in her seat while I cringed. I knew nothing of the lingo. "Poor baby," she crooned.

As soon as we got to the house party, I could not help but feel disappointed. Because I tied everything exciting and outside my own household into KISS, I had expected this to be a celebration of them. I expected *everything* to be a celebration of them, complete with "Crazy, Crazy Nights" playing ceaselessly in the background as theme music. But there was no hint of KISS, no KISS music, even. I had *not* walked into the party world of a rock video.

Instead groups of people hunkered around the television watching a World Wrestling Federation match. Big men in bikinis shaking their fists and stomping on each other's necks. This party had no wild lights, no live music, no sumptuous barbecue, no gorgeous ladies, and no bikers like I had expected. I brightened to see that one man did eventually pull up on a motorcycle. But he was the only one, and it turned out, after all, to be some kind of scooter. There was a case of bitter beer and even a large bong from which people were inhaling. When it came by me though, this strange machine of bubbling water and intricate tubing, I knew a telltale coughing fit loomed before me, inevitable and embarrassing. So I did not bother making a virgin attempt.

Finally there seemed to be a turn for good. I saw Lynnette approaching from the hallway with her friend, Steve, the Paul Stanley look-alike, in tow. Through the dim lights at that end of the house, I caught my breath. It could have been Paul Stanley, in flesh and blood, on his way over. As they got closer, I began to notice some differences. Steve had a longer nose. Smaller eyes. He was a bit chunkier. But still, I mustered up all my imaginative powers. Steve has dark hair, too, just like Paul Stanley, I told myself. He also appeared to be a similarly brooding type, in a RATT T-shirt and jeans. I felt myself sweating as Lynnette introduced us. "Meet Steve," she told me, then disappeared.

"So, like, what do you do?" I asked him, barely containing my excitement before this metal-man.

"Well, I'm looking for work," he told me, taking a drag from his cigarette as he perched uncomfortably on the arm of the couch. "You know. I dropped out of school and all. Yeah. And I can't live at home forever." His eyes wandered around the room. Flustered by his lack of eloquence, I started picking at the pilling couch skin.

And there was silence. With a lump, I realized that no matter what imaginative acrobatics I turned, this was certainly no Paul Stanley. In a last-ditch effort, I asked him: "Do you sing at all?"

"What? No. Why?" he asked, bewildered and clearly unaware of all he needed to live up to. Then he said, "Look, I'm going to get a beer, okay?" and wandered off into the kitchen.

After the party, Lynnette and her boyfriend and I drove around for a while. "This is what we usually do," she told me, excited to be introducing me to a life so different from my own. "You never know what you're going to meet up with." That night, as it happened, we met up with absolutely nothing. We drove to the next town. Then we drove back. We stopped for gas. We stopped later so they could buy cigarettes. At the very end of the night, we sat at a twenty-four-hour diner and devoured a plate of French fries and pancakes with berry syrup. Then Lynnette's boyfriend drove us back to her trailer home. He parked just outside it. "Try not to wake up my mom," she told me as I got out of the car and closed the door behind me.

"You're not coming in?" I asked her through her rolled down window.

"Just get in bed and I'll be in soon," she said. "You can find some extra pajamas in my dresser."

I tiptoed inside and brushed my teeth and changed into a pair of her pajamas. When I came out of the bathroom, I expected Lynnette would have kissed her boyfriend good night and come inside already. But she still wasn't in. I went to the window and lifted up the curtain draped over the screen. Under the lamp light I saw her still in the car parked just a foot away.

She sat on her boyfriend's lap in the driver's seat, facing him, her eyes and nose buried in his hair. His hands, all knuckles, were fumbling inside her shirt. I saw her move up and down, up and down on top of him, and through the still-rolled-down car window I heard her telling him softly, "Fuck me, please." It was too far away to hear exact intonations or breathiness or ecstasy. Instead it sounded like she was, rather impatiently, placing an order at McDonald's. Her face turned slightly and through his curls, she saw me at the window, my face pressed into the screen mesh. I could swear she winked then. Startled, I let the curtain drop and crawled into bed.

When Lynnette came in finally, I pretended to snore. She smelled of the saltiness dripping down her legs and that was the first time I ever fell asleep to the scents of sex. It was not what I expected.

When my father picked me up the next morning, I was utterly bewildered. I came out of the trailer into the sunlight, blinking. Could it be that I had so misjudged everything out there? Was this what KISS was in fact about? Were these Paul Stanley's "Crazy, Crazy Nights?" There had to be more. I could not accept that disenchantment.

A week later, I learned that Paul Stanley would be performing a solo concert at a club in our very own town. I was ecstatic. He has come to redeem himself, I decided. I knew in the concert at that club there would be the lushness, the insanity I was dreaming of. Perhaps I would even make eye contact with him onstage, and like a lustful lord he would summon me to him as he'd done to hundreds of girls before.

The only problem was that I could not get into the show because I was too young. I had to be at least eighteen to get into Club T. I had no extensive underground network, no backlog of wily ways. Even Lynnette did not have the resources to get me a fake ID on such short notice. So, in the end, desperate, I swallowed my bristly wannabe wild-child pride and asked my father to take me as a legal chaperone. He loved me so much that he actually did.

That night inside the club, we split up. My father climbed into the balcony, taking an unfortunate place by a pair of speakers that stood taller than him (for weeks afterward he could hardly hear from his left ear). I went down into the pit in front of the stage. Worming my way through the crowd, I got as close as I could to the front and then held my ground, waiting for Paul Stanley to emerge, romance me, destroy his guitar with a frenzy of music.

Finally, in a crush of lights and screams, he came out on stage. He looked exactly like he did on my cassette cover, long black hair, tight pants, open shirt. The music started with a smash of drums, and then I was caught up in the craze and singing and dancing around me. Worshipping the man on stage, I melted into the motions of the crowd, breathing and moving insanely as one, like a massive, spastic rhino. I never made eye contact with Paul Stanley. But there was a man behind me—I don't think I ever saw his face—and somehow in the random movement of all the many bodies before the stage, ours were in synch. When the music made me dip, he was dipping, too. When I arched up to the lights and the beat, I felt him arch, too. In the same moment, we discovered our corporal harmony, and he took my hands with both of his and pressed up against me from behind. He wore leather gloves with the fingers poking through, and I could feel the sweat from them. Such a strange and amazing thing, to be so intimate so instantly, even wearing his sweat and not feeling bothered by it. It did not matter that my father was up there, cautious, on the balcony. He could not possibly spot the top of my head out of the many others, discern my hands intertwined with someone else's and my body a breath too close to another. It did not matter. Finally, I thought, dizzied, this is what I have been waiting for. And I begged Paul Stanley, as though he had some godly power: Let this all be mine.

In the end, this new-found universe was short lived. The concert finished, the man behind me disappeared, the lights went up, and I met my father outside in the parking lot. Driving home, he was stunned and silent. He stopped for a takeout cup of coffee, then turned on the big band radio station and rattled his finger in his ear once or twice. Horrified by all he had seen, and fearing for me, my parents began to sift through all aspects of my life, my friends, my outings. As a burnout, a head-banger—or even a sorry attempt at these things—I could never become what Nana-bai expected me to be in our family and community, an obligation which at this time seemed repellent to me.

Struggling between the world of my home and the world I wanted to live in outside it, I turned to my diary to voice my frustrations. I wrote about anger. I wrote about music. I especially wrote about sex. I wrote about fantasy and edged through the clumsiness, defying G-d. I also questioned the strict ideas of sexuality that my family had always tried to convey. Because now, in my confusion, they all began to boil over within me. There was the essence of India that Nana-bai imparted in her stories, where breasts could balloon overnight from just looking at a boy the wrong way. And then there were the methods of Judaism, which my parents enforced in the rules and edicts and bits of Torah and clichés I'd heard since childhood. "Remember the three R's: respect, responsibility, and the right decision," they told me again and again. These philosophies seemed at odds with each other now. Nana-bai's drama would not understand my parents' sterile words. Their words would not approve of the voluptuousness in hers. And so the truth of sexuality could not possibly be both of these. Where was I in all this? I asked my diary again and again, as if expecting an answer.

I was caught between gross intellectualism and Nana-bai's boundaries that were deliciously tangible and teasing, at times cartoonlike, at times magical, somehow always stunning. So, as I grew into my sexuality, I was, at different times, a prude, a slut, a flirt, an awkward schoolgirl, and a eunuch. I was an exhibitionist, thrilled to be caught in a white T-shirt during a downpour, where beyond all control, my curves slowly materialized for the world out of sheer, drenched cloth. I was a big talker, leading conversation back to things like blowjobs and sadomasochism before I understood what the words meant. I was even a schemer, playing innocent in order to not appear innocent, in order to hide my innocence, in order to finally seduce by it. And sometimes I was all of these things at once. In my diary, in my awkward accounts and pages of fizzing experiments, there was a joining which I could barely understand, the emergence of a physical presence in words to something that seemed so impossible, so forbidden to exist it could very well have not existed at all.

Dear Diary:

Last night Lynnette and I had a party in the basement. Somehow when mom and dad were upstairs for a while, we got a game going, where you spin a bottle and then go into the closet with the person it lands on. And I went into the closet with Brian Tonelli, and we were on the floor in the dark and he touched my breasts, under my shirt, under my bra. It was the first time anyone's ever done that! He held them and rolled them between his fingers. And the whole time he was saying, "I can't believe it. I can't believe it." I don't know what it was supposed to feel like. But it felt good, it was just very soft, so I'm even shuddering just now from writing about it. Isn't that strange?

One day, shortly after this entry was written, my parents called me into their room, their faces made up of more pain than face. My mother said: "I was in your room and I read your diary. I know it wasn't right, but I wanted to see what was going on. . . . Look, I know it wasn't right and I'm sorry, but I read about the party and we're so upset. My G-d, how could you do this to us?"

My immediate horror and fury at this invasion eventually faded into years of resentment and mistrust, and finally evolved into my own reluctant understanding of a mother's good intentions and hard mistakes. My perceptions of a lust-driven party game and the roles of parents have taken on different shapes in the passing of years, even as I can now imagine more clearly how I, too, will someday hesitate at the thought of my future daughter discovering the pleasures of breasts. But the one thing I have felt consistently, since that day in junior high all the way through today, was that my actual expression of truths was wronged—truths that for once were not Nana-bai's and not my parents, but mine. The encounter, the first feeling of being a woman, the desire, the soft soft hands, all came from my teenage core and were therefore beautiful.

Finding out about that party game was the final infuriating push for my parents, after which they closed ranks around me. No more concerts, they decided. And, indeed, I would not be returning to the trailer park or Lynnette. (Soon afterward she was caught inhaling Dust-Off fumes behind the school. A year later, I heard, she got pregnant. Then she found Jesus.) Perhaps in some other household it would have been possible to sneak past my parents. But feeling an ethnic and weighty entitlement to determine— even own—my very personality, my parents became insurmountable, forcing upon me all the things from which I had run. Religion. Family. The many layers of my heritage.

I could have continued to love KISS in a vacuum, I suppose. But without some invigorating and renewed access to them, without even Paul Stanley look-alikes named Steve who looked nothing at all like Paul Stanley, my passion wilted. I washed the spray from my hair, and, piece by piece, I took down the magazine cutouts from my bedroom walls. So that soon there were only empty, Scotch-tape scars where once there had been a rock star.

*When I was a child, sometimes we used to go to cinema. My brothers liked to go to comedian movies, like Charlie Chaplin and more. But we used to go see classical music also and my parents used to go see drama, though not we children. Until we were adults. Then we saw drama.*

—Nana-bai's diary, page 13

*I*mmediately after they put an end to my feeble rebellion, my parents confined me to the boundaries of home. Hoping the synagogue would be a short leash for me and that I would absorb the sheer morality of the place, my parents said to me: If you want something outside school and the home, if you want any friends at all, you have to find it in the synagogue. In its youth groups and classes and prayers and volunteer work. I felt like a dog brought to spread newspaper and told sternly: If you're going to make, do it here.

Despite my parents' admonitions I did not try to find a place for myself at the synagogue. Instead I grumbled, and locked myself sullenly inside my room. The stench of depression and slow madness spread throughout the house and the rest of the family, soaking their pores and chilling them, too. If I could not live the life I wanted, I decided, I would rather just barely exist. Let *that* be on their conscience, I thought.

One day, in order to brighten the whole family from this, my parents found a good deal on tickets and decided we would all six of us go to see a musical at a small theater in New York City. Though we could still rarely afford to go to the movies, somehow theater was deemed to be a form of entertainment more worthy of our scarce money. I sighed upon hearing our plans, picturing grouchy gentlemen with opera glasses and a stuffy orchestra. But because we would dress up in our finest clothes and drive two hours into the city, for our family this was a heralded event.

That morning, Nana-bai and some of the aunties visiting from Israel came to help prepare food for the trip, chapati and okra and curried drumsticks, so we would not have to spend more money to buy expensive food outside the house. While the rest of the family got ready upstairs, I came into the kitchen, already dressed and bored and fully set to go get the theater over with. The women had just finished cooking and the aunties were already moving into the living room to talk, reminding one another of the days when they went to the theater. Nana-bai was left to pack the food away in recycled margarine tubs and plastic bags. I sat down at the table and watched as she wiped grease stains and crumbs off the counter. Then she turned on the hot water and started washing dishes.

Every now and then I chipped away at the crossword puzzle in that morning's newspaper. But from the other room, I could hear the aunties speaking, discussing what was best to wear for the theater. A silk gray sari. A high white collar. Perhaps a brooch. In the kitchen Nana-bai and I were wordless, with just the sounds of steel wool under running water, and my scratching pen. The smell of lemon dishsoap rose like fancy perfume draining down the sink. Then Nana-bai clattered the last pot into the drying rack, shut off the water, and wiped her wet hands on the striped back of her housecoat. "That's it," she said at last and turned to look at me. "Tsangla. Tsangla. You look nice." I mumbled something in return without even looking up and crossed out a clue in the puzzle. "Really you do." She came and took my face in her hands. I know I must have seemed sour, even then avoiding her eyes. But she continued to hold my face, her hands still soft from the water and finally I looked up.

"What?" I asked her, as if I had just noticed she had my cheeks between her palms.

"Nothing," she said evenly. "I just told you that you look nice." She knew about all that had been happening in our home and why the family was disjointed right then. She knew how I had tried to break rules, how I had been hauled back by my ear. But still she looked at me kindly, saying nothing about these things. Usually Nana-bai had no problem giving her opinion in any situation: That girl looks like a bad character; Sit quietly in the car or your Daddy will get into an accident and it will be all your fault; You are ungrateful children. But at that moment she just held on to my face and smoothed the scowl with her fingers and looked at me lovingly. "Just one more thing you need."

From her hand-stitched pocket, she pulled a gold necklace. It was a heavy woven gold, with an intricate Star of David dangling off it. "This is for you," she told me.

For other families, wealth was gauged by cash, stocks, diamonds, real estate. But in my family, as though we bargained in ancient bazaars, gold was our richness. We knew all about gold karats and gold yellows, cataloguing our chains, bracelets, rings, cufflinks, and earrings. Some were dotted with rubies and emeralds. Before every big occasion or holiday, my mother would take us to the bank to look through the gold. She headed for the safe deposit box with key ready in hand. Glancing furtively around her, she moved too quickly, bustling us along with her into one of the private rooms. Then she locked the door behind us so we could look through the tangles of gold in the jewelry box, away from prying eyes and imaginary enemies. We could choose one or two gold pieces to wear. Fat gold bangles. Or necklaces with our names in thin gold Hebrew script on the charm. Even when we had no money, we held on to each piece of gold as an heirloom, refusing to sell it and recounting as justification its specific history: I had these earrings made for Batsheva the day she was born; My great-auntie gave me this bracelet, feel how solid it is. I always thought this strange, that we did not have enough money for this or that, but then like Ali Baba and Captain Cook, we kept a mound of shiny riches hidden in a bank vault.

Walking behind me at that moment, Nana-bai circled the necklace around my neck and clasped it shut. "There, now you look perfect."

It felt clunky to me, and I wanted to say no thank you and give it back. But just then Leah auntie walked into the kitchen with an empty glass in hand. She saw the necklace around my neck. "Aiaa. What a beautiful necklace. Where did you get that? Isn't that the necklace that papa gave to my mama?"

Automatically—but without even understanding my reaction— I locked my fingers around it, away from her, possessive. Then I turned for explanation to Nana-bai. "Nai," she said. "It was given to me."

"I'm sure you must be mistaken," Leah auntie told her, sugary. "Such a fine necklace, such a weighty gold. Surely he would have given it to my mama before you."

"Well, you are wrong."

Leah auntie called the other aunties into the kitchen. They pointed to the necklace on my neck and discussed it among them, nodding, trying to remember it and claim it from many memories of many gold necklaces. Nana-bai just watched them and waited, and when they finally stopped talking, she put both hands on my shoulders. "This necklace was mine and now it is hers." With a wry curtness I had never before seen in her, she told them, "We old ladies do not dress up and go to the theater anymore. But our girl here will. And she will look beautiful." For a moment, Nana-bai's strange presence made me suspicious. And even the aunties' arguments seemed to make sense. I wondered to myself, was this necklace in fact Nana-bai's to give? But I remained silent with my doubts, as she only peered at them fiercely. They pressed their lips together, petty, looked at each other and finally returned to the other room, talking loudly about how in Bombay they had lived in the big, beautiful house, while *other people* had to live in a shack. I was to be reminded of this day, long after Nana-bai's death, when the family's tug-of-war and attempts to reinvent history would continue, even, dreadfully, as she lay in her grave. Nana-bai smoothed my hair and adjusted my collar, and that's how I was made ready to partake of high culture.

Seated and waiting for the show to begin, Gertie was on one side of me, leaning forward and talking to the woman she had just met in the nearby aisle. "Did you hear?" she asked me, animated and glowing with interest. "Mrs. Engel has just come back from Poland. What do you think of that?" Gertie was excited so she tried to draw me in, assuming I would be excited, too. But I resented being led and, even more, I could not speak easily like she did with this adult stranger, this Mrs. Engel with her perfect rust lips and professor eyes. Also, nursing my brooding like a patient reptile, I did not even want to make that human leap. Instead I just nodded dumbly, politely, while they talked, and poked Gertie with my foot. Understanding the poke, distinguishing it from the hundred other pokes of different caliber and meaning, which we had accumulated over the years, she moved the conversation away from me.

Eventually I turned to Tzvi and Batsheva sitting on the other side of me. They talked seriously between themselves, looking like male and female shadows of one being. With unconscious style in their clothes and skins. With their lankiness and strong legs. They talked about the school sports they each played, hockey and baseball and basketball. Friends from his junior varsity and her middle school team. The tough coaches. The team captains who were real hams. All of us were in the very same public schools, yet because they had sports and street talk between them in a way I'd never been able to harness, they lived worlds away from the solitude I knew. Sometimes, if I saw them in the halls after class, I was even afraid to say hello. But in our house, in the world of the family where we overlapped, I knew people's buttons and weaknesses and secrets. I was in on all the jokes. So then I nuzzled my way into their conversation, "Remember the time when you said that thing at breakfast and we all died laughing?" In home territory now, we laughed again together.

The show we were seeing that day was a modern variation of Shakespeare's *Julius Caesar*—set to dark humor and the lyre music of one man in britches. Certainly, I did not think I would be moved by this unlikely theater. But soon, peering into the expanses of an ornately carved ceiling, settling into the sumptuousness of the red cushioned chair, I began to feel awake as I hadn't in a very long time. The ushers busied in the aisle below me and people milled about, tossing scarves and hats onto the chairs next to them and rifling through playbills. Then the lights dimmed, and on the square of a stage, something happened. Music, voices, costumes, faces, and dance came together. So that each person, Gertie to my right, Tzvi and Batsheva on the other side, Mom and Dad further down, and everyone else in that theater, myself included, watched breathlessly and ready to shed tears at even the slightest prompting. In those hours, it amazed me; nothing mattered more than the fate of these imaginary characters. And though they were over-the-top, they made me feel suddenly alive to the senses, the smells of cologne next to me, the rustling of cotton, the weight of the gold necklace at my throat.

Driving home that night, I lay in the back of the car, watching the neon placards and the lights of New York City fade behind me. Something had moved in me, almost like the physical displacement in birth-water breaking free. And I felt hungry still for that excitement. But more than wanting to observe it, I wanted to generate it in some small way. I could never comfortably be a receiver. The few times when I had been to restaurants, and a waiter pulled out my chair for me or cleaned up a spill, I fidgeted. Even more in a theater, having such transcendent things done around me, I loved it, but also twisted and turned and wanted to do it myself.

Of course, I had had dreams of being a star. Like most every child, before I even knew my personal quirks and terrible shyness, I wanted to be the flawless center of attention. Under lights, on stage, glamorous. So years earlier, when a theater company came to town to perform *The King and I*, my parents brought me to audition to be an extra, one of the many children birthed from the King's harem.

Standing between rows and rows of other hopeful children under the inspection of the casting directors, my eyes must have been perfectly round for wanting the part so badly. Praying to G-d, I tried to remake myself so that I might appear, genuinely, like the child of a harem. I wished away all traces of the century I lived in, of America. Any plastic or Velcro or denim that might be on my body. If I were the child of a harem, I pondered, I would probably be serious. I adjusted my face, trying to appear deep in thought. But also, I realized a moment later, I would be fat and lazy, too. I let the flesh of my cheeks hang loose and fidgeted with my posture. Certain I had finally gotten it right, I held this bearing stiffly, uncomfortably, for several long minutes, waiting for the director to look my way.

He seemed to be looking at everyone but me. I began to sweat, coldly, in a line down my back. Then in a sudden movement, unaware of what I was doing even and how I had broken my pose, I fidgeted with my sweater zipper and just at that moment, the director saw me and passed me over. Breezy, he snapped his fingers in my direction and a gentle woman ushered me over to where my parents and all the other parents waited, drinking coffee. I pretended to be brave, reminding myself that that's how a real actress would be. But for years after that I berated myself, certain that that zipper was my downfall from stardom.

Watching *Julius Caesar* that night though, brooding and disillusioned, something returned to me, my saving grace, still pressed and packed from childhood dreams of stardom. It was a bit of the thrill and hope from when the bigness of Hollywood cast its beady eyes over me and my zipper—in the split second when he saw only me and not yet my zipper. And somehow this energy evoked in me a desire for life, where before there had been only apathy.

Eventually this excitement prompted me to join our high school theater group. And to my surprise, I found that amidst all my vague awkwardness with the world, here was a great equalizing force. Suddenly students with premade lives and expectations had to begin from scratch. Of course, we all brought some scraps to the table, some talent. But then after that, our stage identities were rebirthed and reconstructed by luck and pluck and the far-reaching hands of the director, Mrs. J. No matter what we were at home with our families, or when we walked through the fickle school halls, once we entered Mrs. J.'s dank theater, we became something else entirely. Something she concocted after eyeing us and stretching our vocal chords and making us pirouette. And there was a whole circle of people, budding thespians, eager to be there and work there, too, who wordlessly agreed to take part and buy into this masquerade.

In the long hours we spent backstage together behind the scenes, we did schoolwork to pass the hours, and bought pretzels and cold cans of juice from the vending machines for dinner. There was a camaraderie in it all. In the fund-raising bake sales. In watching the painted evolution of scenery. In waiting hours and hours to spend just three minutes in the spotlight. No matter how many times I reminded myself that our performances took place on just the ratty stage of the high school auditorium, still, staring out into the audience, it felt as big as Broadway.

I was never the star or center of attention. But at different times on this stage, I played a little girl, a nurse, a concubine, a fairy. I shed my own clothes and replaced them with costumes that dictated in their sheerness, in their crepe and wiring, exactly what I was to be. I drew my eyes with a pencil, my cheeks with a brush, my lips with a cake of paint. I could choose the colors. And pushing twine and feathers aside to peer at myself in one of the brightly lit, makeup-streaked mirrors backstage, I saw that when I wore Beautiful Mermaid #3's crown, I *was* in fact Beautiful Mermaid #3, and no one could dispute that. Hell, it even said so in the playbill.

Possibly I was just naturally and on my own beginning to emerge from an age of awkwardness. In learning to dress simply, with flattering makeup. In learning to speak some of my opinions and feel happy. In learning to let the unkindness of the world only touch me so much. But I think, also, I had found something significant there in what lived backstage. Where I was given a role, and I put into it, and took out of it, and made it into what *I* decided. Until this point, I had not been able to see far past certain foreign and uncomfortable borders. I fought them, as a desperate measure, in KISS. But I simply did not have the means or the bold, cool language of others around me to carry it off. Like those who argued with their parents in public and who owned their own cars to race off with in a huff. Such vocal selfish expression from a girl could only go the way of quick defeat in our home.

But now there were other options before me. Legitimate options. Not just what was dictated by my Indian Jewish family. Not just what directly, purposefully opposed them either. It was more subtle and individual than that. It was something I could create and fine-tune. And it might just have power, too. A kind of power in which a story dreamt in the pulsing crevices of one human brain, could make people dance like puppets—and could make those watching believe in the puppets, in their importance, beauty, bad jokes, and deaths. This was not for the meek.

Somehow the empowerment of *Julius Caesar*, of all theater really, moved me to be active myself. To look for inspiration and a voice. To make the best of the bare stuff I had. And that day, when Nana-bai stood up against the others to give me a necklace, when I suddenly saw that a world of power existed outside my small problems and KISS, the bare stuff I had turned out to be just my parents' strict boundaries and the place they pushed me to, ill at ease and prickly. The synagogue.

Still dewy, even sparkling and energized from the theater, I decided to try and embrace the synagogue, not reject it. In fact—especially since I had no choice—it did not take much to transfer my enthusiasm for a rock group to a religion. After certain misgivings, I accepted the idea of the synagogue community. But then I discovered in it a universe of complications that ran more deeply than I had ever imagined.

*This is the prayer I taught the children to say before sleep:*
*Shma Yisrael Adonai Eloheinu Adonai Echad. Hear O Is-*
*rael: The Lord our G-d the Lord is one. Praised be his glorious*
*sovereignty throughout all time. G-d, give me and my family*
*long life, health, wealth, and happiness. Amen. Good night.*
*Apple dreams, honey dreams.*

—NANA-BAI'S DIARY, PAGE 29

*M*y quest for a place to sit and pray should have been simple and spiritual. Finding a chair, a book, a quiet room. But though I tried to make our synagogue home, it was never this straightforward. Inevitably there were clashes. That is the nature of religion. (My father always tells the one about the Jewish man and woman who were stranded on a desert island, who built a synagogue where the man could pray, a synagogue where the woman could pray, and a synagogue where they could both *refuse* to pray.)

A modern-day CEO can snap her briefcase shut and turn off her cell phone for several hours of worship as if it is just anything else—a workout or lunch meeting—scheduled into her daily planner. But she is, in fact, in that time, agreeing to be just as humans were thousands of years ago, paying homage to supernatural forces and accepting a certain blind faith. Something primitive is called upon. Something with traces of Eve's awe and idolatry and the Crusades. Because religion is vulnerable. It inspires fervor and always needs to reassess itself with others around it. "Are you with us or against us?"

No matter how this may be softened by a new-age philosophical acceptance of others, there is always still a speck of a wish that the particular culture embraced will be undisputed. Cutting off a part of the penis, depriving the body of food, and humbly begging some invisible entity for help, all seem much more sane and justified if the vision behind it is reaffirmed. That is a good reason for seeking out a community of like minds in the first place. That is why a variation is so ruffling, why even between an ultra-Orthodox Jew and a reform Jew, there is embarrassment and prejudice. My local synagogue's Judaism, too, had certain expectations that kept it grounded. But when I found I did not fit in to them, I kept religion at arm's length. I tried to believe instead that its truth lay beyond my reach, somewhere far away in Israel.

Growing up, I was always keenly aware of American synagogue politics. Granted, most members of the community were warm people and wonderful friends to us. I remember hungrily the brownies and berry punch after prayers. The kisses on the cheek and the murmurs of "Shabbat Shalom." There was something about celebrating a holiday in this place, in an institution that had been momentarily disarmed in the festivity. Where all faces were, if not friendly, at least familiar. Where we spent long afternoons in prayers, in frying potato pancakes for Chanukah or packing lunches for the homeless. Where we knew even the building itself intimately, chatting with the janitor, wandering upstairs into the closed-off rooms and into the kitchen. Where Hebrew school and bits of Torah wisdom made stories flit by, alive for just an instant or an evening. But, despite all this, in many ways still, my family was on the outskirts of synagogue culture.

Our move from America to Israel, and then, crushed, from Israel back to America, risked much financially, and even after the initial recovery, for years we stood precariously. When we first attempted to reenter American Jewish life, by general standards, we could have just gotten by. But because my parents chose to place us into Jewish society and wanted us to be accepted by a certain element of that community which happened to also be affluent, in that circle we were poor.

My parents stretched our money to its absolute limit so that there was enough to eat, and we patched and repatched clothes from Kmart. Once we had the basics, aside from their regular jobs, they fixed cracked windshields and did babysitting for extra money. Then they used their savings and went into debt so that we could be competitive and compatible with our peers in this circle, with piano lessons and tap dance class. *We* were their investments— not stocks or properties. They wanted our future to be assured there, so that we would not bump and bumble as they had. And we also took out scholarships through the synagogue in order to attend the private Jewish day school, Jewish summer camp, and youth movement trips. My parents took these monies reluctantly, grateful, but enduring this ruffle to their dignities only for our sakes. As a result, we were surrounded by children who were always fashionably dressed, who went skiing every weekend during the winter, who had cleaning ladies. We cautiously tried to befriend them and idolized them but were jealous of them and never fully trusted them, since after all, we sat next to them because of their parent's donations to the scholarship fund. So instead we siblings became best friends to *each other*, fiercely protective of one another and intimate—in the end, our parents' sincerest hope for us.

Oversensitive at the inequalities between us and them, we also felt certain that in a small community, nothing could remain a secret for long. Our financial situation was embarrassingly apparent from the fact that we did not have enough money to pay hundreds of dollars for seats at high holiday services. So for many years we sat in the side room where a tiny television was set up, watching the rabbi in the main sanctuary sing the prayers through the screen. We felt we were obvious, in that our rusty old station wagon sat in the parking lot near their shiny new imported cars. And in that we did not frequent their polished hairdressers, country clubs, gyms, and restaurants.

We stood out also in that when my parents opened our home and tried to befriend the community, they were blind to its politics, and even to their own aspirations for us. They wanted for friends—and often had—the educated, the refined, the established. But, idealists still, and always believing in people's endless potential, they also could not help themselves, and were good-hearted and perfect hosts to anyone and everyone. They offered their friendship to whoever would give genuine friendship in return. To whoever needed hearty conversation and a tasty meal. And so, though we ended up bringing into our home many people of quality, we also brought in the genius misfits, the families who were rough around the edges, the crusty immigrants who could not find other friends. We gave just as much a chance to the pillars of the community as we did to, say, the Fleisher family, scrappy and moldy as they were, coarse and loud on the outside, but seemingly genuine on the inside. In part, this welcoming, accepting, unquestioning goodness is what makes my parents extraordinary. In part this naïveté—bringing in strays and wild mutts—would also be their weakness. Because eventually the oddball types they brought in, even the Fleishers, turned on them when they found some richer offers. And all the time along the way, growing up and seemingly linked as we were with these indiscriminate choices, our own precarious and not-so-impressive position was only that much more apparent.

Our family was also exposed before the community, in the way we learned to present ourselves in its circles, always proper and overdressed and well-behaved, always humble and outdoing ourselves with gushing gratitude. For everything we did that could seem inappropriate, my parents reproached us. "What will people in the community say about that?" A skirt might be too short. A conversation might feel too loud or vulgar. A silence might seem unfriendly. Even if some others made little effort to include us, or invite us to parties, we had to always be polite and friendly and open and ready *in case* they decided they wanted to. The hope was that if we compensated and swallowed our pride, if we went enough above and beyond the others, they would in no way suspect we were not worthy of their association—or the money that trickled down from them to us. But of course, these efforts only made us more obvious and strange.

Aside from the issue of money, our family also sat on the fringe of our synagogue because we were not white. For my parents, spirituality was more defining than just skin color. But some others were not of the same thinking.

"Why don't you look Jewish?" people often asked us.

"What does Jewish look like?" we wanted to say in return. "Judaism is a religion, it is not a look." But they asked this because most of the Jews they saw around them in America were descended from Eastern Europe, and they assumed that those people defined Jews all over the world.

When we explained there that we were the mixture of an Indian Jew and an Eastern European Jew, people automatically identified us by the brownness and what made us nonwhite. Their assumptions drew a distinct line between us and them. "So," they said, after hearing about the thousands of years of history, "I guess generations ago, the Jews in India must have intermarried with the Hindus. That's how you have that beautiful brown color." They said this theoretically, as though they were students of human civilization figuring out how white Jews could have evolved into brown. They even said this laughing admiringly, as though envious of our tan. But in making such a statement, they—the people who even believed in the same G-d we believed in—were also pointing to us as the others and claiming, the skin says it all. We, Ashkenazi Jews, are the pure originals. You, Indian Jews, are mixed products.

Sometimes, as our parents had instructed us, we said to the people who questioned us: "The ancient Hebrews were Semites out of the Middle East, so they were dark themselves. Where then did Ashkenazi Jews get their pale skin and blue eyes, if not from mixing with the Russians and Poles around them?" We recited this dutifully, as though from a well-crafted script, hoping it might make others stop and realize that intermingling was inevitable for Jews around the world throughout time—if not from active choice, then because of human nature and tragedy even. But instead we were pointed to as the peculiarities simply because our interbreeding had resulted in brown and theirs hadn't. It would have been impossible, I think, to not read into the nuances of such conversation, to feel tested and obligated to prove ourselves. So as a result, we walked around, always on the alert and a bit paranoid, ready to fend off accusations at any moment.

Many people simply did not know about our history. And when we explained it all to them, they were delighted and fascinated and thrilled. They embraced us, as if we were their own, and long lost. But a few people were outright cruel to us because of the differences, and these were the ones who branded our minds. They offered cool disinterested small talk and barbed comments, passing by quickly as if we had somehow offended them. At first, we lived in fear of their behavior, so far away from our world of gentleness, of eagerness to please. Eventually, however, we became scornful of them, because they thought we could not see through their poor offerings. They thought we were grateful for their morsels of condescension. These were individuals who couldn't accept Jews who were not part of an elite, plastic formula. To them we were poor oddities, variations of the truth, and exotic in a way that recalled colonial ideas of Orientalism. We were Jewish culture as they had never known it. And to see our family, in brown skin and hand-me-down clothes carrying on inside their synagogue, called all the norms of their religion into question. At best, as we grew into ourselves, we seemed to them to be lovely novelties, like bit sculptures or native handiwork carted back from tax-free foreign ports—souvenirs of some vacation abroad.

Absorbing these sentiments at that young age, I could not help but second-guess myself and feel distanced from the religion that housed them. When I was told we could not afford Benetton clothing, I mourned a little bit. And when my classmates asked me: "Where is your family's summer cottage?" I had to say we didn't have one at all and I braced myself with resentment. As though things like Benetton and summer homes could ever be necessary in any other part of the world. I knew in many ways we had it good, that we always had some kind of food, that we were warm at night. But nonetheless, the reality we were placed into and told to embrace had different standards, and it would not have been possible to live in utter denial of these.

One day, getting dressed in the locker rooms after swim team practice at the Jewish community center, I peeked at the girls around me stepping out of towels. And to my surprise, I saw that they all had lovely pink nipples. I had never looked squarely at someone else's nipples before. I had never even thought about this, that nipples could come in any other color but brown-toasted, like my own. But there they were, twirling before me, girly, dainty, rosy, like rice paper parasols plucked from a tropical drink. My eyes widened, my mouth opened slightly in awe as they seemed to taunt me, superior. And I sighed, thinking enviously, this is how nipples were meant to be. I wanted pink nipples, too, I decided, not my plain old burlap ones.

Had it been possible, I would have somehow changed them myself, coloring in delicate pink Barbie doll circles from a box of Crayolas—not the cheap 8-pack but the full motherload box of 120 crayons, so I could use shades of salmon and carnation and peach.

Instead, for weeks I negotiated with G-d, fantastically, illogically, asking to trade my own nipples in for pink ones. As though nipples were ornamental clip-ons, to be dug up from bargain bins, worn once, and then exchanged with proof of purchase. Upon receipt of one set of shiny pink nipples, I agreed as though by contract to a) Pray for unselfish things like world peace every night before going to sleep, b) Stop arguing with my mother about doing the dishes, and c) Wear wool sweaters, which I loathed—though I fully expected the itching and suffering that resulted to stand in as a testament of my goodwill. When I finally accepted the fact that my wish could not come true and no new nipples would ever appear, another small part of me detached from the world of typical American Jews, saying this is not mine.

As we grew into teenagers, my parents became more financially stable and more at ease with the community themselves. They sent us off to Jewish youth groups and camps so that we could be with other Jews and come to that sense of easiness ourselves. Possibly, also, they were pushing me to fulfill my own private promise to Nana-bai, to ally myself with power and happiness, and then return with these to the family and community. At the very least, I might find a nice Jewish boyfriend.

I know my parents could envision the beauty in these Jewish retreats. Many children of one religion gathering together in rustic cabins, beneath chilly green forests and pine smells and sky. Praying and wondering about the meaning of community. Eating barbecue and drinking cherry bug-juice. And even I felt part of the excitement there, removed from the rest of the world, singing songs and pounding the table in our enthusiasm. So much so that for the first time ever I took on roles of leadership, like chapter president and regional secretary and counselor and teacher. But I don't think when they sent me off, my parents fully understood the inevitable lustiness, too, in these gatherings of young Jewish souls.

Perhaps at home, the parents of these other children also nagged, find a good Jewish boy. Perhaps in public school, where there were not many other Jews, some were teased for having big noses and thick glasses. But, when they came together at these retreats, Jews of all kinds were abundantly collected, nerds and beauties and rebels. Names like Jew bastard and Jewish American

Princess could be thrown out safely now, with ownership. Stereo-typed features could be laughed at safely from the inside; even more, they could be appreciated, and seen as the norm. There, a boy could be handsome even if he wasn't muscle bound. A girl could be swarmed by admirers regardless of the kinkiness in her curly hair. Suddenly freed, there was a frenzied sampling from this smorgasbord of Jews. An orgy here, some marijuana there. A sneaky late night swim naked in the lake. The opportunity to be feverish and vulnerable in faith. And a final dance party bash, where if all else failed, the loners might find each other in the fray and hump to the sounds of Led Zeppelin.

I could have embraced all this and joined the rows of bikini-clad bodies on the grass, the endless, luxurious backrubs and flirt-ing. One night, it beckoned me with a long seductive finger. As everyone sat around a campfire singing and laughing, I met a boy named David. Of course, even before actually meeting David, I knew all about him. Everyone did. He wore trendy but deliber-ately indifferent baggy pants and flannel. He played on the camp baseball team. He had had four girlfriends that summer already. All his older brothers were once campers there before him. And rumors birthed in the nakedness of showers and scribbled on bunk walls had it that the whole family was generously endowed. David and his brothers were legendary.

Though David and I had only been talking for half an hour or so, soon, feeling caught up in the music and the marshmallows, he leaned in to me and touched the skin of my arm. "You're so . . . butterscotch. Can I kiss you?"

His breath was slightly sour and he leaned too close. But he was so confident in his question, so casual and unconscious of these boundaries and smells, that I knew that he had a more experienced comfort with the nature of bodies. "I don't think so," I told him, shaking my head and pulling back. "You don't even know me," I said, attempting a light note.

He sat back for a moment to think, spreading his legs and placing a hand on each knee. "Okay. So tell me about yourself," he decided, as though a kiss should be that easy. I could have kissed him that night. I could have sneaked back to the boy's bunk and gone down on him in his sleeping bag, which in the end he did instead with Shana Goldbaum. But at that age, trained by my parents' principles, and expecting that every relationship would be like their own glorious example of perfect people and perfect commitment and even camel races, this camp-culture shocked my sensibilities. The anxious, oily bodies growing and groping and exploring each other were so much more free and brazen than the few awkward, hopeful pecks and caresses I had experienced thus far. And though this boy was a virile, walking, talking embodiment of the much admired white Jewish world, I knew I was out of my league. So I turned my back on it all and the experimentation and held out for something more, something breathtaking and consuming that would claim me instantly forever.

Frustrated with American Judaism, I remembered and idealized what it was to be Jewish when we had lived on the kibbutz in Israel, where even secular life was intrinsically religious. Though so many Israelis claimed to not believe in G-d, just being Israeli and serving in the army to defend a Jewish State was a religious act in itself. There, instead of answering only to the awkwardness of synagogue institutions, just the fact of living in a Jewish country and speaking the ancient Hebrew language and repopulating the "promised" land with new Jewish babies, made for a profoundly Jewish existence. It was the difference between learning to paint in a college course, and being an artist by instinct and nature.

On Shabbat and the holidays, the country reached a quiet calm. Stores shut down, buses stopped, so that even someone who did not go to synagogue passed the time with family and friends, and indirectly observed the occasion. That person could make the religious motions of lighting candles, and then do something entirely out of the religious formula. Like wander down to the beach in flip-flops for a swim—though in truth there is not much that inspires more awe of G-d and nature than sitting salty on the sand, eating watermelon and watching the sun melt into stars over the Mediterranean. People in synagogues around the world could easily recall the ancient Jewish kingdom with their prayers. But, ah, to be living in Israel as a modern, vibrant incarnation of that kingdom . . . that was something else entirely.

I remembered this revolutionary religion especially after we returned from Israel to the United States. Though our move there had been trampled, my parents clung to bits and shreds of Israel and its ideology. It still managed to be the gauge on our lives. If we complained about how hot it was or mosquitoes or about mowing the lawn, my parents would say: "Come on. Buck up. You're kibbutz kids!" As he grew older, my father would even fight his aching limbs by saying: "Put me working back in the banana fields three days, and I'll be like new again." They wanted, even after everything we went through, for the good of Israel to continue to form us as people. So while I was in high school, they sent Gertie and me back to the kibbutz each summer to visit friends.

But I found the kibbutz system changing. Israel was no longer raw frontier, dotted with dreamy pioneers, so it did not need its many kibbutzim as it once did. Families living on the kibbutz wanted privacy and personal profit. They wanted to own glittery, seductive goods like microwave ovens and laptop computers. Kibbutz children who were born wet and pink into the system never made the decision themselves to live there or embrace the ideology, so they grew up feeling isolated from the MTV and Nike culture in the city. Eventually they tried to leave the kibbutz behind. And it remained, wrinkled and hunched over, each day moving further away from the place where I once hopped barefoot from one bomb shelter to another.

When we lived on the kibbutz, my best friend there was a girl named Kineret. She was a strange child, never fully accepted by the others in our class, with a mass of curly yellow hair and sharp eyes. She called her parents by their first names. And after her father came back from working in the fields, took off his sweaty socks and rolled them up into his boots, she plucked them out and sucked on them. Kineret did this even in front of me, while I sat at the edge of their couch, watching uncomfortably.

"Disgusting," he told her, as he came out of the shower. "Stop that."

"They're good and salty," she told him, hooting, and chewing ceaselessy.

Despite her oddness, I liked Kineret better than most everyone else there for little reasons. Because she always had chocolate in her house and stray cats visiting for weeks on end. And she had an uncanny talent for drawing pictures of the gorgeousness around us, flower bouquets and beautiful women.

Kineret and I barely stayed in touch during the years after I left. So I was nervous when I first saw her on my visit, thinking that it would be awkward. Instead the moment I arrived she embraced me, excited for something "imported," trying to keep the novelty of me all to herself. I remember seeing her, the same face grown up now, with her rolled blue jeans looking like everyone else's out of the communal warehouse.

By then, like all teenagers on the kibbutz, she did not live at home any more, but she had her own room in a dorm. Kineret took me back there and put on Bob Marley songs and offered me a sip from a bottle of vodka. I refused it, so she drank alone while we talked. Kineret told me all the gossip of the kibbutz. About Yael who was sleeping with Zevi. And why no one liked the Katsh family. And about the ballsy Aussie volunteer who was systemati-cally making it with all the kibbutz girls over arak shots and snooker. "I'm so bored with this place and the same people all the time," she confided in me. "I can't stand to see their faces any-more. After the army I'm going to move into the city and get a job or maybe I'll travel to Tibet. Or Sweden. I think that must be the most beautiful place on earth," she said. It amazed me when she said this, that Sweden must be the most beautiful place on earth. It seemed to me that she already *was* living in the most beautiful place on earth. A place where religion was as natural as the stun-ning mountains.

Uncomfortable with American Judaism, I tried to reclaim this part of Israel, this beauty, as my own religion. Every Saturday morning, Shabbat, Kineret and I, and often Gertie, made a simple but delicious breakfast and sat to eat it outside on the patio. We cut up Israeli salad with cucumbers and tomatoes and onions chopped up tiny, topped by lemon juice and oil and salt and pep-per. We made yogurt drinks with rosewater and mint. We had fresh bread with cottage cheese and white cheese and yellow cheese. And olives. And cakes. The patio overlooked the hills be-tween Israel and Lebanon. So those mornings as we ate, we also breathed in the smells of dry flowers and thistles blowing to us in the wind. They beckoned us, and once we were stuffed, we climbed into the hills and explored.

So many things were hidden between there and the mine-covered no man's land of the Lebanese border just a few kilometers away. Amidst the rock badgers, barbed wire, and dried greenery, my relationship to G-d had nothing to do with annual synagogue dues or who my family voted for in the last community board election. It did not even matter if the cantor's son, who had always tried to kiss me, murmuring "gorgeous" and "exotic," in the end only dated nice marriageable Jewish girls whose religious identities were stockly white and familiar. It didn't matter, because on those Shabbat afternoons, we ventured with bursting bellies into another kind of godliness, wandering through the layers of that land.

We found our way into the original bones of the kibbutz. The tower and stockade its first settlers constructed overnight to claim the territory, despite British rule and Arab violence. An army tank that was stranded on a hilltop overlooking Lebanon, harmless, broken, and empty of shells, but left there anyhow, so there would be a vague military presence to shake its fist in warning across the border. We delved into the remnants of ancient people who had passed through that corner of the earth. The winding, voluptuous spread of pools and waterfalls and grass, mythical birthplace to Pan, the goatlike Greek god of fields and flocks. Relics of a caravan resting point, a biblical olive oil press, pieces of Byzantine mosaics and Roman glass begging to be dug up. We even found ourselves touching upon the primitive. Natural rock bridges formed through-out millions of years, arcing over frightening plummeting empti-ness, and blues and greens and divine air all the way down to the sea. And cool wet caves where stalactites grew drop by drop, patiently dank, stony and somehow in their quiet, superior to the passing of eons. Reveling in the spirituality of these encounters, I believed in Israel as the utopian Golden Age religion that Jews for thousand of years had dreamed of in the Diaspora. And modern American Jews, I thought, with the judgments inherent in their petty complications and gaudy synagogues, could not even imagine something so straightforward.

There were, of course, moments when I doubted this flawlessness, when I saw in some Israelis I knew elements of vacant atheism and brutal honesty—enough to tell someone, boy you've gotten fat, or, what is that, a pimple?—and it made me cringe. If G-d had a more defined presence for the Israeli masses, I wondered, would this same harsh culture have emerged? Sometimes, too, I myself felt the need for more than a picnic to express all the turbulence of my spirit, something shapely and collective. And yet, when I had these hesitations, my stubborn idealizing and old grudges always allowed me to cling to Israel as a religion, despite everything. Because it was easy to believe that religious perfection lay there, across an ocean, and, oh, if only it were in my reach, everything else would follow!

Finally I was in Jerusalem, the holiest of all cities. That rare piece of land whose torrential history makes a person feel humbled and tiny. Whose congestion of spiritual searches, at the same time makes a person also feel that she and her own searching have significantly and finally come home. I found myself amidst colorful fruit stands, bakeries steaming with new bread to be dipped into paper pockets of zaatar spice. There were dreamy art vendors around me, and winding streets, musky with piousness, and gold with old brick. This might have, easily, been an ideal scene for some greater understanding of the Israel I had come to worship. In the direction of a wise, bearded rabbi. In the frenzy of the masses praying at the Wailing Wall, the remnant of the great ancient Temple. And yet, in the end, instead of finding an awakening, this is where I first began to suspect that my self-proclaimed religion was not what I once supposed. And it was just because of one crass Israeli nearby me at the bus stop, who leaned up against a pole, smoking a cigarette.

He was a slightly graying man with a tight potbelly and strong arms, probably in his late thirties, but dressed in army fatigues, so I knew he was in the midst of his reserve duties. He seemed tired, and was probably fed up with the reserves. But something about being away from routine and work, and cracking fart jokes with his friends on the base, liberated him. So that now as he waited for the bus, he grinned and glinted like a young boy.

"Hello," he said in Hebrew, eyeing me. Not wanting to encourage him, but even more, not wanting to endure an uncomfortable, unfriendly silence while we waited half an hour for the bus, I nodded and smiled tightly. "So. Where are you from?"

"Guess," I said in Hebrew, short.

He grinned, took a deep puff on his cigarette, thinking. "Emm. Let's see. Ramle?" I shook my head, surprised to hear this particular city suggested. "Well, you're Yemenite, right? So I would guess Dimona maybe."

Now I followed his line of thought. Well-off and educated Israelis of Eastern European descent lived in the nice suburbs. But early on, the Israeli government had filled these particular cities that he was suggesting with large populations of poorer Jewish immigrants from the African and Arab nations. Clumped together, this perpetuated a cycle of little money and lots of crime, with not many opportunities in work or education to even the score. Because I was brown, this man assumed I had come from that world. Perhaps he even herded me into the class-genus-species of the chach-chach. A chach-chach was usually seen in its natural habitat, making a living by selling sandwiches, cheap barrettes, CDs, and authentic discounted Israeli brassware in one of those neighborhoods or at the central bus station. A chach-chach spoke with guttural slang and listened to the kind of oriental music in which voices wavered and whined and shuddered themselves into a high fever. The male wore gold chains and had slick hair. The female birthed often and early. And she could usually be spotted wearing a plumage of bright lipstick.

Part of me could appreciate, even yearn for, the hominess of this culture that was forever being put down. The loose language. The spicy foods and songs. But another part of me also shied away from the name chach-chach, as if from country hick or ghetto girl. And I resented this man, too, as I imagined him, this once-upon-a-time paratrooper. With the comfort of his clean Tel-Aviv existence. And his university education. And his redheaded wife and children. And his graying, bespectacled grandpa, sitting in the breezy library of his aristocratic Jerusalem home somewhere—where he regularly had tea and wafers with Israel's greatest scholars and founders and, once even, with Golda Meir. Because this man looked at me now, and—the audacity!—judged me just by skin color alone.

"I'm not Yemenite. I'm Indian," I told him. Funny that to identify myself, I had to clarify what it was that made my skin brown. No matter that I was just as much white.

"Ah," he said, then after a moment smiled knowingly and chanted in a sing-song, "Itchikidana. Itchikidana."

Itchikidana. This word came from a popular Indian movie, and for some reason it has stuck in much of Israeli culture. Whenever I told someone there that I was Indian, they responded with Itchikidana. Even my mother told me that when she grew up there years ago, Israelis would greet her with Itchikidana. The man at the bus stop did not mean to be cruel with this word. He only used it to try to define and expertly pinpoint, "Aha! Indian. I know what that means!" But like anything attempting to capture an entire civilization in a few syllables, the word simply minimized.

"You must live in Lod then?" he guessed again.

I drew myself up, now taking pride in America, though usually I tried to melt seamlessly into Israel and claim it as if it were my own. "Actually, I'm from New York."

"What! I don't believe you." Casual Hebrew comes naturally to me, so it often takes a while for Israelis to notice the traces of my American accent. "Speak to me in English," he demanded.

"This is absolutely one hundred percent true," I told him in English.

"Rrright. Rrright," he now said in English, in exchange, exaggerating the R's to sound generically American. Then returning to Hebrew, he offered me a cigarette. I refused. He leaned in and told me, "You know, my younger brother is planning to come to New York next year, to work for a few months and make some money. Emm, maybe you'll give me your number and I'll tell him to call you when he is there." He spread his hands wide and explained, "It's always good to know people, to have protectzia and connections. Plus," he winked at me, conspiring, as though he knew exactly what I needed, "he has some nice muscles!"

I looked at him, wondering about the transformation I had undergone in his mind within five minutes. From poor minority, to trite Indian, to a potential connection with American richness.

And it struck me that even in Israel, in the Promised Land, in what I thought was a de facto religion, a natural unconscious religion that transcended such pettiness, I was being judged as I was judged at the synagogues back home, by wealth and appearance. If I could encounter these standards in both countries, was there any possibility of a world that was free of them? What's more, could I honestly claim that I was innocent of my own set of biases—about those Jews back home who were born into money and their expensive brand names, even about chach-chachs?

Worried at this flaw in my perfection, I immersed myself in life at the kibbutz instead, so I would not have to think about what it all could mean. Kineret and all my friends were still walking around barefoot, and so I began to do this again, too. Though I had not built up the comfortable calluses that they had, being barefoot seemed wonderfully free to me—and sometimes I went a step further and left my bra behind, as well. During those summers we went to the ocean and made picnics. Though Gertie, always the commanding big sister, scolded me, I drank beer and tried to samba. We wandered along the boardwalks, meeting soldiers, talking to soldiers, more and more soldiers everywhere. Everyone in Israel becomes a soldier at the age of eighteen. And in the end, idolizing, awed, I could not help myself: I fell in love with the whole lot of them. I never had a serious relationship with one, though I shared a flirtation with one soldier from Jerusalem, a dance with another from Haifa, an innocent kiss, that's it. No frenzied unbuttoning-unzipping-unraveling. Nothing that lasted into winter and long-distance phone calls. Nothing even that prompted empty words destined to fall short, like "I'll miss you" or "I'll write." Most I loved from afar, only becoming easy friends. Just one turned into something more.

I met Ari when he was stationed at the kibbutz for two weeks, to stand guard at the gates and look out over Lebanon. On a day when he was off duty, he introduced himself to me at the pool and we sat together in the sun, in two orange beach chairs. Ari taught me all sorts of Arabic curse words, incorporating "your mother" and "your father" and some kind of shoe. He also taught me some of the choice Arabic phrases he'd learned to use in the army, like "Open the door!" He talked in slang, dirty, motioning with his hands in crude twisting gestures, shocking me but making me laugh, too. We spoke of his girlfriend, and I said to myself, content, so we'll be good friends. Ari invited me to come and keep him company one night in the guardhouse and I agreed, excited.

I walked to the guardhouse that night along the border, barefoot. There was the smell of dried grasses and night and sweet dirt and I felt myself a patriot, a Zionist, thinking wistfully that this is what my life would have been had we never moved back to the United States. The night was beautiful, more meaningful and alive than anything back home, and I could hear the distant voices in Lebanese villages, feel the ancient terrain around me, the fearless souls tromping through it that had once been conjured up in childish songs.

But here now I found myself approaching a real Jewish warrior. I could see him through the dark in the small guardhouse with the door propped open, all lit up and white. He sat with his booted feet up on the desk smoking a cigarette thoughtfully and talking to the other guard. Ari looked painfully young, but there was a machine gun by his feet and he sucked on the cigarette in his lips with an old, driven need.

When he saw me, he sat up, beckoning happily. "Look what I have," he told me, opening up the dusty minifridge in the corner even before I'd walked in. "I have some meat here and Coca-Cola and we can make a barbecue on the range outside." I think I was surprised that there was a fridge in there, and a fan and a radio playing Pink Floyd. I had expected something more spartan, more dangerous, and so I hesitated for a moment. But a barbecue was irresistible, so I was happy to pitch in and pour cups of cola and get the coals going. We laid out steaks and ate them charred inside cold pita breads, pulling pickles from a briny can to munch on every now and then.

"Come walk with me," he said when we had finished, motioning to the other guard that he was leaving for a bit. We walked together silently for a while, till we reached a bomb shelter, one of the bomb shelters I long ago danced over. He climbed up it and then extended a hand to pull me up too, and we sat side by side watching the stars. It was a moment of complete quiet and bliss between a boy and girl, so I should not have been surprised that he would lean over to kiss me. But when he did, putting needy, wet lips on my lips, in truth I *was* surprised. "What about your girlfriend?" I asked him, pulling away. A part of me did not care. He looked at me with wanting and as we sat on top of the shelter, under a majestic sky that was both familiar and still profoundly moving to me, it seemed natural, even glorious. I trusted him. But something in me had to ask again: "What about your girlfriend?"

"Come on," he said, nudging me. "Really."

"No," I told him again. "What about her?"

He moved back then an inch or two and looked at me. Who knows what he saw? A tease, perhaps. Or maybe a fourteen-year-old, slightly plump and awkward, chilly without her shoes, annoyingly not as easy as American girls were reputed to be. For a moment, I felt fear in my gut, the truth of the situation. That I was far from others, alone in the dark with a man who might be feeling trifled with. But then he let out a loud breath and said to me, "You know, most guys would not take no for an answer. You need to be careful. You're lucky that I am me," he said and patted my back.

"But," I told him, still confused, "you have a girlfriend. I thought you just wanted to be my friend."

"You can be like my little sister," he reassured me, hopping off of the bomb shelter and helping me after him. "But you should know," he explained, no apologies, "a hole is a hole."

Though that night I followed Ari back to the guardhouse, mortified, I remembered this encounter even years later wrapped up in the romantic, tragic urgency of war. I thought of him when I listened to Israeli pop songs about boys on the battlefield. And I could swear that I saw his face in a news clip about the Palestinian Intifada uprising the next year . . . and then again in a magazine photo spread on more uprisings years later—G-d, will it never end?

I could still feel the fatigues, khaki and dusty, slitted for air but nevertheless thick with a musty smell. I remembered the heaviness of an M16 carried casually by a strap, and the sense of a body near me that was trained and powerful and important to the country, and still with me, with me! This was my reality, too, I tried to tell myself. After all, I had lived in Israel before and I might live there again someday. I was practically fluent in Hebrew. I was *not* just a dumb American snapping pictures, having a summer fling. The few words between Ari and me—figuring out where we stood—could have been serious intimacy, as though they were part of an ongoing dialogue for people with infinite possibilities before them.

Though I returned to America and my existence became more and more rooted there, still I pored over my photographs, and reminisced about moments that were so raw they had to be religious encounters. I remembered the days I spent in the desert, without showers or plumbing or civilized contact. Just hiking and sleeping on the sand, till I burnt and froze and dried up, and finally beaten by the desert, was seduced by it. I remembered what it was to sit inside a giant crate of freshly picked grapefruits, with the smell of soil and citrus like pillows around me. I remembered the many delicious soldiers and their persuasive words. Some words were so absurd and transparent that they were poetic. Other words were too farfetched, like when one curly-haired boy proclaimed to me, "You are one of the most beautiful creatures in the world." And yet, he uttered these words so sincerely that he managed to startle me and even himself with what he said. Of course, especially, I remembered with adoration that one soldier that kissed me on the mountaintop, Ari. And all this reaffirmed the connection for me. But eventually even I saw that it was much to ask of a poor, horny soldier, that he be a symbol. Certainly, it was not a new story. A uniform that somehow turned a homely man handsome. A sense of patriotism and wonder. The age-old line desperately whispered at the edge of a cot, who knows what will happen by tomorrow? And yet, it was the kind of story that could keep a young girl feeling spiritual.

Back in the States, I stubbornly tried to restore religious authority to my idea of Israeli life. But sometimes I caught myself, fiercely American, wanting personal credit for my accomplishments. Or getting caught up in rich synagogue politics. And then I reminded myself of the chanciness in the muscled twists and fated stardust that brought me away from the kibbutz and Israel to where I was finally in the United States. I scolded myself, forced myself to think about what it would have been like had I stayed at the kibbutz, gone through the army, and lived on like my classmates. I would probably not have had an extensive education or expensive tastes. I may not have even missed them. I might have spent forty years working in the communal laundry feeling perfect contentment.

But I, too, changed. Not just in the usual growing up, but in a way that brought me far from the basic qualities of the kibbutz and the world that would have been mine if I had stayed there. And I realized that though it was easy to believe in and live through the faraway clouds of Israel, it lay before me to find a part of Judaism that in all its complexities could actually touch me in the life that was mine.

Part of me could never be a kibbutz adult. American cities, American Judaism, academia, and the luxury of a surplus culture, all molded my lifestyle and expectations—so deeply that I even tried to pour the hard, pure line of adult abstractions into my reflections on the kibbutz. I tried to delineate it all: A utopian society. An independent religion. And young bodies, never purposely trying to create complexity, but somehow organically restless in anticipation of growing up, feeling the turmoil, seeking it out. I tried to recognize myself—starkly and with adult meticulousness—as I was then, choosing, unnecessarily, to expose bare feet to adventure. To the elements, the frosty grass, the wonderful slide of mud. Even to stones and the unbearable heat of the pavement.

And yet, in many ways, another part of me, stunted in growth, continued—and probably always will continue—to be an original kibbutz child. For good or for bad, sharing made me overly generous with myself and my few earthly belongings. After living off waterfalls of flowers and vegetables so closely, I was left primitively connected to nature and the imagination forever. And most of all, that piece of life and world remained beautiful in my mind, no matter what. I felt it all caught up in a breathy whirlpool of salty ocean spray and cold mountain air, fruit spilling off the trees and a dangerous olive-skinned soldier turned brotherly.

And I remained that kibbutz child at heart because despite all the grown-up jumble of ideas I tried to impose upon Israel, still when I thought about that place, that home, it was with utter longing. And what puffed out in the end was just this impossible simplicity. A picture of me, dancing barefoot on a bomb shelter.

# PART THREE

# Kin, Not Kind

*"Most husbands are docile and only attack when provoked. Like other domestic animals they respond to kindness more than anything else. They do not understand the actual words so much as the tone of voice. You should try using a friendly tone when addressing your husbands. You will find that it will make him almost human and life will become much more cozy for you both. In fact, before long you will be glad you married the man."* —*Anonymous*

—NANA-BAI'S DIARY, PAGE 28

T he bruise over Nana-bai's eye was healing rather quickly. It was a good sign. In the last few days, it had gone from angry red to black to blue-green and then a faded, puffy yellow which could almost blend in with the brown of her skin.

The night it happened, Solly came to dinner acting gruff. But still, Evie had been anxious to help serve her papa's meal. Carefully she had carried heavy plates out to him, weighed down and bracing the chubby legs beneath her night shirt. She was happy to have even this small part of him. Then she went to sleep and Nana-bai came to him to clean up after the meal. But he was in an evil mood that night. So he looked for an excuse to be mad, baiting her into a discussion on the ideology of Zionism.

"Why shouldn't we Bene Israel leave India and go to Palestine someday if it is possible?" she asked. "Isn't this what we have wanted for hundreds of years?"

He picked his teeth and shook his head, as though it was obvious she was wrong, and she knew it and must just be saying these things to anger him. "We have our own kind of life here in India. We do not need to begin changing to match the rest of the world." But then, nastily, he stretched, as if welcoming her to speak more on the subject.

It had been several weeks since Solly last came by, so Nana-bai who had gained an ounce of her natural courage back, did not see this trap. Instead her quick mind entered eagerly into this debate, even before she could think to stop herself. She started to speak, "I disagree. Because it is fortunate, really——" but after just a few moments, Solly stood up and came to her and her voice faded out in the middle of a word.

"Do you dare?" he asked her in even, fuming tones, dangerous in their quiet. "Do you dare to contradict me?" He was quiet because he could not be bothered with Evie waking and peering at them from beneath the blankets, as he knew she sometimes secretly did. Then he hit Nana-bai, his blows coming slowly, methodically, as if he were performing some kind of duty. Afterward, as usual, he washed his bloodied hands in a bowl of water and left without a word. Nana-bai waited till he had left, holding her face for the pain, and cringing as the salt of her tears burned into the open cuts.

She did not bother to ask him: "What did I do? How did I disobey you?"

When he beat her the first time, not long after they were just married, she did ask this, crying into her hands. He put on his shirt and shoes, and only told her, "I don't know the reason. But I'm sure there is one." Then he smoothed his hair before the looking glass and, catching sight of her reflection in the room behind him, added, "So it's for that. Whatever it is you may have done. And also for whatever it is you're going to do next."

She knew she was lucky to even be alive. Wives were killed every day, for overcooking the rice, or if her family could not collect the promised dowry. Their own husbands and mother-in-laws doused them with oil and set them on fire, then pronounced the death an accident as they looked to start over with a fresh bride. And Nana-bai knew she was fortunate that such a terrible thing had not happened to her.

At least, she sighed, Solly no longer seemed interested in spending the night there after beating her. Mostly he just returned to Rebecca's home these days. And that was a gift in itself, that she then didn't have to tolerate him touching her, that she didn't have to pretend to not feel the pain of where he had hit her. As though noticing her cuts and bruises was an acknowledgment of some embarrassing thing they had both witnessed, which would be best forgotten.

She turned her already swelling eye to the corner where Evie's bed sat, and felt relieved that she did, in fact, still seem to be asleep. Thank G-d. She did not want her to see these things. She did not know that Evie was only pretending to sleep, with her eyes just barely open, standing guard through the shade of her lashes. As though if things got too bad this time, she would hold up a small, protesting hand to her papa.

In the following days as Nana-bai lay on the bed, Evie took her bloated head and nestled it into her lap. Then she tried to make her feel better, tracing the blooming parts of her face with light fingers and telling her of all the lovely colors that could be found in the bruises around her eye. Blue like the sky in the split second between night and day. Then green like okra, but only half-cooked. Finally, when there was yellow like rice with just a pinch of turmeric, Nana-bai decided it was time to leave the house. Solly had not given her any money recently. But luckily there were still some coins left over from her payment for stitching petticoats for the Reuben family. She would use this to buy food, since there had been almost nothing to eat while she lay in bed recovering those days.

Nana-bai applied powder to her face, hoping to camouflage the bruises. She wrapped a plain brown sari around her, and scooped a few rupees into a kerchief. Then, taking Evie by the hand, they emerged into the sunlight. It was pleasant to be outside again after so many days. To be surrounded by crowds, and for just a moment, to not think about the problems of her husband. Bombay smelled of people, all people. Rich, poor, filthy, perfumed, newborn, dead, even rising to the sky from their funeral pyres. Often she felt constricted by this and dreamed of what it must be like in Palestine, where there were lonely mountains and desserts and groves of oranges and olives. There, a woman could talk to her echo and live in peace. But today, the smells of Bombay were invigorating. She and Evie wound through the streets wordlessly. As they approached the marketplace, the growing throngs, the fat ladies and sharp elbows and wide baskets, all going in the same direction, began to carry them by sheer force. And then the market was before them, a mass of colored cloths and sticky sweets and golden trinkets and fruits and vegetables, displayed as if for kings.

Nana-bai bought a kilo of rice, then some vegetables and fresh chili. "What do you say we make the two of us a lovely little vegetable dish tonight?" she asked Evie. "I feel suddenly like I have the appetite of a pack of hungry wolves."

But Evie was not listening. She had her eye on a giant red mango at the very top of a pile of mangos spread out before a vendor. She crouched over it, leaning her hands on bent knees and peering at it intently as if looking another little girl in the face.

Nana-bai saw this and reached immediately for the fruit. Presents were too costly usually, so if ever she saw that Evie wanted something within her means, she was happy to snatch it up. She bought the mango and allowed Evie to carry it back herself. It was so big she had to hold it in both her hands, but she was delighted by it and as they walked home, every now and then she brought it up to her nose to sniff at the fragrant skin.

Passing the synagogue on their way home, Nana-bai and Evie came across a small group of Bene Israel women gathered outside it. On their way to or from the market, they also carried parcels of freshly bought food in their hands, and packages, and business papers from just finishing their husband's errands. Her own sister Rebecca was there with her young daughter, Leah, who would someday be one of my great aunties. Rebecca was holding up many beautiful yards of foamy green cloth, displaying it for the other women, allowing them to even touch it between two fingers. "He is such a dumpling," she was saying. "He gave me the coins and said, 'Darling, go buy yourself something.' And as soon as I saw this, I knew he would love the color on me."

Leah, with one arm circling her mama's thigh, stood in the middle of the crowd of women, enjoying the oohs and aahs from above her. "Mama, you said from the leftover cloth you would have hair ribbons made for me. Isn't that so?" Rebecca beamed down at her, nodding.

Curses. I should not be out here, Nana-bai thought suddenly, frightened the women would see her bruises. Even muted under a layer of powder, they might betray her shames as no rumors could. She knew she had been foolish to leave the house in such a condition. Nana-bai would have liked to just nod and smile and continue home but that would have been insulting. She was obligated to stop and speak with them, for a moment at least.

As Nana-bai approached the group, she angled her face so that the still-healing bruises might not be seen. The women quieted down uncertainly when she neared, and Rebecca, feeling magnanimous, as the liaison between the community's circle of ladyhood and her poor sister, told her coolly, "Hello."

Nana-bai nodded in return to her and to the other women, inquiring quietly about one of Rebecca's sons who had lately been ill. Seeing these formalities exchanged between the two, the other women relaxed. Rebecca began to speak more intimately with one of her friends to the side, while some of the other women exchanged a few polite sentences with Nana-bai, and one even stooped down to speak with Evie, who clung to her mama's arm tightly. But then, sensing the dispersal of attention, little Leah gave a shriek and pointed at Nana-bai. Pulling on her mother's sari, she declared loudly, "See mama, isn't that a boo-boo she has?"

The women quieted and directed their attention to Nana-bai who blushed hot and murmured, "Nai. It is nothing. I fell."

Rebecca gave a sticky smile. "Leah, dumpling. You are always such a sharp girl. She does not miss a thing," she told the others on the side. "Go play with Evie for a bit and we will see how to help with these boo-boos."

As Leah led her away, Evie heard Rebecca tell the others, "Little girls are puzzled by boo-boos. *Women* know what they are and how to keep their husbands happy enough to not get them." She laughed, sensing the cryptic cleverness of this. And the other women, seeing that one sister could say this to another, felt permitted to laugh, too.

The women freely began to discuss their husbands then. And Nana-bai standing among them, was forced to listen courteously. "It is all in the curry," someone said. "If you make it too spicy, he won't be able to open his mouth to you."

"Never be the one to bear bad news. Send the children with it. Send the maid. Send his mother even. But never let it be you."

One young woman leaned into Nana-bai confidingly and told her in wispy tones: "I empty my head of absolutely everything when he is around me. Of all my own worries and interests. That way I am completely open to all the things he needs from me. I can tell exactly when he wants his feet rubbed. When he would just like to read a book and not have to hear the children running about near him." She smiled widely at Nana-bai, thinking she had been helpful. She also quietly congratulated herself on her tact and refinement, in making no direct acknowledgment of the ugliness of beatings.

The other women drifted off into separate conversations and soon Nana-bai and Rebecca stood by themselves a pace away, face to face. Rebecca turned a chilly look to her and said, "The whole family will be coming to my home to celebrate Rosh Hashanah." Playing the part of the gracious but burdened hostess, she nodded her head and said, "I suppose you and Evie could come, too. It will be many, many people. But it is natural that we should all celebrate in my home since it is by far the largest house in the family."

"Thank you," Nana-bai replied, grateful but suspicious.

As an aside, Rebecca told her, "You should probably also plan to come early to help with the cooking. Two of my servants have left me recently and I have had a most trying time looking to replace them."

"Ah yes. The cooking."

"And of course, you might also want to plan to leave somewhat early. Returning to your house at night is probably quite dangerous. I don't know why anyone would live in that part of the city." As if Nana-bai made a choice to live there. As if the finances of Rebecca's own rich household had nothing to do with the finances of

Nana-bai's poor one. "If only some man would be able to escort you home, that would be one thing. But everyone else will be enjoying until late at the party. And certainly my husband will not be able to help you out. He will have to work early the next morning and even such a thing as this party will be difficult. What with all the important meetings there have been these few weeks." She enjoyed throwing out such details as meetings at the office. They showed a day-to-day intimacy with Solly that Nana-bai, who only saw him once in a while, could not possibly have. It proved a comfortable, reliable exchange between Rebecca and Solly each night after work, something to envy, something that made their relationship legitimate: Tell me about your day, dumpling. Tell me, how was your work. Let me have some tea brought for you.

Biting her tongue, Nana-bai told her, "Evie and I will be happy to help out while we are there."

Then one of the other women leaned in and picked up the conversation on husbands again. "Mine has such a sweet tooth. I find if I put a spoonful of carrot halva in his mouth as soon as he walks through the door in the evening, he is a happy man." She added slyly, "Sweets also make him turn rather loving . . . and generous, if you understand me."

"It is good to be loved," Rebecca agreed, pointedly, running a delicate hand over Nana-bai's discolored eye.

One of the elderly women hooked her arm roughly through Nana-bai's. She had a round, wrinkled face but her arms were covered in gold jewelry. She told her: "Aiaa. If an old lady like me can make her husband happy, what can you possibly be doing wrong?" Her age and riches entitled her to talk plainly and the other women burst into laughter at her outspoken words. The sounds of it were shrill in Nana-bai's ears.

A few minutes later, Nana-bai came to collect Evie from where she sat under a nearby tree with Leah. Nana-bai was flustered and red-faced and she looked as though she had many things to say which would not come out of her mouth. She walked with teary, shoulder-humped traces of humiliation, wanting only to return into the hiding of her home. In a distracted daze, she took Evie by the hand, as Leah waved good-bye with a stiff, practiced smile, the kind young royalty is accustomed to giving. And it was not until they were home that she noticed Evie no longer carried her huge delightful mango.

"Where is your big mango?" she asked.

Evie avoided her gaze. "It was not *so* big."

"What happened to it?"

"I gave it to Leah."

"Kai-bug!"

"She told me papa would want *her* to have it. And I think she was probably right." She looked up hopefully then, as if Nana-bai might tell her differently, that this was not true and papa would want only her to eat the fruit.

But Nana-bai could not look at her through a still puffy eye and say this honestly. Instead she poured the newly bought raw rice into a flat tray and, taking it upon her lap, sat to sift through it with her fingers for insects and hulls and stones. "I know I tell you to be good and forgiving, and to share. And that it is not right to make fusses and be disobedient." She spoke thoughtfully, digesting the words herself even as she said them. "But at times it is right to demand some things, some happiness for yourself." Evie came closer, listening cautiously to her mother and running her fingers also through the fine grains of rice, not to sift it clean, but for the massage of its texture in her hands. Nana-bai considered her own words for a moment, feeling something rising and aching in her. "You are a very clever girl. Big enough even to watch over your young cousins and run errands. And probably it was wise to give Leah that fruit. There were many people from the community around us and perhaps it was best to not make a public scene. There will be many things you cannot get in this life. But some things," she paused, feeling all the skin of her body awakening. "Some things, the important things should be as you want them." Reaching through the rice, she took Eliza's hand. "Did you want mango?"

Evie nodded, uncomfortable in asserting herself. "I did."

"Then I will get it for you."

"But mama," Evie said, open mouthed. "What will you do? Will you go back out there? With them?" She swallowed the word "them," because of all its unspoken implications.

"Of course I will." And hearing this, Evie gave a wide grin of surprise from behind the gaps in her newly grown teeth.

Energized by her daughter's awe and almost unaware of what she was doing, Nana-bai stood up in a thrill, in a fury, and seated Evie where she had been sitting with the tray of rice. She told her: "Be a good girl. Stay here for me and clean this rice for supper." She took a few last coins with her, and marched out of the house, reminding Evie to latch the door behind her. She made a calm, determined show for her daughter as if this was only natural, to be forthright, to demand and then pursue.

But outside on the street, the momentum left her in an instant and she stopped short, quaking. Even to take one step further meant she risked coming across those women again, or Rebecca, still wandering about the city and shopping at the market. It had already been terrible enough once that day to endure their teasing, their arrogance, their patronizing advice. She had just barely walked away with a scrap of dignity. But to encounter them yet another time, to have the bruise scrutinized again, to be treated to more of the same brittle behavior—that would be too much. It might very well break her.

I could just pretend I went to the market, she thought. I could simply wait here in the shade and after some time return home and tell Evie there were no more mangos left in all of Bombay. Her bruised eye pounded now, hot. She could feel its grotesque obviousness, distended, how it would precede her as she walked down the street like some body part chewed and tossed out sloppily from the mouth of an animal. Nana-bai wanted nothing more than to do just that, wait in the shade and then creep back home to make her excuses to Evie. She knew Evie would accept them easily, forgivingly. She would ask no questions. She might even believe her. And Nana-bai could wait a day or two more till her face fully healed. Then she would buy not just one, but two or three mangos for Evie.

But then she considered her daughter sitting behind the wall of the house, sifting through the rice. She could picture her obedience and patience in it. She could see how doing this for years and years would form her nature to be thick, plodding. She could, easily, see her sifting through rice like this as a mother, as a lonely wife, then someday as an old lady. And knowing there would probably only be this one moment in her daughter's life in which attaining a mango might seem powerful, she braced herself. She pulled a corner of her sari as a veil around her, and hiding half her face, walked down the street asking for strength under her breath, "Please G-d."

At every corner, she expected the women to be lurking. She pictured them laughing, pointing and staring at her bruised face. She could hear their screechy voices, their breathy whispers saying impossible things: "Make your husband happy, lady. Aiaa. Make him happy." The streets of Bombay had never seemed so frightening to her as they seemed now, because of these women who had been her schoolmates, and even her own sister whose hair she had herself braided and oiled lovingly as a child. Fighting the urge to run back, she instead continued on toward the market.

The women were not on the street. They were no longer outside the synagogue. When she finally came to the market, she half expected them to be lurking like demons just behind the next stall. But they were not to be found. At times, she felt sure they were just a step away, as if she could see their dark faces puckered in pettiness, poking into the business of their neighbors and bargaining over melons and squawking chickens. And yet, they did not appear. Instead she just pinched and squeezed and smelled the many mangos, finally selected one and bought it in peace. Not such a giant as the last one had been, but a good-sized one, perfectly ripe, its juiciness ready to burst from the skin.

That night after supper, they sat to eat the mango together. Nana-bai cut the pieces, long slices that hugged the pit. There was silence between them as they sucked the pink peel for every bit of its stringy meat. Maybe from Evie, glowing, even dripping now with a new, brazen relish, there was a bit of unladylike slurping, too. "Umm. It's good," she muttered from a full mouth.

As she ate, Nana-bai could imagine the coveted piece of fruit Evie originally picked out. Just bits of its flesh left, skinned from the mango, and then dropped somewhere with bones and papers and other rubbish from the big house. It burned her blood to think that probably Leah took three bites from it and tossed it away. But watching Evie wipe at the sticky corners of her mouth, Nana-bai felt a small satisfaction that despite herself she had returned to the market and bought the fruit that rightfully belonged in their meal. Even more, she was glad that Evie had witnessed it.

*"Don't complain about the snow on your neighbor's roof when your own doorstep is unclean."* —*Confucius*

—NANA-BAI'S DIARY, PAGE 74

*A*fter years of following a predetermined path, for me college was a candyland. If I thought to try politics, I could put up a few posters and run for student senate. If I had dreams of being a dancer, I could enroll in ballet. If I changed my mind and decided to be an astronomer instead, then I could shuffle classes like cards and soon sit for hours stargazing from a chilly observatory. With such easy access to knowledge, those years were rich with epiphanies. But they were also vulnerable to self-righteousness. To the reduction of lives and detachment at the theoretical end of the microscope.

During one particular stage, enamored of the exotic and enchanted with the politically correct idea of reaching back to one's roots, I studied anthropology. This was not a surprising choice, since even as a child, I was an avid voyeur of the lush and naked photographs in *National Geographic*. I had an intellectual fascination, but it was a warped fixation, too.

I must have been six, when flipping through the pictures in an old *National Geographic*, I discovered the ancient Chinese practice of foot-binding. But after hearing an explanation of it from Daddy, more than feeling horrified at this cruel ritual, I marveled at the circuslike spectacle of preserving tiny feet. And I wanted to mimic it. Taking two cloth bandages myself, I tied them as tightly as I could around my toes and ankles, even cutting off circulation. Then I sat back to wait for baby-doll feet to appear, as though it should happen immediately and at will. In the end, my mother made me take the bandages off so I could get into the bath. And I had to give up on the whole idea, realizing sadly that I had started too late in life to successfully achieve authentic bound feet. As I grew up, of course, I could recognize the terrible injustice in wrapping the feet of little girls, all so that as grown women they could have tiny broken-boned balls at the ends of their legs thought to be dainty. Nonetheless, shadows of this kind of curiosity followed me to college. And so I found myself in Anthropology 101.

Someday, I planned during class, like a Victorian heroine in well-pressed khakis, I would travel far away to live with the Kung of the Kalahari or the Trobrianders in New Guinea. I would hold native babies and work the land and hunt. I would learn to speak with guttural clicks, absorbing the intricacies of the community's witchcraft, circumcisions, family structure, and yam exchanges. I would even master the erotic secrets of other cultures, the way to bite a lover's eyelashes, the potions, the methods of stretching lips and necks to wide, lofty lengths.

In this period of my life, moved by the vastness of civilizations as I had never been moved before, I rediscovered India. Since my brief flirtation with traditional Indian dance as a child, my interaction with Indian culture was limited to how it played out in the small Indian Jewish community. But in college, surrounded by Indians of all kinds, I was surprised to find I longed to connect with them and the larger Indian culture. People who in skin resembled me, who others automatically likened to me. People who grew up on some of the foods I grew up on, and for whom the temperaments, philosophies, and sensibilities that formed them were birthed in the same landscape as those that formed me.

Every year the South Asian club on campus celebrated the Hindu Diwali festival of lights. The deities honored were not mine, but I went anyway, following the smells of spices and the tinkle of anklet bells, familiar to me as if from babyhood. There were performances of songs and dances. Sometimes, sitting in the audience, I was a spectator. At other times while I watched, I felt it was an intricate part of me being acted out onstage.

Afterward, there was an immense table of Indian food, and I wandered through the crowd filling up my plate once then twice, sometimes more, enjoying the experience of the throngs. Because as I was pushed in line, as I hunted for a free chair or a clean napkin, and nodded knowingly at others, I had an amazing feeling of appearing ordinary. In synagogue, though I was surrounded by other Jews, I always appeared to be different from those around me. But in this public gathering, where many local Indians collected, my hair and skin and features were normal. My body itself seemed to remember and understand theirs. Clearly I was Americanized, there was no denying that. But I was not the oddball. Instead, the few white people there were eyed doubtfully—especially suspicious were those white people wearing traditional Indian clothing that day, meticulous and straight-faced in their crinkled cotton and braids, as if they *always* dressed with the Diwali festival in mind. Like the way my own family must have seemed when we sat at an Irish pub on St. Patrick's Day. A pack of big-eyed Indians, tapping our toes to folk music, as though each jig would bring us closer to Celtic roots we'd never had to begin with. But miraculously that day, in that auditorium, honoring a Diwali festival that was not mine by religion, *I* looked like I belonged. That alone was reason to celebrate.

One year at the Diwali, I met a girl named Anujah. She had long coal hair and brown buttered skin, with eyes so full they seemed to boil over each time she smiled. She was beautiful and kind and collected in her Indianness, my first Indian friend. But for some reason, I never tried to move beyond her beauty and sweetness, to find something concrete and profound in our friendship. Instead, I only watched Anujah like the Hindi movies I saw on television. I did not understand the words spoken. But the flicks were pretty and flashy, and the men and women seemed to have emerged straight out of brilliantly colored *Kama Sutra* drawings. They chased each other around pillars, singing and crooning, shimmying their shoulders. I imagined what he sang to her—your lips are like pieces of papaya, and what she sang back to him, giggling—you are greedy. But I did not have any true understanding of the depth that might have been there. I was content with the shell of this connection.

I took every anthropology class I could. I went to festivals, lectures, and even performed in a folk dance troupe, waiting to be transported back in time to the more genuine calling of mankind. But all the while I worried that this world was not waiting on me. My textbooks were littered with photos of tribe members whose traditional jewelry adorned blue jeans, whose ancient mud huts stood right alongside pickup trucks. The part of the population that still had primitive mammoth roars ringing in its ears, was rapidly progressing, disappearing into city life and Coca-Cola.

And I could not understand why it would want to. If I had the choice, I told myself, I would give up all I owned to live in the rhythms of season and body and instinct.

I saw myself on a direct path, studying and soaking in experiences that would allow me to be both spiritual and savvy. Some absurd Wonder Woman combination of Peace Corps mastermind by day, earth-loving hippie by night. But, instead, I was like the fragile medical student who has no concept of what she is getting herself into, who diagnoses herself with every ghastly disease she learns about. And so, in studying ancient, fading cultures, I became especially aware that my own heritage of Indian Jewry sat somewhere in the dying ranks.

At that time I knew little of the history, and Jews are simply Jews in many ways. But because a shipwreck isolated them from the rest of the Jewish world for centuries, I recognized that the Bene Israel of India have their own significant story. Instead of being transformed by the overlapping movement of Jews in the Diaspora in Spain and Poland and Germany, Bene Israel culture pulled the major part of its identity and inspiration from a G-d and prophets and image of Israel that were frozen and fixed for them in the world of the Bible. The Bene Israel clung to an ancient form of religion that was passed down in stories of what their ancestors had last known. This was a religion, surrounded by paganism. It had in its backdrop King Solomon's great Temple, with incense and pilgrims and sacrifices, and at the heart of it all, the holy ark and the slabs of stone that bore the Ten Commandments.

After the destruction of the Temple, much of Jewish culture moved to focus on synagogue life and the new communities they formed around the world, seeing the Temple as part of a former era. But for Indian Jews, the Temple and their last interaction with that larger Jewish civilization was still vibrant in a collective memory, too, and it flavored another kind of religion. There was a special use of incense and symbolic sacrifice in religious ceremonies. There was the Malida, a singular celebration of the prophet Elijah, which may have been common in the context of India's other cultures. But to other Jewish ways of life, it seemed to almost border on a worship of him. There was a uniqueness in the prayers, folklore, and observance of the Sabbath. There was even a set of mating rituals that somehow allowed these few Jews to remain distinct in a vast subcontinent for hundreds of years. Now, however, scattered and interbreeding, Indian Jews had become an endangered species.

The suggestion of finding a mate within a small group of several thousand Indian Jews dispersed around the world today could seem to be farfetched. Nonetheless, each individual making choices, marrying and creating new families, was inevitably either feeding the larger destiny or allowing it to be weeded out through some Darwinian selection. This culture, in danger of slipping away, was tied up with faded memories of Nana-bai grinding flour by hand, eating food with just a graceful basketing of her fingers, demanding that the girls in our family dutifully serve the boys. Growing up, I was uncomfortable with these things. I wanted clean white flour from the store packages. I wanted her to be like the elderly relatives of my friends, eating with a fork and knife, and having her hair frosted. I wanted my brother, just once, to clean the table after a meal.

Living in this antiquated culture myself years ago, I rebelled and tried to push it forward. Yet in college, idealizing the quaint, I minimized this awkward friction and instead wistfully mused that, but for some random moves and choices, such a simple, hearty life might have easily been mine. Just like the people in my textbooks—only before they had discovered deodorant. I thought about the picturesque nature of the culture a great deal. But fancying myself just an academic observer now, on the verge of great hypotheses and dissertations, I imposed the actual, living responsibility of perpetuating Indian Jewry on others, never on me. And in the back of my mind, I started to congratulate myself, since it seemed here I might be coming close to fulfilling the promise I made to Nana-bai in my childhood. If this wasn't an illustrious return to the family and community, then what was?

Then, one summer in college when I was visiting Israel, I found myself smack in the middle of this way of life again and everything, especially the way I saw myself, changed. My parent's friend Shimshon, also an Indian Jew, invited me for dinner with his family. I had never been to their home before. But they gave me directions that night, and I took the bus to their neighborhood. As I got out at their stop, I could not help but stand still a few moments, absorbing the crowded street before me. The sidewalk was lined with small brown grass patches, and sand that spilled out and piled up around the tires of the parked cars. At one end of the road lay a playground shell, a rusty jungle gym. At the other end sat a small kiosk, its few colored rows of candy bars and gum and snack chips giving a lonely bit of polished color to the street. There a group of Indian men stood arguing, holding a newspaper open flat between them. Further off, where the street twisted into an alley, several prostitutes in bright red lipstick and high heels waited around for business, bored. I looked up at the apartments looming over me, underwear and bras and heavy paint-speckled blue work pants laid out to dry over the window sills. At the entrance to each building, groups of kids and chach-chachs and even grandmothers, Indians, Ethiopians, Yemenites, sat talking over the loud music that poured from different windows. Making my way through them, between wolf whistles and friendly hellos and curious stares, I entered the building Shimshon had directed me to. Nodding my head, I tried to commit it all to some scholastic memory on the lives of Indian Jews. So this is how they live. So this is an Israeli slum.

"Come in, come in," Shimshon told me, greeting me at the door with a warm hug and smells of paprika. He motioned me over to join the rest of his family. "Have some pita and hummus in the meantime. We are just waiting for someone else I invited along." Here he pulled me aside. "He's a nice boy and your mummy told me you had no boyfriend right now." I started to protest, but he put a large hand on my shoulder, winking. "No, no. He comes from a nice Indian Jewish family, that's all you need to know." I started to say something again, but sighed and gave up instead, noting crisply to myself that well-intentioned matchmaking was still quite common in this culture.

My mother was guilty of matchmaking, too. I had to admit it. Despite her efforts to get away from the Old World in matters of love, my mother was an unrelenting matchmaker. For as long as I could remember she always tried to make matches between the single people she knew. As though the survival of humankind itself depended upon her efforts. She cut out marriage and engagement announcements from the newspaper, highlighting the names of the couple, verifying who was no longer available. On the phone with some lonely woman, my mother nestled the receiver to her ear, rubbed her hands together, and dug through our family address book like an inspired spelunker. "Well, let's see. We have a divorcé here. But I think he's still in legal battles. How about a widower? A young man. Still has most of his hair. Eh?"

My father teased her about this. "Sweetie," he told her. "Can't you leave well enough alone? We don't want to meddle or make any trouble." She just ignored this and inquired if anyone had recently become single at his work, making checks alongside the names of any new potentials in our address book.

Following my father's lead, I became wound up, too. "You're not Cupid. You're not G-d," I felt I had to remind my mother. She acknowledged this, but secretly waited till I myself was of age and then turned her powers on me.

Then, without even noticing, I myself began to set up matches. It started slowly, where almost subconsciously I looked through the newspaper and made casual comment of who had just gotten hitched. Then I started to bring my single friends together, ducking out rather suspiciously as soon as possible so they could get to know each other alone. I was mortified when I finally recognized my own tendency for hennish, groping interference and I tried to suppress it, like a primitive tic. So even in Shimshon's home, I feigned patient tolerance at his matchmaking, as though it were foreign to me.

Soon, we all sat down to dinner and with abundant generosity, Shimshon ushered in a short, cylinder-shaped, bug-eyed boy, who gave me a floppy handshake. He lived one building over, and worked as a mechanic. I could have been open-minded to him and warm and kind. I could have even just academically observed him, made mental notes on the thoughts and experiences of an Indian Jewish handyman. But because of the circumstance, because he had been brought here for me, I immediately shut off to him. A snob now, I asked myself: What could this boy know of the world? Shimshon and his family tried to begin conversation between us. But when the boy asked me in timid English, "How is it, to be in New York?" I brushed him aside and used words he would not have learned. Phenomenal. Intellectually stimulating.

Over the next two hours, seated next to him, I rolled my eyes and reached for the potatoes across him as though he did not even exist.

Suddenly, my academic fortress, and all my cool objectivity and observations disappeared. I could not even bring myself to form pretentious, charming pictures of this old-fashioned world, running parallel to my own universe. Instead I felt uneasy with it. Where the lack of brilliance and even clean teeth meant nothing. Where all that counted was a reproduction of those same few Indian Jewish neighborhoods and apartments and meals and children. When I could imagine myself for a flash nightmare moment in that life, I panicked. I glorified the static when it was abstract, when it was documentary material. But when it applied to me growing up with my grandmother, when a tie to it sat before me unadorned even now, I cringed and turned away and judged mercilessly. Despite everybody's hopes, I was haughty. Shimshon and his family, too good to even recognize my cruelty for what it was, felt deflated, awkward. And that boy—short, cylinder shaped, and bug-eyed as he was—by the end of the night, slouching home, felt these things as he never had before.

Ashamed of my bad behavior during that dinner, it occurred to me later that maybe I missed something important in all my anthropology classes and all my self-moralizing. Something that would allow me to look at individual lives without judgment, without reduction, without an agenda. Perhaps, of all the vast opportunities available, that was the one thing I could not find in the privileged candyland of university. Certainly no textbooks ever covered it, no exams ever tested for it. And while I could do all kinds of accomplished things—talk politics, dance ballet, and stare dreamily at the stars—much would have to happen before I could give any true meaning to the rise and fall of civilizations. Especially my own. So my promise to Nana-bai would remain for a while longer unfulfilled and beyond understanding. And in the meantime, I began to feel that in my small place in this big world, the preservation of a culture could not be about a tribe in its entirety. I wondered if instead, it could be as simple as being genuine and gracious to a homely boy sitting cornered across the table.

$\mathcal{E}$ ventually, as poetic justice would have it, I fell—hard—for someone myself. I found Noah, a good Jewish boy in the next dorm over who seemed to embody everything I should want. He was Israeli, too. And it felt inevitable that I should be with an Israeli. I was, after all, still my parents' daughter. Noah had just enough rugged sexiness, intelligent humor, and charisma to make me think there was something special between us. Certainly, fresh out into the college world of independence, I came upon so many wonderful firsts through him, it seemed what was between us simply had to be unique, too. The first time I had a big American city—lovely Boston of chowder and beans—at my own adventurous disposal, with subways and street performers and bars. The first time I locked myself endlessly in the library and studied all the things that truly fascinated me. The first time I had close Jewish friends, and still felt easy and happy around them. The first time I could spend whole candlelit days with these friends in bed, napping, talking about the world, and listening to folk music. The first time I lived on cafeteria food and order-in pizza and a man who roamed the dorms with a cooler of food hawking: "Chinese-food-man. Is anybody hungry?" The first time I went to a fraternity party. The first time I lasted so long without my parents, going for days and days without speaking to them on the phone, not angry, but stolidly trying to assert my independence. And of course, the first time I ever saw a man, Noah—giddy for being satiated—parade around the room to reggae, bare and unabashed.

Noah's freedom never ceased to romance me, even one day while I vacuumed the refrigerator. Most refrigerators don't need vacuuming, and certainly the one in our dorm room, of the midget variety and only reaching knee-height, should not have required much maintenance. But decades of girls passed through that college, leaving trails of their perms and combs and picks. So hairballs abounded in the dorm. They rolled through the halls and under the beds and even into the refrigerators, like tumbleweed through a Western landscape, so sometimes we were forced to employ a vacuum for harvesting. As I vacuumed deafeningly, my roommate Karen sat on her bed amidst a pile of books, unwrapping tinfoil packs of homemade gourmet food that her mother had sent. Hamburger meat with currants wrapped in dough. And cherry brownies.

"You have to try this. It's delish."

Turning off the vacuum, I sat on her bed, too, and took a bite of brownie. "Yum." Now, in the sudden quiet, without the roaring and sucking of the machine, we could hear, not surprisingly, the sounds of sex coming through the walls. Our plump neighbor Jenna-Ann and her still plumper boyfriend, Lou. I looked at my watch and rolled my eyes. "Of course. Right on time."

It was not that Jenna-Ann and Lou were excessively loud or

ferocious lovers. It was just that they were ceaseless. Their soft moans drifted through the thick concrete of our dorm as consistently as the bang of the heating pipes and plumbing. Since we heard them constantly, Karen and I almost felt ourselves to be an intimate part of their lives. From even the slightest fluctuations of time and temperament, we could tell if they were quarreling or ill or reaching a second wind. Early in the morning. Late at night. And of course, every day reliably, at just this time in the afternoon, when they finished class, and came back to her room for a full hour of sex—or else they skipped class and made it two hours. Then they put on sweats and went down to the cafeteria for an early dinner. Sometimes, thoughtfully, they called us to join them, considerate that we, too, might be ravenous after having a small part of their frolic. "Don't they ever stop?" I wondered mildly.

Just as we considered this question, there was a knock on our door. Then it crashed open and we started at the noise. But there behind it stood Noah and several of his friends, frozen, silent, as though waiting for the smoke to clear. Noah held a guitar in his hands, eyes cast down for several moments, and began strumming softly and angelically. As though on a signal, one friend dropped to his knees and pulled out a tambourine. Another took a matador stance and whipped a flute from his pocket. Then all at once there was furious improvised music, a bit of Bossa Nova and Trance. Strumming and hopping and cawing, they conjured up a melody that could probably never be replicated, a tune that was musically impossible, but graceful, hypnotizing, and very likely dangerous to the ears of small children.

From our place inside the room, Karen and I giggled and gave an appreciative wolf-whistle now and then. Still in the hallway, Noah grabbed one of his friends to lead him in a moment of country dosey-doe. With dramatic tango-intensity, he dipped him and planted a fat kiss on his forehead. At the end of their serenade, he stiffened like a gymnast after a complex hurtle and landing, waiting for our applause and then collapsing into a sweeping bow. The crew came tearing into the room, then, proud of themselves, brandishing our vacuum like a sword, scattering the stuffed animals off our pillows and plucking hairballs from the floor to wave threateningly. Noah jumped onto my bed and pulled me to him from where I had fallen on the floor in mock disbelief of their spectacle. "Here, we brought some drinks," he said, producing several purple bottles. And I felt his hand wandering to me already, under the covers.

The phone rang then and I could hear Jenna-Ann next door, talking to us through the phone, echoing in the walls. "I heard some kind of fuss. What's going on over there?" As if *she* required some kind neighborly explanation for next-door disruptions. "So? Are we going to dinner?"

"Sorry," Karen said into the phone, giggling as one of the guys pretended to make love to her teddy bear. "I guess we're having wine tonight instead."

This world and all these small, senseless moments around Noah charmed me, so I was devoted to them. And yet it was as though I was trying to learn a new language. Only, before actually knowing its grammar and vocabulary, I already had preconceived and mistaken certainties about its equations. I pulled from my parents' ideals, and what was passed down to me, filling in the blanks. Love equals wonder and awe and groping and serenade. Boyfriend equals the amount of intimate time spent together, and charm, and the beginning of all things permanent. I could not fathom a relationship of kisses and friendship in which two people did not demand and fight to keep it infinite as my parents had done and as they had preached to do throughout my life. Their guidelines on sex and love had been so stiff and rigid, that though in my teenage years, I fought against them, still subconsciously I believed myself to be fighting the truth. The obvious, G-d-given truth. That was how I defined it—almost as if it were a legal matter—though many others couldn't, and of course, Noah did not. When the serenades stopped, when it became too heavy and complicated for him, when it became so bitterly consuming for me that I could not even bear to bring words out of my mouth—except just once, choked, "Do you know how much I need you?"—it ended between us.

Within the framework of my family's culture, and even in the context of all ordinary girlie preparation, I had, a bit pompously, a bit uncertainly, plodded devotedly through the necessary steps toward someday finding my supposed ideal, a manly and complementary reflection of me. In the process, I tried to resist sidetracking temptation. Like a campground of orgies. Like a sweet-talking soldier. Even like the consuming time warp of an Indian Jewish mechanic. At times in the process, I was intrigued by the religious men, with their paraphernalia. The knots of tzitzis hanging from their pants, and knitted kippot, worn just to the perfect careless angle on their heads. I saw the intensity of their closed eyes and bodies rocking back and forth in prayer, and I admired it, wished I could be so myself. Also, I could not help but wonder selfishly, how would such fervor worship me? At other times, in the process, I imagined myself with a standard Jewish husband, the kind we had seen and secretly envied at synagogue growing up. A wealthy businessman who jogged forty minutes every morning and owned three cars and was admired by everyone in the community. That infatuation with Noah in college, then—a solid Jewish, Israeli boy, perhaps a bit macho but all in all good-hearted, a boy my parents themselves might have chosen for me—was the next natural step.

But broken by it, and purged of the ideals that once caused me to secretly moralize over others, now I locked myself inside a darkened room, picking at shreds and scabs of disillusion. Once, still before I was ready, I shakily stepped out. And then I met Noah's brother, by sheer chance in a nightclub. I brought him back to my dorm at three in the morning, to eat Chinese food and then grimly get to business, hating myself the whole time. But when I finally, truly emerged prepared for the world and rubbing my eyes, too many months later, I found that I was a little bit tougher and cooler, a little less self-righteous, and a lot more open to the experimentation that I had once passed over. I think if I had been able to let loose early, when I was younger, or in the enclosed camp of Jewish teenagers where my parents originally sent me, my trials would have had a limited influence. I might have eventually embraced the whole package of the strict Jewish circuit and continued to move within it. Those same people who once felt each other up behind the tennis courts were now perpetuating a new community, just two small steps away from the one that forged them. I, too, might have grown and been content within it. With straitlaced adults in business suits, marrying amongst themselves, planning to send their own children back to that same camp.

But instead in my backlash, I found myself again where I once started out, sitting in the backseat of our station wagon staring out into an America that was beyond my reach. And what began as a prideful struggle against the shadow of the ordinary self-hating Jew emerged as a jungle fever of sorts. My body itself craved the "other" and shied away from the upstanding examples of "my own kind." The nice Jewish men who were doctors and lawyers seemed to be caricatures, ambitious but without creativity, only groomed to be such from birth by overly doting mothers. I thought I could sense their smugness over accomplishment, their calculated spontaneity, their contrived attempts to carry success with a casual air, in carefully assembled fashion and notions of beauty. I found myself wanting a man who did not have thousands of years of chosen-people baggage behind him. I wanted a man who did not need to consult Zagat's restaurant guide every time he wanted to dine out simply because that was how sophisticated people *should* make plans. I wanted, just once, to not play Jewish Geography: "Oh, you go to school in Boston? You must know the Lemberg family then. We used to have many Shabbos meals by them." Instead I wanted a man who was refreshingly different from me. I wanted a man who was rugged, who played country music on his radio, who ate ham sandwiches.

My ears pricked up when I heard one Jewish professional complain to another about the Jewish woman he was dating: "She's so hairy, so dumpy," he whined, in a trendy, comedic-tragic way, as if straight out of a sitcom. "Too many of them are, you know. It's tough to be a Jew." Of course he would say that, I told myself. I cringed because they cringed, and so my rebellion, in the end, was predictable, really.

I went out of my way to date all kinds of men and I had no intentions whatsoever. I saw that there was something wonderful in just going to dinner with a man, then wishing him good night and never having to see him again. I could be picky also. Too skinny. Too bald. Too poor a sense of humor. Too spoiled. Too by-the-book. Too vegetarian. Too politically correct. Too sterile. Too good-looking, so he'd never developed a personality. In this new world,

I kissed a West Point cadet and a rather dashing circus clown. I picked up an Irishman in a bar, and dated an immense basketball player, at my full height only reaching up to his belly button. I backpacked through distant countries with visions of the Coliseum and Shakespeare leading the way. And drunk on foreign liquors and ancient history, I had a wild flirtation in London and another in Greece. I kept a pen pal in Canada, who was half the time my confessor and half the time the object of all my lust and devotion. I learned to salsa dance. I lay with a perfect American boy on the downy couch in his Connecticut home—a down of unbelievable richness, a Connecticut of picture-book gardens and Colonial recipes. And folding my hands behind my head, I listened to his stories of golf and early retirement, pretending to consider these things myself—naturally, as if they had always been part of my paradigm, too. I hungrily partook of a lover's family Christmas, stepping into the pictures I had imagined for years, the gorgeously decorated tree scents and lights, the eggnog, the turkey, the exchange of gifts, and the sweet, intoxicated grandmas on the couch.

One night in Europe, I even danced with a skinhead. I was in a nightclub, surrounded by spilling wine and bared bodies. He was dancing on a small stage just above and spotting me, picked me up with thick hard arms, pulling me to him and inside his legs. The music seized us like a tongue and we moved as a single body in a masturbating rhythm, dressing ourselves with one another, his sweat glossing my lips. In all the noise and crowd of that club, we only exchanged names. So I could not, in fact, be sure that he was a militant anti-Semite. But feeling conscious of my Jewishness as I traveled through an area loaded down by its history of atrocities against Jews, I thought I saw traces of this everywhere. Quite possibly, the man just enjoyed the feel of a clean-shaven head. But he was German, with a muscled bare chest, and in my own prejudice and inexperience he looked to me like something from an old WWII movie, frightening in its suddenly fleshy dimensions. He conjured up Auschwitz for me, piles of breathing Jewish skeletons with just a hint of face smudged on, and all the nameless family from my father's side who perished. I remembered my parents' good friend, a survivor who would limp through our home for Sunday coffee and cake, branded with concentration camp numbers on his arm, and grossly maimed by the Nazis. And it is enough to know that though I had these baseless pricklings of suspicion and sickness, still I was drawn to dance with that man, self-absorbed, as though in a ritual of fertility, as though in a display of birthing hips.

I followed whims and lived out driven fantasies, at times, especially this once, to surprising end: I have always loved books to the point of being greedy. But unwilling to leave my favorite characters behind on the last page, I insisted that they follow me back to reality. First came Georgie Porgie. Then came King Thrushbeard and the Wizard of Oz. If I faced hardship, I summoned up Siddhartha to lean down and whisper, patience. If I was meek, Tom Sawyer made funny faces and the Musketeers dared me on. Sexy dreams especially left definitive Romeo fingerprints up and down my body.

I loved the gorgeousness of books so much that I even loved the teachers who brought them to me. There was Mr. Simmons in middle school, who described the thick feel of book page parchment with such sensuality that he made my mouth water. There was Mr. Donahee in tenth grade, who upon finding a rare book that was torn and mistreated in the public library, then diligently, defiantly checked it out every two weeks for the next thirty years so as to keep it safe. The man was a literary vigilante, bumbling and plum-shaped, but my hero nonetheless. Each semester, as though my teachers were themselves chalk-wielding, mind-blowing creatures out of a book, I grew attached and willed them to spring to life beyond just classroom walls. Eventually one did.

Scott taught a workshop of contemporary poetry during my last year in college. Witty and lean, with a striking redwood face, he had read, published, and lived through things in the world that I could not even imagine. But from the beginning I knew that he saw me as more than just his student. When he lectured, I nestled each sentence lovingly against my ear, picking out the specific words I hoped were meant for me. Eroticism. Power. Intimacy. When we spoke, his eyes always demanded more. "You're on to something," he would say, at once encouraging and probing, convincing me I was right. Through him, I was eloquent.

My body churned when I thought of Scott. I pictured us as Anaïs Nin and Henry Miller, or as poor writers from a book. I could move in with him, I decided, and we would sit up long nights writing poetry in a mess of metaphors and coffee. We would eat cheap jelly sandwiches and freelance in order to pay rent. While I learned from him, he would be rejuvenated by me and my admiration. We might argue sometimes, and I might leave him during one terrible fit of jealousy. But then we would meet one night in a bar to make up over brandies. And I could imagine us the next morning, restored, our caramel legs tangled up inside the sheets. Rolling over, I would wake him with my tongue, lapping up the salty textures of skin and hair and muscle. With the secrets of *Lady Chatterley's Lover* and D. H. Lawrence at his beck and call, he would take my hips and pull me close, watching my face as I melted, coiling around him. Perhaps already transforming this moment into the erotic spirit of his next book, he would unfold my legs and hide himself in all the pink of my insides, first slowly then hard, till I sobbed, biting his shoulder, rocking in plea-sure and disbelief. Sitting in class, watching Scott pull back more and more new layers on the world, this was how I imagined it would be.

After that semester ended, Scott invited me to have dinner at his apartment, a small studio perched over a pub. It was sparsely furnished, and its grayed wooden floors were misted in dog fur. But he had rich bookcases covering the walls with hundreds of books: red, fat, brittle, thin rice paper, weighty hardcover, some rusty and gold-edged. "I built these bookcases myself," he said proudly, running his fingers along a shelf. Scott put on Bob Dylan CDs and boiled a pot of spaghetti. As raw poetry unfolded in the music, and the smell of garlic rose off the stove, Scott came out of the kitchen, wiping clean wet hands on his jeans. He walked right up to me, softly took my mouth and kissed me. We parted for a moment, my glasses steamed at the corners, and he murmured, "Is this okay?" I said yes and we kissed again, breathless, till he drew away to fry the mushrooms.

Scott came back in a few minutes later, weighed down by steam-ing plates, and as we sat to eat, suddenly everything changed. I could see clearly from just the gentle way he served me spaghetti that all I ever wanted to pull from the fantasy of books was now made flesh and could be mine. But suddenly I knew that if I let myself and Scott enter the world of real lovers, with sour morning breath and comfortable silences, we would also chip away that fantasy. Over spaghetti, this truth hit me and I froze, awkward, causing Scott to become awkward, till we spiraled around each other in the silence that followed. Even Bob Dylan, ill at ease, wound down the last song and then packed up his guitar. There was a quiet clang of silverware throughout the rest of the meal, a fuss over dessert, and finally a question put out there, almost casually, "Maybe I should go home now?" Too young to be able to delight in a man who could make good spaghetti and write poetry and also just sit there at times, very unpoetically cracking his knuckles, I wanted to keep Scott as just a delicious abstraction. So cringing under his hurt look, and panicking as he grew limbs and tried to climb out of my book pages, I hastily gathered the shreds of whimsy around me and fled.

Suddenly in my trial and error, I learned surprising things about myself, and I got to know men of all religions and cultures and ambitions. The very strictness of my upbringing, the traditionalism of my ideals and the inevitability of my heartbreak led me to awaken at a more serious point in my life, with a momentum and diversity that was not part of the formula. And when I finally found genuine love for the first time, it took me by surprise. Love could be called, I found, simply Matt, husky and warm and sometimes sarcastic. Love could be me and Matt, eating cereal in front of the television together. And intimate jokes launched by just clearing the throat or raising an eyebrow. It could be me baking him bread, or hanging out in a seedy bar to watch his second thrilling hour in a video game marathon, or me saying, did you remember to pick up your medicine? It could be him taking me home to his mother or feeding me pudding after my wisdom teeth were pulled or touching me so knowingly it was as if I was touching myself. Love, it turned out, was not the loftiness of fantasies I had pursued, or even the extremism I had forced myself on. It was just something plain and solid and good.

And so, in all my explorations, there was no dramatic climax here. The salty, maddening amazement of braided, glossy bodies, so convinced in the moment of their own perfection and originality, turned out, really, after the juices settled and the breaths evened, to be nothing new in the history of sexuality or romance. My parents through their rules, and Nana-bai through her cartoons and stories of ballooning breasts, had passed down everything they could, to form in me a specific kind of girlfriend, wife, mother, and sexual creature. All three had tried to steer me toward a straightforward, old-fashioned relationship with an appropriate Jewish man. But in the end, bumbling and tripping with my own trials, mistakes, and adventures, it seemed possible that my life could go in a very different direction, and my eventual marriage might never be like my parents' perfect one. I could marry an African, a Catholic, a poor artist. I could just live with some lover in a mountain hut forever. Or I could end up in the exact same place they wanted me to be, but for reasons they never could have imagined. My parents would never fully understand the complexity or path of my odyssey and experimentation. And I would never truly believe that theirs was anything but simple and biblical and flawless, even down to the legendary camel races that colored the story of how they met.

Their example always seemed tough to live up to, of course. Not only because their marriage was so extraordinary, but also because of their expectation. Even before I was born, even before my parents began guessing whose smile I would have and what I would be when I grew up, they already assumed that I would someday replicate their own lives to a certain extent, that I would marry much like they did, and have my own children.

They never figured on a roundabout path. They never calculated my differing ideas on sexuality or my chances of divorce or of marrying between religions and cultures into a myriad of problems. They never even questioned the idea that two people can be everything to each other in the context of marriage. That modern, constantly evolving individuals can be happy inside an ancient institution which for centuries served as a mere bartering tool between families and communities—but which today is presumptuously and perhaps naïvely declared to be romantic.

But still I risked everything, my heritage and family, as children have done throughout time. I risked it for that one humble moment of truth, the kernel of which I had once found in the softness of breasts and a party kissing-game, which I confided to my diary. That moment before conscience and orgasm, where his flesh is almost-inside-me-not-completely-but-just-enough, where limbs are wrapped together, like animals mating, like children hugging, like dying people grasping at wet bedcovers.

I risked it, even though I knew I could very well find myself someday exposed, one of Nana-bai's story images from long ago come to life again. A spoiled girl, walking through the crowd naked. With giant breasts before me like mounds of wet clay, and only yards and yards of hair like a veil.

But then, please G-d, I thought, let me at least walk with grace.

*Mango Chutney:*
*Peel six raw mangos and scrape for meat.*
*Add one teaspoon chili powder, a flat tablespoon salt, three*
*cups sugar.*
*Mix all this, fill in a jar, close tight and keep for 15 days in*
*the sun.*

—NANA-BAI'S DIARY, PAGE 20

After college, I had a roommate, Shelly, who was a crazy chemist in the kitchen. She cooked chicken soup and beet-juice borscht with an offbeat eccentricity that the typical woman usually does not achieve until she has silvered, shriveled, leathered, and then reemerged, ballsy, with a fetish for purple. Shelly began each morning with a bowl of oatmeal, always in her big porcelain white bowl with the handle. She added to her oatmeal eggs, cottage cheese, wheat germ, spices, tofu, tuna fish. Sometimes she varied the spices, maybe adding cinnamon or oregano, or just a simple salt and pepper. Sometimes she omitted the tofu altogether. "I need my oatmeal," she often said to me or herself or anyone who would listen. Then she popped the concoction into the microwave for five minutes twenty-five seconds at breakfast time, and most days at dinnertime as well. Because of all the oatmeal, the entire apartment had an earthy smell that didn't quite belong in the middle of the city. It hit you immediately upon walking in, as though the door had just been opened to a grain storehouse sealed in biblical times, so thousands of years of overripeness and sweet baking were rolled into one breath.

Shelly possessed a remarkable haggish majesty as she worked amidst the pots and pans. Padding about in fuzzy slippers, and wearing—even during the summer—a pom-pom woolen hat with ear flaps, she heated up whole, unpeeled grapefruits and glasses of water to drink straight up, like tequila shots. She cooked an entire sack full of Japanese groceries in one great steaming pot, adding what seemed to be prehistoric roots and leaves that she had snuffed and foraged for herself. She even made homemade dishes for her dog Tico, a long-haired Chihuahua who looked like a rat dragging around in a too-big fur coat.

Tico followed Shelly around the apartment, standing around her legs when she cooked, even joining her in the bathroom. Sometimes, as we sat to eat at the table, he dragged out his humping pillow to put on a show for us, and with great intensity, pushed it inch by hurried inch across the hallway under his tiny straining legs. When she was ready for bed, she called, "Here Tico!" and he came running and jumped up on the bed and got comfortable on the second pillow, waiting for the door to be closed, as if they were a couple and wanted their privacy. In the morning when they woke up, he sulked if she didn't cook eggs for him. But, of course, Shelly did this happily.

When Tico was really good, Shelly fed him doggie biscuits from a canister, sniffing at them and eyeing them as though tempted to try a bite herself. I recognized her instinct. As a toddler, I myself had crawled into the garage and taken several swallows of puppy food from a greasy bowl—the crunchy kind of food, like thick, meaty pretzel chunks. And though I was pulled away immediately, disgustedly, dog food after that never seemed entirely unattractive. Until years later, that is, when I worked for a stint bagging doggie biscuits to make some extra money. You don't ever truly appreciate the difference between dog and human until you have donned chalky latex gloves, dug through cartons and cartons of crackery bones—cartons which stand taller than yourself—and counted out hundreds and hundreds of baggies, with exactly seventy dog biscuits each—no more, no less, and no broken bits, besides. Yes, I'd known what it was like to have dog biscuits up to the armpits and then to go home smelling like them. So I was sure to warn Shelly off the stuff. But still she was enamored of Tico's Milkbones. "See puppy!" she'd coo, pretending to eat. "See how yummy!" And she'd almost convince herself.

Watching Shelly from a distance, I never knew what to eat myself, deliberating back and forth between elaborate recipes and canned food. Being around food has always made me happy. Even the fresh pepper display at the market with red and yellow and green peppers stacked like a mountain of marbles has often struck me as one of the most beautiful sights in the world. There is nothing quite like it. In fact, I have always been fixated on food.

In the first dream I can ever remember having, I was locked in a grocery store, running wild through the aisles, tossing new bread and chocolate cake and roasted chicken legs as big as my own into a shopping cart. I danced through the bakery and skated over the ice creams, sampling a blueberry muffin here, a spoonful of vanilla fudge chunk there, then galloping off into a sunset of brilliant cheddar. Someday, I worried, I would wake up from this dream at four hundred pounds, with a series of chins running like stairs down my neck. But still nothing could keep me from poking my head into the oven and breathing in garlic or warm apples like oxygen.

Food has always been my weakness. Normally a quiet type, I

have discovered that at meals, I am strangely loose of tongue. Like an anxious lover willing to confide almost anything to seal the deal in the dark of night and blankets. So when I am seated at a table, waiting for the waiter to appear, open and giddy in anticipation of what foods are to come, I have found that I am capable of revealing all sorts of insights and secrets previously unknown to even myself.

I have also found food distracting me in the experiences that should have transcended it. On the holy fast days, for example, I've often sat in synagogue thinking about food, rather than G-d and repentance for all my sins. Others around me, even those who were there to merely make their annual duty call, seemed to be lost in pensive prayer. Meanwhile, I was pondering what fish would be served when we finally broke the fast, and whether or not we would have cheesecake. Or at other times, enjoying the lazy, flannel-wrapped early afternoon glow with a lover, I was already planning in my mind what we should do for dinner, if I could convince him to go for Ethiopian food, or if we should just go to the diner instead.

After much worry and self-berating, I decided that these things didn't necessarily make me less spiritual or less loving or even a glutton. It was more that in my family, the most striking and memorable exchanges happened at the table, and that is where I continued to seek my wisdom, if only from sheer habit. That is where the truth emerged, both hard and beautiful. That is where a family's ethnicity came to light, where my friends' parents could say, We trust you and no matter what you do we will love you, and where my own parents said, Everything you do, every choice you make must first answer to our family and community. That is where judgment was given.

When it was just me and Shelly, I returned from the grocery

store with mustard sauces and Camembert cheese, and I made huge batches of chocolate chip cookies, surrounding myself with more and more choices. And yet, still, when I was hungry I rummaged through my shelves, past noodles and bowls of spicy leftovers, never knowing exactly what I was in the mood for. I saw us like this: Shelly, naked without culinary inhibition, and me, instead, fixated—and, okay, picky—staring for long minutes at a time into the open refrigerator. And I could not help but think to myself that how a person cooks and eats is the most intimate thing in the world.

I don't remember the first time I ate solid food, not mashed or baby-strained or milk-washed. When I imagined it, though, I saw a meal that was typical to my home, something steamy and rich, served proudly by Nana-bai and my mother from heavy, green-stained pots that had been carefully packed and carted from India to Israel to America. There would be rice, made yellow from the turmeric and studded with cloves. There would be potatoes and cuts of chicken or beef in an orange curry sauce. There might also have been lentils or chutney or okra or chapati bread made from scratch. Afterward, as a special treat, there might have been any number of desserts—pancakes like crepes rolled up with coconut or soft creamy perda cookies or syrupy gulabjamun.

For this first meal, I was probably brought in from the sunny yard, young and plump, in just a big diaper or shorts. A pair of strong brown arms must have scooped me up and into a high chair, then put before me a plate and a small plastic baby spoon. Holding the spoon in any conventional form would have felt awkward to me, instead I must have gripped it in my palm, tightly, reflexively, as a gorilla instinctually makes a stick into a digging tool.

The tingle of spice on tongue would have seemed ordinary to me for its original place in my knowledge of foods. Unconscious of the boundaries of lips, of fingers and spoon, bare arms and chest and table, each morsel must have found its own direction, chewed and swallowed or mashed into my hair or dropped a few feet away for the pleasure of a plop sound. If pieces of food got caught between my stray teeth stubs, or if even the thick smells of curry lingered all day on my skin, so what? I did not notice or blush or choose to wash. These messes were healthy energy for shaky fat legs. They were as much a given to me as need, as hot and cold, as sleep.

At that age, I simply ate.

Then there was a time when I was learning new things every day. I learned by following those around me. Fork on the left, knife on the right. Close your mouth when you chew. Put dirty dishes in hot water and soap. I also learned by asking questions. Why does Kelly's family get to eat bologna sandwiches and Twinkies? How are vegetables born? Who is G-d and why doesn't he give everybody in the world enough to eat? Why don't boys have to wash dishes?

I sat at the table, eating obediently, showing good manners, eager to please. Dab napkin to mouth. Eat all the greens. Still, I studied the plate before me, and could not help but ask more questions. What is this food? Why is it more spicy than the food at Molly's house? What are the green things in the sauce? Picking at the food in order to reach its core, I discovered the chicken was not Shake 'n Bake, the rice did not look as it did on Uncle Ben's box. There were extras here, things that made this food different, flakes of spice in the gravy, sun colors, bits of onion and garlic softened and sautéed in the curry and oil. Curious and thorough, I pushed the cloves out of the rice, the pieces of onion and garlic from the gravy, and piled these up at the side of my plate. I pulled the slick skin off the chicken. With a finger delicately crooked in tea-party fashion, I squeezed each piece of meat inside a folded napkin and soaked off its glossy gravy coat.

I wondered, complained, compared, and dissected, but still I was content. The food at friends's houses and school cafeterias and drive-thru windows was exciting and exotic, powdery as sugar, enmeshed in foreign crowds and noisy barter. But Nana-bai warned me against it. "Nai. You never know what they do to the food in restaurants," she said disdainfully. "Roaches and pig meat and they don't use spices. And cooks not washing their hands after going to the bathroom. In India we almost always prepared our own food at home."

"They have health rules here," I assured her, not really knowing what these rules were, but relying on their authority. She just shook her head at this attempt to take something simple and turn it clinical.

"So? In India, the right hand was used for eating, and the left hand for wiping after going to the bathroom. Haa. But what does that mean?" She stated this with finality, as though it should settle everything. And, indeed, I found that I could not argue with a standard I did not understand, which for millions of people was dictated by the fact that toilet paper was an extravagance.

The food in our home however was above any such controversy or speculation. It beckoned warmly and commanded a primal respect, like the draw and heat of the tribal cooking fire. I could watch it evolve from a pile of beans into a simmering curry. I knew exactly how each spoonful would taste and I could lick the bowl. For this food there was no need for further identification—

Italian food, Greek food, Korean food. What my mother cooked
for us at home defined food.

When my mother began to work all day, she did not have time to
make homemade food very often. When she could, she made her
curried potatoes, perfect yellow roasted, and brought them to dinner parties. But often in these high school years, Gertie or I began
to cook the family meals instead. I was glad to do this because I
did not want my mother's food. I wanted to be different. Chili
powder smelled funny. When we ate it, it made *us* smell funny,
too, and I was sure everyone noticed and secretly held their noses.
So I made pasta and meat sauce, or else we had cold cuts and
thawed bagels on the go. Every now and then, when I decided that
I was really a very religious person, I baked challah bread. Two
monstrous five-pound loaves with honey and raisins.

With teenage certainty, I concluded that I understood things
my mother could not possibly understand. I had cast aside the
oily heaviness of the Old World and acquired an appreciation for
a new, sophisticated food. Food that you did not need to sweat
over while it was cooking. Food that you could dress up and leave
the house for. There was nothing ancient about this food. It did
not involve musty spices that were bought from small Indian grocery stores. It did not have names that most people would stumble
over. My tastes had matured, I decided.

I wanted the sophistication of potato chips instead. Or hot
dogs and hamburgers and takeout. People in the movies always
ordered takeout. Even the word takeout was magical. It conjured
up a pink Barbie car, a laughing group of people obviously head-
ing somewhere glittery. Or two people cuddling in candlelight on
the couch, placing bits of sushi and rolled-up grape leaves on each

other's tongues. Ethnic food that you were not ethnically attached to. I knew with certainty that the world of pop-star magazines and short skirts and guys with blond hair were intrinsically connected to mall food, pizza, and French fries. I saved up my baby-sitting money and tried to buy them all. And then, if one day it left me bloated, I resolved to eat healthy. I wanted to be beautiful. So I went on diets and biked for hours in front of the television. For a while I ate only canned vegetables and crates of grapefruit. Then just sourballs for a week. Or else I drank Slim-Fast chocolate powder shakes. Once I devoured an entire fat-free pound cake, simply because it was fat-free.

I was hungry.

During college, there was an Indian restaurant off campus that had a $5.95 all-you-can-eat buffet on Sunday mornings. If we had a ride into town, and if there was no hangover in need of nursing, this was the place to go. I went sometimes, when my friends dragged me along, scraping up the few dollars here and there. After months of overdosing on cafeteria food, a change was welcome. It was cheap and plentiful. Besides, it turned out, Indian food was trendy.

At that time, also, a number of my first dates took place at elegant Indian restaurants in the city. These were hushed, low-lit rooms with soft Indian music playing in the background and attentive Indian women in gold saris waiting on the tables. In the spirit of these places and this trend, I imagined that the American men who invited me there were swept up in the exotic India-feel of the place. They seemed charmed to have a tie to the culture sitting across the table from them, and eager to prove a certain fluency in ordering foods by their knotty names off the menu.

An Indian restaurant would not have been my first choice for a date. It raised all sorts of complications. If noting my mix of facial features, the busboy eyed me curiously and asked, "Are you Indian?" I would hesitate, tense. How to explain it all as he pours us glasses of water—Jewish, Indian, American, Israeli? So I might just tell the busboy no, to be done with it. And yet, still, I would feel the need, the pride, to explain our family history to my date and to inform him that I had not yet found a curry as delicious as my mother's. I wanted to be able to stake a claim in India, but I could not yet easily let it stake a claim in me.

We would order together and share. Two different kinds of bread and samosas that came with small glass bowls of red and green and brown chutney. We would get a number of different dishes, too, maybe curried cauliflower and peas, or cheese and spinach, and lots of rice and mango lassi. There would be something very sensual about our exchange, over heaping plates of food, with both our breaths scented by the same herbs. Fingers brushing, leaning in close to whisper or pass on a forkful.

This was glamour. This was Indian food I had never tasted before.

When my roommate after college cooked, she was healthy, generous, loud. Shelly's concoctions spilled over into the grates, and whenever the stove was lit thereafter, the apartment would smell like sweet burning seaweed and spinach. With this same exuberance, she found the humor in almost anything, in burping, or in a bad pun. She laughed, and it was startling, at once loaded with a hearty, fat jelliness and the shrillness of what sounded deceptively like terror. Our neighbors mentioned that they heard this through the walls, and even after years of living together, when I heard her laughing on the cordless phone as she washed dishes at the sink, I was alarmed and ready to rush over in case she was in pain. I never held her up as an oddity, though. Instead I marveled at her, at something I could never be. I was served something different.

When I finally started to do my own cooking, in the end it was just me and my own pot. This was not a pot with history, but a regular American-made Revere Ware, a nonstick type that did indeed stick. One day I pulled it from the cupboard to prepare a small dish to bring to a Shabbat meal, the first that the whole family would share with Gertie and her new husband, an everyday American Jew. I was uneasy even to enter their four walls, where rules and relationships as I had always known them would never be the same. Here a piece of the outside world had now been brought in. And nervous, my culinary attempts on this occasion involved a flurry of utensils and eggshells, a spill or two, and one thumb slightly diced by my own butcher knife. So much fuss that it seemed inconceivable that when I entered their home that evening, all I brought with me was a simple, square platter wrapped tightly in tinfoil.

By the time I arrived, Gertie and her husband were already laying the table with polished silverware and glasses. They scurried about the kitchen, making salad, setting the Crockpot. The others trickled in after me. Batsheva flew in from Montreal. Tzvi rode the bus in from medical school. And my parents, with their old habit of avoiding the extravagance of public transportation, made the nine-hour trip by car.

As sundown and Shabbat approached, the tempo picked up. We raced for the showers, for clean clothes, to set out a last minute bottle of wine. Then, finally, with the lighting of candles, the mystical Shabbat bride seemed to sweep in, like a breeze of cinnamon, and at her invisible bidding we all sat finally to rest and eat. While

I found my place at the table, through the screen door I heard other Jewish families in the neighborhood walking home and into the plenty of their own Shabbat dinners. There were blessings. There were murmurs. There were clinking glasses and steaming bowls, Twelfth-Century prayer books and silver spice holders. And as we dug in, ripped challah, and forked chicken, my offering, the small dish I had prepared, was just one of the many in the spread with a serving spoon buried halfway through it.

For so long, I had known intimately and exactly what I would see across the table. But now I did not. Now among the faces beaming at me, bearing the familiar mix of my family, there was one new face, a stranger's face, rosy and kind and joking in the candlelight. Gertie's husband. Different as he might have seemed at first, soon, however, I forgot the strangeness in that he grew charmed and chewed and laughed and sang Shabbat songs just like us. Also, the features and colors in his face would be in the faces of my future nieces and nephews, babies with chubby thighs like perfect croissants. And already I loved these imaginary children, so nothing else could matter.

So I ate a fat slice of meat and noodles and two servings of potatoes and squash soup. Then I rested a few minutes and had another helping of noodles. From one corner across the table, while full stomachs were being patted, I heard a smattering of compliments over my small dish. Words like delicious. And spicy.

"It's all homemade," I could not help but tell them boastfully.

After that I cooked a lot. I cooked with a random collection of spice boxes. I cooked with garlic bought during a stay in Israel, labeled in Hebrew script; a small tub of chili powder that I took from my mother's cupboard; saffron from Price Chopper.

I cooked with a Hare Krishna cookbook that I bought in the train station from a man hawking Indian food and philosophy. "Are you Indian?" he asked, sizing me up and trying to make a connection. "Do you want to buy our cookbook for just a dollar?" I looked at him a moment, transfixed by the tambourine melodies he jangled against his knee. Perhaps there was an answer there, in the luscious orange of his robe, in his large hopeful gaze. I am Indian enough, I thought to myself, and I could certainly use a cookbook for a dollar. So I bought it.

I cooked also from my mother's scribbled recipes. Some she noted herself for me, others I copied down as she told them to me over the phone. Her trademark potatoes. A sweet rice that Nana-bai used to make on Rosh Hashanah. A traditional egg dish. I tried to write her instructions down as one would expect to see a recipe—one cup of this, a teaspoon of that. But it was more subtle and sometimes she did not think in these terms. She'd say, "Be sure you stuff the raw potato dumplings full, but not overflowing. Don't make them big like the puri auntie used to make, more the size of your palm . . . and round like a bangle."

What could all that mean to me? "You're confusing me," I'd tell her, when I got lost down a trail of black pepper.

"See," she'd remind me. "Didn't we always tell you to watch Nana-bai when you were little so you could learn?" Then she'd repeat the instructions for me, and if I was still puzzled she'd say, "You tell Nana-bai you're confused. I keep asking her to write down all her good recipes clearly for us, but you know she'll probably never do it." My mother herself had no measurements, no formula to read from. Instead she judged using these countless generations of reference points, using smells or the bubbling of liquids or a particular texture of meat. For her, this cooking was natural. She knew curry her whole life. She watched her own mother do this for so long.

While my roommate bent over to feed the dog some fish from her own bowl, in my half of the kitchen, maybe too thoughtfully, I burned and overspiced and watered down. Still I reassured myself, I have also known curry my whole life. I, too, have watched my mother. So I stirred patiently then, and tasted, and waited with certainty for my own gut instinct.

*When Jacob-bai came to visit me, he brought:*
*1 pair home-wear chuples, 2 cakes pear soap, 5 pounds for*
*pocket expenses, 5 kilos coconut oil, 1 box tooth powder.*
*When he returned to Pune, I sent with him:*
*1 pair gold earrings for cousin Julie, 2 caps, spices worth*
*58 rupees, 1 bottle cologne water, hand made puri.*

—Nana-bai's diary, page 63

*E*ventually, after college, I reached a point where I had a respectable sense of comfort with who I was and how I came to be.

I was fortifying my mind with postgraduate work. I had big plans for corporate America. I could pinpoint my mood swings. I knew exactly how I hit my limits, who my true friends were, when I had enough food to eat and enough wine to drink. I could humbly acknowledge that if I thought I knew everything, in fact I knew very little, and that each day, freshly blinded to myself, I reenacted my ignorance in new ways. I took earnest baby steps in my spirituality. Someday soon I planned to go back to Israel. Maybe to live there, maybe not. Maybe just to visit it again, and let the place jolt me, as it had once jolted me and generations before me. After all, I admitted to myself, what would I be on this earth if I did not pursue the few eternally bewildering and powerful riddles that inhabited me? All in all, I loved and felt inspired and on the whole I was at peace with the many cultures inside me, as they seemed to swirl together in a melting pot of contemporary self-awareness. In short, I felt ready to return to the fold and fulfill the half-hearted, finger-crossed promise I made to Nana-bai in my childhood, the day I learned about our terrible family split.

Lulled by the even keel in my life of late, it seemed clear to me why in the first place Nana-bai had extracted that promise from me long ago, why she had wanted me to return to the larger family and the Bene Israel community, despite the fact that it was fraught with difficulties and baggage. Everyone there knew about her hardships and shames as second wife. Many in these circles, especially those from the other side of the family, doubted her line would ever climb out of that lot. Probably they believed that we, her descendants, would still be living in the slums of Bombay, not in our haven of clean American suburbia, already in itself an achievement. At times I had a vision of myself, visited from this world of where I might have been. One of the millions of children in Indian documentaries. Perhaps a scrawny little girl with a bloated stomach and pierced ears. A wily beggar. This possibility would always be my shadow. And though its heaviness, following us around, made Nana-bai severe and prickly, keeping her distance from the others, she wanted me to promise to come back to them, so they would see me as something else.

She did not plan, as I had believed with irritation when I was younger, that I should be exactly like her. There was too much sense in her. And she didn't just want me to disappear into the anonymity of that culture. Instead, I realized suddenly, she wanted me to transcend it, be successful and beautiful on her behalf, so I could float among them, righting the past, or at least proving it wrong. She was like the haunting matriarchs I read about in books, who passed on painted, cryptic, purposeful messages to empower the women who came after them to rise above where they themselves once were. That, it seemed, was Nana-bai.

I decided to go back to a place which for a long time we remembered as an American echo of Nana-bai's trials: a local community of Bene Israel, a dwindling congregation of people she knew from her childhood in Bombay, in which some of our family had for a long time been active.

So often growing up I heard these people say, "We've always loved Nana-bai. We've always respected her and tried to help her out. She was the clever sister, you know."

My father said he one day wanted to take aside all these people, who said they loved her so much and respected her so much and helped her out so much, to ask, "If everyone loved Nana-bai so much and respected her so much and helped her out so much, tell me, why was her life so damn hard?" Because years ago, even this community, so far away from India's shores, had snubbed Nana-bai. Their insult was not obvious, but we recalled it in our family for a long time after.

On the day that Nana-bai was slighted, I was still a child. Only a few months before I had learned that she was a second wife so I was still trying to even understand what it meant. The community was sponsoring a grand picnic festival in the park that day and everyone was meant to pitch in with the preparation. In the end, however, Nana-bai herself did most of the cooking beforehand, on her own making lots of spicy delicacies and pots of potatoes and sweets and puddings—even a whole tub of homemade mango juice. During the festival, while most other people sat around talking or playing cards or wandering between arts and crafts tables, she made sure to keep the food hot and found clean forks and served up platefuls for everyone.

In the meantime, I ran around with my brother and sisters and the other Bene Israel children, playing on the grass. The day was wonderfully sunny and I wore sandals and braids. We were so free together in the plenty of the picnic that we played catch with vegetables we found in crates under the tables of food. We tossed whole zucchini and small pumpkins to one another and caught them in our arms as though gardens were exploding in the sky.

In the midst of the festivities, the leaders of the community at that time stood up on a podium, and with the microphone screeching every now and then, proceeded to thank everyone that contributed to the day. They thanked the rich old banker who donated three hundred dollars for groceries. They thanked the friends who flew in from Bombay and London for the occasion. They thanked their wives for contributing all their delicious recipes. Yet no one thanked Nana-bai for actually cooking and sweating and bringing the food to life.

She was not the type to demand excessive gratitude. But clearly, as the leaders' glances swept across the crowd, unable to avoid seeing Nana-bai cleaning up behind the food table a few feet away, they simply did not deem her work worthy of public acknowledgment. She was an old woman by then, with a precarious history behind her. She was a second wife back in India and therefore not enough of an important figure to praise here in America. So they took her for granted. Even the people standing at the side, applauding politely and flimsily upon cue, passed chilly unseeing eyes over her.

After noticing the omission of Nana-bai's name, I tucked the gourd in hand beneath my arm, and stalked over to her. "Nana-bai, they forgot to thank you."

"I don't think they forgot," she told me simply.

"Then say something to them. Don't just take this."

"Look," she told me, holding up her hands to calm me and

close the matter. I could see in them the veiny years of labor. "Look, they know they were wrong. There is nothing more to say." She straightened her hair and returned to her work.

Years later when I decided I was ready to return to this community on her behalf, I came home for vacation from graduate school with grim determination. I polished my nails for the occasion and wore my most professional-looking suit. I even combed my hair with special, premeditated care. I meant business.

They were meeting in a small rented hall for the evening prayer and they had already begun the service by the time I arrived. So I took a prayer book from the stack in the lobby and slipped into the back of the hall. I expected to perhaps feel old anger stirring, but instead, stopping short immediately, I was touched to be there. It had been a long time since I had purposely collected in a community of Indian Jews that did not include just family. I looked around me, with distance and newness, realizing we, the people in this room, shared something extraordinary. We all were descended from survivors of an ancient shipwreck. We all had crept out of the tangled relationships in our small circles. We all faced the same things each day when we walked around America, brown on the outside and a myriad of cultural influences and tugs on the inside.

I was calmed to find myself there, surprised by this fact, but reassured that despite everything we all emerged with pride and tradition and the will to come together from time to time in a small run-down building. The melodies the cantor sang had a hint of old-world murmurs, and I listened to them with eyes closed, feeling at once the hints of lullabies Nana-bai once sang to me.

After all the years of living under promise and expectation and disappointment and brief encounters and bitter memories and funneled details, to sit at that moment surrounded by Bene Israel was a nudge. Not a hard jolt, not a pointed whisper, but just a casual, off-the-cuff nudge, reminding me that other real people existed behind the stories and battles of our past. I felt as if I was seeing the vicious high school bully, twenty years later, balding and tubby and chasing his toddlers through the furniture department of Sears.

These people—who once made Nana-bai cower, who held our family secrets between their clenched knuckles, who seemed to prance through our history hand in hand with the snide descendants of the first wife—they were smaller than I had always pictured. And whatever these people once were, with slurs and pushes and insults relegating Nana-bai always to second wife status, now I could see they were frail and mellowed. If there was a once upon a time wife-beater in the group, these days he minded his own business, went home and soaked his teeth in water, and sat beside his wife to watch the evening news.

I looked at the people around me praying, and I saw that today they were flawed more with weakness than with cruelty. One couple bickered in their seats even in the middle of the service. A man in the corner slyly picked his nose. And with the younger generation moving on, most of those still left were old. When they saw me, a young newcomer, clearly one of their own, but whom they did not recognize after all these years, they looked to me with eager, friendly eyes. This was what they had become.

After the prayers, everyone gathered for desserts in the foyer and people ambled up to me and introduced themselves. When they learned all about me and that I was related to Nana-bai, they sighed happily and talked about the good old days back in Bombay and asked, upon wandering off, that I be sure to remember them to her. As if there was no doubt that she could only have sweet memories and ties to them.

I met a historian, by the coffee pitcher, who had written several books on the Jews of India. She herself was not Indian but was an outside observer and, for a moment, I felt resentfully territorial that she came here to merely study and write about the culture that we actually lived. But I saw that she had been with this community decades longer than I, and looking to the old grannies for example, I recognized that they trusted her and loved her as one of their own. They knew, also, that only through her studies and the few babies waddling around and perhaps drifters like myself, was there any hope for continuation and immortality.

Warmed by the earthiness of these softened people, I felt sure that Nana-bai would be pleased with the peace that had come when I met them again after all these years. Looking back, I could admire the strength it took her that day long ago to pull a reluctant promise out of me that would someday return me to the Bene Israel. I honored the bravery of her past, held it up as a bible of sorts. But it also seemed clear to me that she was speaking into a very different and very ancient dialogue.

In the years that elapsed, this had become a new world. And step by step we were coming out from the shackles and oppression Nana-bai once lived under. There was a politically correct peace with history—I felt it, had worked through much of my life to achieve it, saw it that very day within the Bene Israel community—and I was determined to celebrate it.

On my way home, I decided, I will write Nana-bai a letter. I will tell her I fulfilled my promise to her. I will tell her I returned to the family and community, that they thought I looked as lovely as she would have hoped, that they were startled and moved by my small successes into remembering her fondly. I will tell her that the community changed, the other side of the family changed, even we changed. Then she could be content and finally the generations of wickedness would all be behind us.

After Nana-bai's death, I stumbled across the letter I wrote her that day saying these very things. She saved it along with her diary and scrapbooks and photographs in the messy pea-green suitcase that I eventually claimed. In the turn of events that followed, my own words soon came to sicken me.

PART FOUR

# Peace by Peace

*In first year of marriage, I received from Solly three and a half meters linen flowered cloth for frock, two petticoats, and one 24 karat gold necklace with star of David.*

—NANA-BAI'S DIARY, PAGE 33

*T*he schoolmaster had requested that Nana-bai come to speak with him.

His note, formally penned on crisp, sheer paper, did not specify why her presence was needed, but Nana-bai knew anyway. In the last year or two, ever since she'd had one unpredictable taste of mango, Evie had become so strong-willed and rebellious that sometimes Nana-bai doubted such a girl could have ever pushed from her own body in a slick of blood.

Oh, Evie was a good-hearted child. Her small mutinies—like fighting on behalf of stray dogs—were always noble. But she herself was brash and oafish, more concerned with rolling up her sleeves and giving a presumptuous street urchin a piece of her mind than with stitching hems into place or primly straightening the ribbons in her hair. As a result, in the schoolyard, in the family, she was on the fringe of all the others. Embarrassed that they were connected to her, the girl cousins reprimanded her and said she might do well to wash behind her ears. The boy cousins who saw her as any other grunt, challenged her to running races and spitting contests to prove her wrong. But she barely listened to any of them. She played with them when it pleased her—whether they welcomed her or not—then easily left them when she was bored, sprinting off with bare arms and wide grins at any small bits of victory.

One day recently, Evie's ways went so far that even Rebecca got involved. "Your daughter," she had begun, storming up to Nana-bai as she and Evie strolled down the street. "Your daughter has forgotten herself."

"What happened now?" Nana-bai murmured then. Evie took a place behind her mother as if for protection, but her face edged around the flat hips before her, eyeing Rebecca boldly.

"She had the audacity to torment my daughter!"

At that instant, Evie had jumped forward squarely, her hands opening up in surprise. "I did no such thing."

"Are you calling me a liar?"

Seeing her mother's wary eye, Evie had caught herself, taking a deep breath. "Auntie, we were passing through the street and a beggar asked us for some money or food. And I had nothing to give him. But Leah pulled a coin from her pocket and held it out to him and when he reached to take it from her, she quickly snatched it back and into her pocket just to tease him." Her calmness subsided and she exploded again, snippy. "So I made her give it to him. So what?"

But Rebecca had just cut in then. "You had no right to make her do anything. She said you pulled her by the hair!"

"Nah," Evie waved this aside. "She's got plenty of hair." She said this not with cruelty, but rather with the matter-of-fact scrappiness of a girl who has yet to discover the vanities of hair. To her, losing a handful of it for the sake of something important seemed like a fair exchange.

Rebecca looked back and forth between the mother and daughter, waiting for Nana-bai to anger at her daughter, to apologize on her behalf, to decree a suitably harsh punishment. But she just stood still and placed a hand on Evie's head instead. "It must be some misunderstanding," she assured Rebecca mildly.

"Well!" she had gasped, fuming. "Well, this is no misunderstanding. You'd better watch what happens to this wild girl. Mark my words, she is becoming more and more spoiled every day." She stepped back and eyed the two of them for a moment coldly. "And you'd both better think hard about whom you sour against you." Rebecca had stalked away, leaving an exasperated smoke of dust behind her. Then mother and daughter continued on their way home, and Nana-bai took Evie's hand in silence.

Waiting outside the schoolmaster's office only a few days later, however, Nana-bai could not help but feel nervous. Maybe I should have said something more to her then, she worried. She is an obedient girl at home, with me and with her papa. But certainly it was not kind for Evie to be hurting and forcing herself upon Leah. Part of Nana-bai did sometimes want to take her daughter aside and ask: What are you thinking? What in G-d's name are you thinking? Very often, though, she held her tongue.

Sitting outside the schoolmaster's door, waiting and wondering at what unpleasant surprises might lie behind it, Nana-bai's fingers tapped the arm of her chair restlessly. She tried to keep busy with thinking about her stitching work instead, so she would not drive herself mad. There was that new dress for the Divekar lady and some baby clothes for the young woman down the road who had just given birth to twins. She made a mental list to buy more buttons and a new packet of needles. And of course, there was also the enormous order of bedding from Rebecca. She had sent over the material only a few weeks ago, offering moderate money in return for this massive amount of stitching. Every now and then Rebecca threw paid work her way to keep an even financial keel in the larger family and Nana-bai usually accepted it because she needed the money, any money at all.

This time it was a delicate job, requiring many painstaking hours. In the end after all her hard work, the final perfect bedding would only go back to Rebecca who every so often spitefully sent her maid over to complain about how long Nana-bai was taking. But despite all this, it was still a work of love for Nana-bai because the material she worked with was simply the softest, most beautiful cloth she had ever seen. Since Rebecca was so anxious to have it back soon, clearly it was precious. And from touch alone, Nana-bai knew this was not the kind of puckered cotton spun here in India. No. It smelled of clean foreign fields and waters to her. And while she worked carefully with this cloth, she held it luxuriously up to her cheek, wondering about where this other cotton came from, the foreign people and lands that could create such softness.

The door opened with a heavy scraping on the floor and the schoolmaster led Nana-bai into his office severely. "Do you know why I have asked you here?"

Nana-bai folded and unfolded a handkerchief between her hands, nervous. "Evie."

"Yes. Evie. Her teacher has had many problems with her. None of which have been solved by caning." Nana-bai was startled for a moment. But when he told her this, he only shook his head, as though the bewildering part was the malfunction of this careful discipline.

Her forehead wrinkled in wonder. "What was the problem this time?"

"Evie was unable to recite the names of all the countries in Africa in the allotted amount of time and so she received a poor mark on that examination—"

"Why, I helped her study for that myself," Nana-bai interrupted. "And when I tested her she knew them all."

"Apparently not. And after not studying sufficiently and learning the material as she should have, Evie had the audacity to stand up and complain to the teacher that she was not given the same amount of time the other students were given to recite their answers. That was how she explained her poor marks and she demanded another chance. Unimaginable!"

"It is possible the teacher made a mistake and did not give her enough time. I know when I myself was a teacher, there were so many things happening at once that it was too simple to overlook such a thing."

"Our teachers do not make mistakes. Now unless you are going to insult this institution and suggest, as your daughter did, that this may have been a purposeful oversight, I think it best we deal with the real problem."

He spoke so harshly that when Nana-bai answered him in return, her voice was quaking just a bit. "I am certain you are correct."

"It is clear that since your daughter dares to argue with her elders and teachers, she simply does not know her place in the world. Frankly, I am shocked that with her position in your family and in this community, she has no gratitude for the fact that she is even receiving any education at all." He took up a ruler sitting on his desk and absentmindedly ran his fingers along the edge.

"Now," he tapped it against the wood of his desk, as though instructing a course. "We brought this problem to you first. But unless you can assure me that you will properly care for this matter, then I am afraid we will have to bring her father in here, too."

Nana-bai paled and stood up abruptly. "That will not be necessary. I will speak to her myself."

"I hope so," the schoolmaster told her and led her to the door. "I hope this will end here."

She assured him again that it would end with this, and returned home thoughtfully. But already by the time she neared the house she had decided she would not punish Evie. She knew she should and that if she didn't, it was just putting off the time of reckoning. But as if transfixed by her daughter, as if amazed and hypnotized by this force that was Evie, Nana-bai could only wait instead to see what she would do next. Long ago she had somehow set this top spinning and now she could only watch it skip and twirl and maybe fall. But no matter what, she was powerless to change its course.

At home, Nana-bai's brother Samuel had unexpectedly called. As soon as she saw him, her pulse quickened and she dimpled and laughed out loud in anticipation of the laughter to come. He sat near Evie pulling on his banana moustache and telling jokes as she made him a cup of tea. See, Nana-bai told herself, catching sight of Evie bent thoughtfully over the brewing cup. See, she can be a dutiful girl.

Samuel's visits were always a pleasure. Very often he was gone, traveling about India for work. But when he returned to town, he came in a flurry, bearing gifts for the family, paying respects to his parents. In the rush, he left before anything could settle down into routine or unhappiness and he did not have time or patience to become involved in the family politics. That was one of the reasons why Nana-bai liked him. "I was worried you would not arrive in time," he told her as soon as she entered. "Look what I have for my sweetest sister."

"What?" she asked playfully, more animated and excited than she had been in months. With Samuel, she was no longer a burdened wife and mother. She was a girl again, and he was simply her brother. That was how they were together.

He hid something behind his back. "Guess."

She swooped around Evie in a hug, drawing her into the game. "Is it an elephant? Is it an army? Is it a leg of mutton?"

Evie turned on her, "No, silly."

"You know also, peanut?"

"Of course. And it's wonderful."

With a flourish Samuel drew two tickets from behind his back and presented them to Nana-bai with a flourish and a bow. "Madame. For your pleasure, a ticket to accompany your best-loved brother at an orchestra concert to be performed this very evening."

Nana-bai's eyes turned bright. "A concert! Aiaa. I have wanted for so long to go hear a lovely concert!" Then abruptly she let go of Evie and turned away. Looking at the floor, she busied herself picking up some stray clothing across the furniture. "But I am not sure I should go."

"What? Why?"

She looked up at Samuel and took a deep breath, clutching the clothes to her chest. "I don't know. I shouldn't just leave Evie here alone too long. And even though she can take care of herself, there is supper to make. Also," she moved toward the pile of bedding that still remained to be stitched for Rebecca. "Also, there is work to be done. A great deal of work." She held up a length of sheet to him, as if to prove it.

But he only looked at her searchingly. "Nonsense. You must come."

"The truth is," she admitted quietly, "Solly would be very angry with me. Such things are so frivolous to him." Nana-bai shook her head, as if nothing could be said now.

"He would never know."

But she just shook her head again, hopeless.

"I refuse to accept this," Samuel told her. With a silly swoop, he grabbed hold of Evie and picked her up. "And Evie refuses to accept this too." He held her as if she were a baby—only she sagged in his arms, a clumsy, giggling bundle, very far from a baby's size. Still he held on to her. "Until you agree to accompany me, I will not put Evie down. I will have to walk down the street with her like this, like a bag of rice. I will have to bring her home with me. I may even be forced to take her to Pune next week."

Evie giggled harder now. "You won't be able to carry me like this all the way to Pune."

"True." He looked pensive, considering the matter-of-fact details in this absurdity. "Then I might have to throw you over my shoulders like . . . like a shawl." With that she was tossed into the air giggling and shrieking. Then he wrapped her around him exactly like a shawl and turned with mock accusation on Nana-bai. "Is that what you want to happen to your daughter? That she should be made into a shawl? And at such an early age too? Shame." Silly, he swung around so Evie faced her mother. "Help me out," he told Evie. "Tell her you won't go quietly."

"I won't go quietly," Evie said.

"Really." Nana-bai looked stern, trying to assert herself. "I simply cannot go to the concert. There is too much stitching to do."

"Please come," Samuel begged her turning a sincere look to her now, as he shifted and strained under Evie's lanky weight, struggling to appear unbothered by it.

"Please go," Evie said too, peering at her upside down and splayed out awkwardly.

The sight of them forced Nana-bai to crack a smile. "The two of you and your pleases. . . ." She hesitated and gnawed on the inside of her lip a moment. "Fine," she said at last. "Fine, I will go."

With a fresh sari on and a puff of powder to her cheeks, Nana-bai squeezed two heavy bangles onto her wrists and clasped over her throat the gold necklace that Solly had given her at the start of their marriage. For an instant it gleamed at her neck like a dagger, then the gold of its Star of David faded into a smooth sheen. She spooned some leftover lentil dahl onto a plate for Evie to eat for supper. Reminding her to keep the door latched and to finish her lessons, Nana-bai swept out, an elegant lady on Samuel's arm.

The show was magical. The music that emerged in slow, then teasing, then extraordinary notes seemed in their perfection to have been destined for existence long before the minds that created them, long before any poor pieces of wood were polished and strung, then plucked in just the right way. Nana-bai and Samuel sat between the high-caste, well-dressed Indians whispering around them, half-awed. Nana-bai, feeling lovely, gleamed and sighed and gasped and closed her eyes to capture all the sounds of the orchestra, then opened them back up to drink in the sight. And Samuel at her side, who had acquired something of a sophistication in his travels, only leaned back and smiled.

Afterward, still floating from the music, they stopped in a pastry shop. Nana-bai had never come to this shop before because it did not have any of the usual Indian sweets, syrup-laden, thick and condensed. Instead, it was filled with foreign pastries, the fluffy, fragile delicacies of other lands. They were terribly expensive, since mostly British ladies and gentlemen visited there, looking for a taste of back home. Even the store itself, looking like any other Bombay store from the outside, was decorated on the inside with crisp pink paint and a tangle of silk ivy and roses that looked like they were pulled straight from a lush, chilly garden in London. When peering in, Nana-bai hesitated before these exotic delights. But Samuel was firm. "It is my treat. I insist."

Nana-bai saw Indian men working in the back under the hot stoves, of course, but at the front, as the bell clanged over the doorway when they entered, they were greeted by a red old Englishman with rolling eyes. "Welcome," he called. He stretched meaty arms out to them and drew them in to the scents of baking, describing his delicacies with pride. There were chunks of marzipan and fudge, custard éclairs and fruit tarts and cakes with cheese or with deep chocolate and cherry preserves. He threw out the pastry names at them, and tantalized, Nana-bai tried to catch them on her tongue, sound them out to herself under her breath. Petit four. Napoleon. Finally she chose a chocolate cream horn, and with tiny, melting bites it vanished into her mouth.

Nana-bai returned home much later than she had expected. All the way back, half-humming under her breath, she fretted over the hour and worried about Evie. Finally she crept quietly through the door and her eyes darted immediately to the sleeping bundle in the corner. Such a wonderful, comforting sight, to return and see her daughter's resting body breathing deeply under the bedding. She sighed with relief, audibly, with a "hah," but then in the next moment she let fly her hand to her mouth in a silent scream. In the dark, just behind Nana-bai, stood a man. For a moment, still barely seeing his face, she did not recognize him. But then she saw that it was Solly. She felt the strangeness of this, that a wife could not immediately know her husband in the dark. How had she not seen his profile, his glinting eyes waiting for her patiently in the blackness?

Like a sudden snakebite in the dark, his hand clamped around her neck. "Where in G-d's name have you been?"

"I was gone." She could barely choke out a word. "Nai. I was gone out on business. Errands."

"Business? What kind of business could you have at this time of night? Only prostitutes are out now." He jerked her by the hair and with a cry, she clutched at her scalp and followed its pull. "Do you think I am stupid?" He pushed her to the floor and sat on top of her chest so she could barely breathe. "You dare defy me? Embarrass me? Running about this city at all kinds of hours?" He slapped her across the face but she didn't make a peep. Then he slapped her again, and the pale sound of flesh crackling in the quiet of the night felt clumsy even to Solly, as though he heard himself passing wind.

Infuriated, he came at her more swiftly, not just with flat palms now, but with full hard fists, as though trying to burrow through her face. She was bleeding everywhere, the edges of her mouth and eyes were ripped and there was no quiet now as she screamed out in pain and terror like she had never before felt. This time he will kill me, she thought. Always in a beating, she felt this way, certain nothing could stop the force on top of her that glared with anger or disgust or cruelty. But now, she felt in the blows that something was different. And she was thankful for the dark so she could not see his eyes, because she knew this time they would be utterly vacant. In the pain, she started to lose consciousness and through the cloud of dizziness the befuddled logic seemed clear to her: she had returned smelling of chocolate and whipped cream and it was *this* scent that had driven him mad.

Suddenly, over Solly's form, came a heavy, clanking thud. He groaned and grabbed his shoulder in pain, then turned to see Evie standing over him with a copper pot in her hands. The pot was as big as her own belly, and weighty, too. But now she held it up again over her head and said, "Aiaa. If you ever touch my mother again, I will kill you."

More slowly than humans were meant to move, as if his every gesture were blurred by snail and sloth and sap, Solly leaned over Nana-bai's cringing body, breathing heavily and hunching toward his own wounded shoulder. Then seeing himself there, between this bloody woman and a little girl with a copper pot, he grimaced and heaved himself up off the floor. This time as he left, he did not stop to wash the blood from his hands.

Panting hard, Nana-bai struggled for consciousness, shocked that her daughter had done something so big that she herself could have never done. "Dear G-d," she whispered hoarsely. At the same moment that she was proud, she was fearful and ashamed of Evie's disobedience. Most of all though, she had a surge of mothering sense, all-powerful and prophetic, smelling musty from an ancient life, where mammoth meat and medicine drinks cook slowly on the fire. With a shiver of Freud and motherfucker and mother Mary and motherland and mother's milk, this feeling spoke to her. It spoke to her as it speaks to modern women today and as it has spoken to countless grunting, hairy-breasted she-carbon creatures for thousands of years.

The instinct told Nana-bai that she would, in the end, survive this beating, too. And that with every bit of life in her body, she would be sure that her daughter and grandchildren and great-grandchildren would make it to a different world. Not now necessarily. Maybe not even for many years or several generations. But someday—though it meant giving up all her own authority in a familiar culture, though it meant that afterward she would always seem to be wrong, backwards, quaint—Nana-bai would sacrifice everything she had to give herself and her descendants a new kind of life, away from all this.

Just as Jews in Europe were starting to awaken from centuries of exile, to feel their very souls (if not the anti-Semitism around them) driving them toward Palestine, in this Jewish home in India, too, there was a yawning, a stretching, a rubbing of the eyes. This family needed the new world of Palestine because they were at the brink of fading into something that within a few generations would be vacant of all its Jewish core. Not just in this family, either, but Jews all over India would soon start to pack up their clothes, their chili, their baby diapers, to seek out a new life. This was the next natural, necessary step.

Lying on the floor, feeling her cracked face, Nana-bai foresaw— not as a vision but as a truth—a time when she and Evie and Evie's children and grandchildren would be safe, eating sugared lemons on a porch somewhere in Palestine. (Perhaps she saw me, too, in the future Israel—driven by her bravery and by my parents' dreams. Free enough there to believe and disbelieve, kiss and tell, come and go and come back again). Nana-Bai saw that they would be part of the masses of dark-skinned people, lost tribes and lost Jews surging to Palestine to build a new Israel, all burdened with similar stories of the Old World, of ancient ways they were trying to move past. And small individual efforts and long-ago struggles would even pale in comparison to the power of Zionism, and Independence movements, and organizations like the Black Panthers in Israel—the Indians, Yemenites, and Moroccans, who demanded rights for themselves when the governing white Jews questioned their basic equality and legitimacy.

But even if one copper pot wielded deftly and one mother's

resolution in the end would be nothing inside the expanses of communal greatness to follow, still, this instant is forever etched into the history of anonymous heroes. Because on that day, with their small determined leaps of faith, there was no true guarantee of life beyond their world. So as Nana-bai struggled up off the floor, and as Evie, grasping in the dark for the nearest thing at hand, took a corner of Rebecca's freshly stitched bedding and wiped the blood from Nana-bai's mouth, in that moment they were extraordinary.

> *"The use of great men is to serve the little men, to take care of the human race, and act as practical interpreters of justice and truth."* —Theodore Parker
>
> *"In the language of the Gita I want to live at peace with both friend and foe."* —Mahatma Gandhi

—NANA-BAI'S DIARY, PAGE 19

Nana-bai died quietly one evening in a hospital bed in upstate New York.

I took the train in from graduate school to see her in those last days. Such an out of the way place for the end of a life that once crisscrossed history and the world. But I was not shocked by her death since I had braced myself for it. I was not angry at G-d since she was almost a hundred years old. She had lived a full life, and was ready to go. I was also not horrorstruck. Because she departed with as much grace as death in its coolness allows, when people are crowded into a sterile room, when the patient offers her visitors orange Jell-O off the supper tray as though it is even possible to eat in such a place, when there is a bedpan and bloated skin and only random moments of lucidity to say I love you.

Afterward, I was just numbed, and I mourned her, aching and empty. But I was tearless. For some reason I could not cry, even after her body was shipped to Israel for burial. Nana-bai had saved up to buy her own burial plot, nestled in the hills near Jerusalem, where all people living and dead would someday come together joyfully in the age of the messiah. This holy resting place was her only wish in her old age. Not a vanity, not a selfishness, just the one thing she saw fit to put money away for in a yellowed envelope. But even after I knew her body was headed there, something in me could not cry because I felt it was not yet over.

We anticipated a small funeral. There were, of course, the relatives from the other side of the family, from the line of the first wife, who all lived in Israel at that point. Every one of Nana-bai's direct descendants had ended up in the United States instead. After years of flurried movements and visiting and exchanges between countries, this was where the different camps had finally settled, finding a new relationship of just sparse letters and phone calls. For us in America, it was just too expensive for everyone to fly to Jerusalem to attend the funeral. So only my mother went, and the grannies and aunties and uncles went. But the youngest generation—me, my siblings and cousins—we were left to make our peace from a distance.

Afterward, when she returned, my mother called me up at graduate school and told me about the funeral and so I lived it through her. The dry heaves and disbelief. An uncle from the other side of the family honoring Nana-bai by reciting the Kaddish prayer for the dead. The awful power of cemetery mechanics, the lopsided lowering of the body, the clunky fall of earth chunks. Then the hushed logistics for a somber lunch after. Whispered directions to the home where everyone should meet, and the questions that, no matter how practically asked, can't ever be appropriate, like who can carpool and were there enough platters of fish and hummus prepared?

A few days after the funeral, the American group had to return home even though there were still many details to tie up and final-ize. They told each other such things as, Nana-bai would have wanted us to go back to work and to our families, to carry on with our lives immediately. But it never fully comforted them. And in-stead they kept themselves occupied in worrying about the details of the tombstone that would eventually be placed over the grave. This would still have to be ordered, supervised, cut, inscribed, and set in Israel, a difficult task to orchestrate from overseas.

"Don't worry about the tombstone," Leah auntie told my mother as she saw them off at the airport, putting an assuring hand on her shoulder. "You just let me know what the inscription should say and send me a check. And I'll take care of all the details here."

"You would do that?" my mother asked from behind her days of tears.

"Of course. We all loved and respected Nana-bai so much. Don't worry about a thing."

My mother composed an inscription and sent her a check. Leah auntie took off a day of work and ran around to different offices to make arrangements for the tombstone. Then, months later, she informed us everything was finished. We, in America, heaved a sigh of relief because now we were assured that Nana-bai finally lay at peace somewhere near Jerusalem. But I still had not been able to cry for her death.

And then, not long after the tombstone was placed, I found that Nana-bai visited me in my dreams. Her kind face looked at me from behind thick glasses and her words were scrambled by strange accents. When I woke up in the middle of those nights, tears streamed down my face. But this was not crying as crying was meant to be—cathartic and conscious and emotional. I was not convulsing. I was not relieved. It was more my sleeping body's reaction to these dreams and her evasive words, which, upon sitting up with a start, I immediately forgot. Bewildered, I wiped these tears from my face and turned my pillow over and tried to fall back to sleep.

Sometimes the most important things happen to us because of a collection of chance occurrences. Like the way Nana-bai changed her daughter's life when she bought her a mango. The most perfect fruit ever seen in all of history, which was then swallowed into a pit of petty family squabbles. What if there had never been such a mango? What if it had not been so large and red and glossy and seductive? What if, an instant earlier, someone else buying fruit had wanted a custard apple fruit, then waffled, and finally bought that particular mango instead? Would all the things that transpired in our family from that day—the rebellion, the tumult, then eventually the moving between countries and cultures—have never occurred? I have always wondered about those small moments that come together, how things might be so different if tying shoelaces one morning had taken a split second longer, if the decision to buy lunch at one sandwich stand versus another had been reversed. It has always frightened me that big life changes can be based on such small things as whimsy and weather and the urge for a meatball hero versus grilled cheese. But in the end, this was how we came to discover the truth behind Nana-bai's grave.

That summer, one of the American cousins traveled through France and Spain and Greece. In Athens, at a sandwich stand, he randomly met up with a friendly group of Australians who were taking a ferry into Israel. So he tagged along with them and did some more sightseeing there, too. Because he was already in Jerusalem anyway, he decided to visit Nana-bai's grave. Had we been

able to afford mass airfare so he could have been at the funeral itself, he probably would have had no need to visit the grave again.
But since he had not attended the funeral, something in him wanted
more closure.

He found the cemetery, and located the specific plot. And
though he could not understand the Hebrew words inscribed
upon the freshly set tombstone, he stood soberly before it with his
head bowed for several minutes. Then, just before leaving, while
digging through his backpack for bus fare, he stumbled across his
camera. As as afterthought, he took a photograph of the tombstone, thinking the sentimental family back in America might
want to see it themselves.

That film was crammed away into his backpack and almost
forgotten. But then, in doing a massive load of his laundry after
the trip, his mother discovered the film. She had it developed, and
while casually flipping through that roll of forty-eight, found with
horror the one critical photograph in there, the telltale snapshot
of Nana-bai's grave inscription, which did not read as my mother
asked for it to read. Trying to compensate for so much of Nana-
bai's lifetime, my mother had asked that the grave specifically com-
memorate Nana-bai's marriage, even though other gravestones in
Israel might not typically do so. The photograph revealed that
where it should have said some Hebrew equivalent of BELOVED
WIFE AND OUR MOTHER, instead Nana-bai's stone read pointedly
just OUR MOTHER.

Planted on her tombstone by the other side of the family, this
inscription moved the struggle for importance between first wife
and second wife even past death. Like a curse, like an insult, it
stripped Nana-bai of any marital legitimacy where she lay for
eternity. After all her unconditional love and their jealousy, after
all her torment and their supposed respect, after all her silent

struggles and their barbed tongues, the other side of the family had taken one last hit to have the final word. We thought she lay peacefully under the sweetest soil and grass on earth. But in a stumbling course of fate, we discovered that the language placed above her small plot robbed her of the old-fashioned anchor of wifely validity and pride for which she always suffered. It left her whole life, even her most-prized moral character, spoiled and open to speculation forever. As her tombstone read, she was only a mother. She was not a wife at all.

"Don't panic," we told each other, as news of this moved between the different homes of our family in America. "Maybe it was a mistake. Maybe the other side of the family did not know about it." As if some lone tomb-carver in Jerusalem just going about his business could have haphazardly left off the specific two words that were the points of contention for generations of our family. "Besides," we assured one another, "we put out the money for the stone. So, as long as we keep within religious guidelines, we can put an ode to Mickey Mouse up there if we want. It *has* to say whatever *we* want it to say."

My mother put in a call to Leah auntie and asked her, calmly, about the inscription. Ruffled, Leah auntie said of course it was just a mistake. She avoided my mother's calls and letters for months following this, changing the subject when it came up. Then, finally, when cornered in another phone conversation, she promised that the inscription would be fixed. And we assumed that it was.

Months and months after, my brother Tzvi traveled to Israel. He was there on other business, but he too wanted to see Nana-bai's grave. Warily, he contacted Leah auntie and she was thrilled to hear from him. "You must come for dinner," she told him. "I will cook you a feast that you will never forget."

"I actually don't have too much time here," he said. "But I do want to go see Nana-bai's grave while I'm around. Can you tell me where it is?"

There was shocked silence on the other end of the line. As if she could never have imagined it would come to this and someone from our side of the family would want to see the grave again. As if we did not have a moral right and obligation to visit it. "Well," she began, drawing out her words to stall for time as her mind raced furiously. "Well. Well . . . sure. I would take you there myself, only I can't get off work. I wish I had known you were coming sooner. And I would have cooked you a meal you would never forget. But now I can't even get off work."

"Can you tell me at least where the grave is?"

"Like I said, it would be better if I could have taken you myself. Because I don't know how to explain the way to get there. Yes. It's too hard to explain."

"The cemetery is just north of Jerusalem, right?"

"No. I'm not sure. I actually think it is just south of Jerusalem."

After more of this circular conversation, Tzvi hung up the phone and found the cemetery himself. Contrary to Leah auntie's suddenly bewildered directions, it was *north* of Jerusalem. After searching through the hundreds of gravestones as if in a desert, where with each step, more and more sand mounds surfaced endlessly, he found the grave itself. And Nana-bai's tombstone inscription was still *not* corrected. It became clear that if that side of the family had anything to do with it, it might never be changed. Tzvi returned to America with further photographic proof of the unchanged inscription, as though the burial of a decent old woman should require such clinical methodology. And I was beside myself with fury.

Even if by some chance the mistake had been honest at first, still the family had agreed to correct it. How could they sleep one night—much less many many months of nights—without changing this affront to Nana-bai over her helpless grave, this affront to our own living wishes for her? How could they be so blasé, so indifferent, as though they themselves had not known and been nurtured by this woman, too? But we should not have been amazed. This had, it seemed, been in the making all along.

If originally having the inscription set from overseas would have been a difficult task, now the prospect seemed a hundred times more daunting. From all the way in America, trying to change something that was literally set in stone by unknown artisans in a faraway country riddled with sluggish bureaucracy. Filled with disgust for the other side of the family and their ways that kept us anchored in old-world pettiness, I saw we were very far from the shiny progress and new-age love I had imagined not long before when I visited the local Bene Israel congregation. Where was the balance of pride in heritage and happy modernity I thought I'd embraced? It was not, it seemed, all that simple.

Instead, suddenly primitive in my rage, I found that I wanted to arbitrarily rip up tombstones from the crumbly Jerusalem soil. I wanted to angrily scratch the correct engraving into Nana-bai's stone with the screeching dig of my own fingernails. I forced myself to feel too far above it all, too haughty and wronged and removed to add to the active dialogue of bitterness and revenge that fueled our clan. Physically shuddering, though, I wanted to sever those strained family ties forever.

But now when I dreamed of Nana-bai, she did not whisper to me incoherently, mysteriously, purposefully. Instead she just kept busy. She sewed petticoats and bedding as she had done for so long to make money. She prepared hot milk and black pepper. She ironed handkerchiefs. She crushed chili in an old brass grinder. She washed pots and pans. She massaged chicken pieces with curry powder. She folded clothes.

Tossing and turning in my sheets, I searched these strange dreams for an epiphany or some kind of eloquent message. But there was none. If Nana-bai had been alive for an insult of such magnitude, there would have been no pivotal turning point for her, either. She would have merely recorded the person responsible in her mind, and perhaps in her diary. She would have decided, pointedly, to *not* send them the treats of homemade mesu she had been preparing for them. But she would probably not have tried to change them. She would just have continued the day-to-day tasks of her life and she would, in the end, have refused to cut off any ties.

With all her wisdom and experience, the only answer Nana-bai could give me in my dreams was her pacifism, her practicality. Why then had she ever made me promise to return into this fold of Bene Israel family and community?

Disappointing the poet and bookworm inside me, I realized she had not after all tried to give me some clean-cut, self-actualized, politically correct ideology of heroines and melting pots. This was beyond the limits of her vision, birthed in a colonial world. Still, she was telling me *something* in my dreams. And she did this in her way, for lack of the right words, by cooking and cleaning it into life. It was not lofty philosophy. It was just Nana-bai's old-fashioned elbow grease belief in the importance of family and community. Because she understood that though it was not at heart bad, it was, inevitably, messy. There would be give and take. There would be stepping on the shoulders of other generations— knowingly and unknowingly. There would be answering to the complicated ties of ancestors about everything from what to eat, to how to live, and who to marry. And though family was every individual's weakness, it could also be their greatest strength.

As her presence gradually faded from my dreams in a flurry of housework and sweet smells off the stove, Nana-bai had no great solution for me. She only wanted to assure me that just as she was once saved by her daughter in the harsh marriage her parents made for her, I, too, would someday be redeemed by my daughter for such ugliness as haggling over the inscription on a tombstone. That was family.

For Nana-bai's sake, we continued to hope it had all just been a misunderstanding—praying and waiting for our suspicions to be proven wrong, for our belief in the inherent good of all people to be restored. Perhaps it really was a mistake in the first place and the other side of the family, planning to correct the inscription all along, was too embarrassed to admit they hadn't yet found the time to do it. But in the end, we could not let things restore themselves as Nana-bai would have. Instead we busied ourselves with a steadfast course of setting things right, trying to correct the inscription in our own quiet, efficient way, without relying on the others—probably more than Nana-bai would have done, but nothing less than she would have *wanted* us to do. And we could not have done it without her.

After everything passed over, part of me still wanted to finally cut off all ties with the family. Not just those directly involved, but everyone around it. Since we would never have a way of knowing who exactly from the family was connected, who was purposeful, who was careless, who was a pawn of the elders, and who, in the end, knew nothing about it. But, torn, I found I could not make this kind of break. And someday, when I am back in Israel, I will probably phone them again, hopeful. Someday soon, too, I will go to India, where everything began, to find surely, achingly, that its world is nothing like I've imagined it to be.

So I would not make the break. *They* might make that break on their own, after learning that we would not protect and obey this secretive old-world hierarchy and viciousness any longer. But I could not do it myself. Because when Nana-bai long ago extracted the assurance from me that someday I would return to the Bene Israel, underneath it she was saying, "Tell me you'll do this. But not just when things are good. That's not enough. Modern, intellectual men and women, with fancy apartments and new cars and edgy wits, will still always somehow be moved to battle like biblical characters over a birthright. So tell me what you'll do *then.*"

Through my dimpled smile that day, through my fingers-crossed promise to Nana-bai, I had agreed that in my way I would do what she asked of me. But family is something you don't get to pick and shop through. And so, as I turned an ear to the ghosts of generations crowding around me, clanging their pots and pans, I was also admitting at that moment that there was no other choice.